Beth McColl has written  for *ELLE, Brooklyn* ... *AskMen, The Big Issue* and *Vice*. She lives in London. *How to Come Alive Again* is her first book.

@imteddybless

HOW TO
COME ALIVE
AGAIN

BETH McCOLL

unbound

First published in 2019
This paperback edition first published in 2020

Unbound
6th Floor Mutual House, 70 Conduit Street, London W1S 2GF
www.unbound.com

Text design by PDQ

Illustrations © Mecob

A CIP record for this book is available from the British Library

ISBN 978-1-78352-876-9 (trade pbk)
ISBN 978-1-78352-719-9 (trade hbk)
ISBN 978-1-78352-721-2 (ebook)
ISBN 978-1-78352-720-5 (limited edition)

Printed and bound in Great Britain by Clays Ltd, Elcograf S.p.A.

3 5 7 9 8 6 4 2

For Archie, Charlotte, Callum, Ray, Julia

Contents

Introduction

This book won't save your life. But you already know that.

Here's what I want from my life and my recovery.

I want to be calmer. Minute to minute, day to day, I want to feel calmer than I've been feeling. I want to process emotions in a way that isn't ruinous, that allows room for sadness, but doesn't let that sadness bulldoze every rational thought into nothing. I want to sleep better. I want to face my fears head-on. I want to be more honest – both with myself and with the people around me. I want to be kinder. I want to do braver things. I want to accept – and perhaps eventually love – all of the odd and harmless things that I do. I want to learn how to cook. I want to put down fear, right now, right here, and live my life in a way that doesn't ache. These are my goals. Some days, I think I come close. I make recovery my bitch. I'm kind to myself. I take on as much as I know I can handle, and I say no to the things that I know I'm not ready for. I take my medication on time. I eat enough food in a day to give me the energy I need, and if I want to eat more than that, I do. I drink all the water that my strange human body needs. I don't ask what it uses it for. That's not my business.

But on other days I don't quite make it. On these days I can't make myself get up out of bed. I lie flat on my back and I stare up at the ceiling. On these days my brain chemistry doesn't allow for any happiness or peace or calm, and getting up for a cup of tea or a glass of water is pretty much the upper limit of what I can handle. These days no longer represent failures to me. They simply are, and accepting this has been as important to my recovery and my peace of mind as anything else I've put my heart and time into.

I know now that some days I do less because my depression is looming huge and unconquerable. But I also know that some days I do less and make mistakes simply because I'm a person on Earth and that's a guaranteed part of this deal. My instinct is still to beat myself up, but this doesn't last as long as it used to. After I'm done giving myself hell, I get up. I dust myself off and recognise that this, too, is a lesson. It's all a lesson.

As a child and as a teenager I really thought my happiest life would be a life of restriction and discipline, a life of watching what I ate and exercising on command. Now that I'm (apparently) an adult, I know better. My happiest life involves no serious restriction. I eat the foods that I think are delicious, I disagree with the people who speak ignorantly, and I give myself a break when things don't go to plan. My happiest life is forgiving myself for mistakes or qualities that once I would have considered sloppy and unacceptable. I know now that my happiness has nothing to do with being quiet and pliant and agreeable. My happiness is an unapologetic animal. A growing, shifting, changing thing. A thing that wants my life to glow.

And this book is what I did to get from there to here, and what daily work I do to stop from sliding back. It's not a panacea or a life-changing volume of ways to never be depressed again. Sorry if that's what you were expecting, but no book (or pill or person) will do that.

I'll talk about mental illness in this book. Occasionally I'll specify that I'm talking about depression or anxiety, but mostly I'll just be referring to the broad and ridiculous nonsense of it all. This is, of course, because I'm very lazy. Just kidding. I mean, I am, but that's not the reason for my not being more specific. I'm not more specific because in this context it doesn't really matter. There are so many things under the heading of 'mentally ill' that apply to a lot of us, regardless of our current diagnosis or presenting symptoms, and

I don't want to make the waters all soupy by throwing labels into the mix.

I also reference a lot of CBT- and DBT-type exercises in this book. CBT stands for cognitive behavioural therapy. DBT stands for dialectical behavioural therapy. They are cousins. CBT is a talking therapy designed to shine a light on the things you believe and the way you behave, and how all of this can affect your mood and how you cope out in the world. DBT can be very similar, but has a more specific focus on helping the practiser accept themselves and their behaviours at the same time as treating dysfunction or illness. Sometimes I jazz the exercises up a bit, put a few tassels on them and make them do sexy little dances. But ultimately they're just the same exercises that any pro-DBT or CBT mental health professional would recommend. I include them because they've helped me. So here I am, giving them to you. This doesn't mean you have to try them all, or even believe in them as tools that can help you. You are you. You know you. You live with you every single day. They, like anything I write here, are just suggestions.

If anything in this book sounds wrong for you, or you feel very, very strongly that it isn't something appropriate for your treatment, that's absolutely fine. Ignore it. Scribble it out. Tear the whole page out, set it alight and use it to set fire to a small log. Have a tiny barbecue, it's fine. You're under no obligation to try anything. The point of this book isn't to give you a whole pile of solutions that will absolutely and definitely make you better. Some won't work for you. Some might even make you worse if you were to try them. So exercise your right to choose and trust your gut here, and always remember that you can ask for a second opinion from a loved one or mental health professional.

Because there's a LOT of advice in this book. A whole buffet. A pick 'n' mix. There's also a lot of advice that I repeat in different sections. This is intentional. Certain advice is very applicable in different situations and I wanted to be thorough.

Often I'll encourage you to practise certain techniques several times a day, or incorporate this thing or that thing into your daily routine. What you have to remember is: I don't want you to try it all at once and take on too much. Pick one or two things at a time to try. Don't attempt to totally overhaul your life overnight and do every single thing I mention. You will literally burst into flames and melt into goop. It's too much. A lot of it I'm still getting to grips with myself, so proceed cautiously and with as much mindfulness as you can muster.

But all of what I suggest is in pursuit of the one thing I *am* sure of: you have to know your monsters to kill your monsters. It's like in video games – except not fun at all. It's the first step on the magical journey of Feeling Slightly Better and Not Wanting to Actively Fall Off the Planet and Into Deep, Dark, Endless Space. Your monsters, of course, are the things that keep you from wellness. It's that simple. Maybe your monster is anxiety. Maybe it's self-doubt. Maybe depression. Maybe all of these and more. Identifying what it is that has its teeth stuck deep into your life and is sucking the joy out is the first step to making life a little more bearable.

I'm personally very much still in recovery. And yes, I'm doing better than I used to be doing. I'm no longer living in denial about the fact that I am a mentally ill person. I'm happy and funny and I really like my life most of the time, and I'm still mentally ill. I get up and go to work almost every day, and I'm still mentally ill. I know what it means to have a good and healthy relationship and yet – still mentally ill. You're not reading the work of someone who's been healed, who's totally mentally healthy now and neurotypical and has absolutely everything squared away and taken care of. Nope. Not happening. Maybe in a few years I'll feel differently, maybe more of my symptoms will be managed and I'll have figured out how to undo more of the damage. But right now, this is where I am. And the thing is, I'm not angry about it. Because depressed people are not a doomed subcategory. They can be the most incredibly funny and happy and joyful people you'll meet. If that sounds like a contradiction in terms, then this might be an important book for you to read. People with depression can often understand happiness and joy in even more acute ways than people who don't have depression. They know the sum of joy and freedom and light better because they've lived without those things for so long.

This book will contain:

- Appropriate trigger warnings.
- CBT and DBT techniques that I've tried in my own recovery.
- Some swear words. Sorry to any and all of my grandmas reading this. I learned these words from you.
- A bizarre and unsettling number of references to aubergines.

This book will not contain:

- Dietary advice. I want you to eat and I want you to enjoy eating. I do not subscribe to any belief system that claims your depression will be healed by abstaining from so-called fatty foods and eating a steamed cauliflower under a full moon. When I talk about nutritious foods, I just mean foods that energise and comfort you personally. Eat.
- Additional flavour sachets. You'll need to buy those separately.

 PART ONE: *Lightlessness*

PART ONE: Lighthouses

You're sick enough

You don't have to be sicker to deserve treatment or sympathy. You don't have to be at rock bottom, barely alive and right on the edge of everything to deserve help and healing. You don't have to prove to anyone that your illness or your stress or your unhappiness is real. You don't have to tear yourself open and show everybody exactly where it's hurting. You deserve help, understanding and treatment right now, wherever you are. If you're in pain, you deserve it to end. If your life doesn't feel good or meaningful or bearable then you deserve some kind of guidance and help. You deserve the terrible time to end.

Don't wait. Take steps now. Make the moves to get the therapy that you know might help you to conquer and defeat what's hurting you right now. Ask outright for the kinds of referrals and treatments that you know could really make the difference. And if your doctor says no, then see a new doctor.

Because you're sick enough now, and waiting to get sicker is a terrible and dangerous idea.

Depression

Depression is an extremely popular mental illness to have. If you're going through it, you can bet that you're not going through it alone. You are not a single malfunction in an otherwise perfect machine. You are one of so, so many. The machine is all of us.

And the machine is not just now breaking; it has *been* broken. It's an irrelevance. None of us are malfunctions – we're people with illnesses. And these illnesses take an incredible toll on how we feel and what we can do and what we're able to endure. They can lead us to self-isolate, to lie to the people that we love, to hurt and punish ourselves, to live a life that's a lot smaller than the one we know we want to be living. They can block our impulse to care about our own well-being, or our future, or what happens to us day to day. They can eat our light and our motivation and our will to try. They might do this for days or weeks or months at a time. They might have done this for as long as we can remember.

Our work, then, is to make it through, to make everything more bearable for ourselves and for other people like us, and to reduce how frequently we feel at our very worst. Our work is to squash shame right out of the equation, one horrible and difficult day at a time.

But it's not easy. Of course it isn't. Even now I get stuck in bad days, in bad patterns, in endlessly failing loops. I'm forgetful and groggy. *Make a doctor's appointment*, I tell myself before I take yet another mid-afternoon nap. When I wake up I've forgotten. In the fog of a depressive episode, it doesn't occur to me to think about things like doctor's appointments or calling a friend or even getting some fresh air or a glass of water.

Depression might mean lying in bed for days in your own filth. It might mean drinking until you black out every single day for months. It might reduce you to your most basic and terrible self. It might make you feel as though all meaningful parts of your personality have been rinsed away; maybe it'll convince you they were never there at all. It distorts reality. It disrupts normal life stresses and makes them into huge, looming, gargantuan messes. Depression is terrible. But you – you are not terrible.

Depression is not

- A character flaw.
- Caused by not eating enough vegetables or standing a bit too close to the microwave that one time.
- Just feeling a bit sad.
- Contagious.
- Ignoring good things on purpose or choosing negativity over positivity.
- Made up for attention.
- For weak people.
- All in your head.
- Better off being ignored and buried and not openly discussed and worked through.
- Experienced consistently forever in exactly the same way.
- Experienced by any two people the same way.
- An incurable, terrible illness and a fate worse than death.
- An excuse for someone to treat you like a burden or an embarrassment.
- An excuse for anyone to manipulate, abuse or hurt you in any way.
- An excuse for you to be manipulative, abusive or hurtful to anyone in any way.
- A type of spicy Ukrainian broth.
- The same as having a bad day or reacting to something sad by feeling sad.

Anxiety

Anxiety has often kept me from joy. It plants itself in my path like an enormous black-coat-wearing bouncer and says, 'Sorry, love, not tonight.' Anxiety demands all of the sufferer's attention and energy. It's like a needy goldfish. It always wants more. If you've ever been anxious, or have a chronic anxiety disorder, you know what I'm talking about. If not, feel free to use these chapters as a learning opportunity. Or just take a nap. Use the pages to make a small paper aeroplane. Fly it to the moon.

Anxiety can make you feel like there's a big foamy hulk-hand squeezing your heart, and you're sweating but you're somehow also very cold. It can make you feel like you're about to vomit your entire guts up, and like you're in severe immediate hideous danger and also you're dying and about to be killed even when you're just sitting on the sofa eating a cracker. It can flood the space between everything that makes you feel like you and leave no room to think straight or act like the person that you're fairly certain you should be. It can make doing anything that isn't totally under your control so difficult that mostly you won't want to bother.

Anxiety and depression often come hand in hand. They skip through broken promises and cancelled plans and unspent opportunities. One can often trigger the other. Anxiety might come first, make the space just dark and cold enough for depression to thrive, and then it opens the door and ushers it in.

Sometimes you get so good at this anxiety/depression combination that you can be feeling all of this terror while sitting quietly in a group with a polite smile on your face. Your body is yelling and begging to run, and nobody knows it but you.

I get anxious about a lot of things. Going to any new place for the first time can trigger a mudslide of terror. Where's the entrance? Where's the exit? What if I get lost? What if there's a confusing door and I don't know how it works and everyone sees me struggling with it and they think I'm an idiot who can't even use a simple door?

So I meticulously plan my trips. The supermarket becomes a potential hazard zone. I imagine my route inside the store. What I'll pick up first, which aisles to avoid, what to do if I see somebody I know. Of course when I get there the plan almost always fails. I get so anxious I forget it. Me anxiously browsing a supermarket is a pitiful thing to see. There's no logic, no game plan. It's just me pinballing around the aisles until I can pull it together enough to grab a few familiar-looking items so I can get the hell out, clutching my bag of batteries and satsumas in a state of terrified alarm.

Anxiety is not just feeling a bit nervous. Let's squash that misconception right now. It's not a fleeting panic that can be corrected with reasonable effort and a bit of time. It's a pervasive, hungry, nasty monster. It doesn't listen to reason. It eats reason. It eats peace. It eats time. It eats joy. It eats the heart out of good days and makes them into rotten things.

Because anxiety settles under the tongue, at the base of the brain, at the top of the spine, all across the skin. It reprograms and rewrites. It shouts loud enough that all rational thought is lost.

It's an absolute bitch, is what I'm saying here.

The physical symptoms alone are exhausting. Anxiety will literally sap the energy out of you and leave you unable to think or talk or stand or fend for yourself. It'll snatch words right out of your mouth and leave you gaping like a carp in a puddle. Thoughts will stand dumbly and hopelessly at the peripheries of your pulsing, terrified brain. Sometimes the body will respond with tears, or with hyperventilation or involuntary physical movements (teeth grinding, fist clenching, twitching or shaking, etc.). Doing anything feels terrifying. Going outside to the corner shop becomes mission impossible. Things that other people don't bat an eyelid about keep you up at night. It's a powerfully confusing and brain-scrambling force. It's also takes its toll on your body and your physical wellness.

Anxious people don't get enough credit for how BODILY the whole thing is. Being this nervous is a sport, thank you very much. The day-to-day undercurrent of it is bad enough, but an anxiety attack can be enough to wipe you out for hours and hours.

It's very different from normal, everyday anxiety in a few key ways. Regular anxiety might mean worrying about bills or relationships, feeling nervous right before a big interview or performance of some kind, or an increase in fear directly after an upsetting or stressful event. These are human responses and are often experienced by people without any sort of anxiety disorder – which is where a lot of the confusion comes from. People with anxiety disorders are not just nervous, or reacting in a typical or predictable way to regular life stressors. Their worries are unsubstantiated and extreme. They're irrational and terrible and totally unpredictable. Anxiety is huge and distressing and plonks itself right down between the sufferer and the things they need or want to do. It doesn't just make them feel a little jittery and nervous, it kicks the world out from under them and can cause overwhelming physical symptoms of terror, nausea and discomfort. It can cause an over-reliance on control or medication, and it can disrupt sleep to the point of serious physical illness.

Normal worrying and anxiety can be controlled, and however unpleasant it gets, it never reaches the point of being so distressing that it interferes with your day-to-day life or your ability to function or provide for yourself. With an anxiety disorder this isn't the case. Your worrying is out of control. It comes on without warning and can last for days or even weeks without any real respite. This anxiety can cause you to obsess about things that have no chance of happening – things that are provably unthreatening or totally imagined. It can cause bouts of nausea or diarrhoea, sweating, trembling and faintness.

This kind of anxiety will try to convince you that normal life blips are actually terrible and fatal and the end of the entire world as you know it. When you make a mistake at work, when you do something stupid in front of someone who you think is cool, when you forget something important, when you get lost on public transport, when you get a fine or a parking ticket, when you miss out on a promotion – your anxiety will yell and screech and give you unrelenting hell for it.

Your anxiety is a liar, though, is the thing. It's also incredibly unhelpful. It'll fill you full of the deepest sense of worry and panic and then give you NO SINGLE IDEA of what you're worried or panicked about. Not a clue. You can ask it nicely to elaborate, to give you some tiny hint as to what the problem is and what you could maybe do to fix it. It will say nothing. It doesn't care. Your pleas won't do a thing. It will just repeat, louder this time, that something terrible is definitely happening and that you should be very, very afraid.

Anxious brain is a real jerk.

Anxiety is not

- Just feeling nervous or apprehensive about something.
- Conquered by 'being brave' or 'pushing through it'.
- Something to be ashamed or embarrassed about.
- An uncommon condition.
- Fatal (though it can definitely feel like it is).
- Something you can control by just pretending it's not happening.
- Ever helped by someone shaming or scolding you for it.
- Incurable.
- The only thing you'll ever feel in a new or unusual situation.
- A made-up condition.

Dissociation

Dissociation involves feelings of numbness or detachment or a sense of not being present or real. Dissociation often occurs in response to abuse or trauma, or a manifestation of anxiety.

Signs of dissociation

- Staring at one spot or object, unthinkingly and for no real reason.
- A feeling of numbness or blankness.
- Feeling like you're outside of yourself looking in, or as though you're watching yourself in a film.
- Struggling to understand what people are saying to you, as though they're speaking another language, or the information is filtering through to you very slowly.
- Easily losing track of what you're doing – e.g. not being able to focus on the television show or the conversation that you're having.
- Feeling uncomfortably aware of your body, like it doesn't belong to you or that you don't really exist within it.
- Having trouble recalling simple details about yourself, like your middle name, age or address.
- Experiencing a kind of floating feeling.
- Not feeling entirely real, like you're part of a dream or another world.
- Feelings of dizziness or light-headedness.
- Feeling as though the people around you aren't real, or seem different or more difficult to understand or relate to than normal.
- Struggling to keep your train of thought, or remember what you were just thinking about.

- Finding it difficult to speak or vocalise any feelings or needs. Feeling a general disconnect from language.
- Not being able to follow instructions, concentrate, or respond when asked to say or do something.

How to help someone who's in a dissociative state

- Remind them of the basics. Tell them who they are and who you are. Tell them where they are and what they were doing before they started to dissociate.
- Help them to regulate their breathing by counting through it with them – inhaling for four beats and then exhaling for six can help to slow their heart and their breath down and help them to refocus on the present.
- Encourage mindfulness of surrounding and senses. Ask them to think about what they can see, smell, hear, etc. Don't press them to vocalise these things if they aren't able, just ask that they try to list them in their mind.
- Don't touch them unless they ask. They're in a vulnerable and strange place and it can be quite alarming and overwhelming to be touched.
- Speak calmly and only say things that are constructive, reassuring and don't demand any immediate response or reaction.
- Be patient with them. They may need some time to return to a responsive state of mind, and rushing them or behaving with urgency will only make things worse.

Coping statements for anxiety

'All I need to do today is make it from morning to evening. I just need to endure this one day and survive it.'

'My anxiety has to peak before it can wane. It will get worse before it gets better. Right now it feels vast and unconquerable and completely out of my control. And right now (DEEP BREATH) that may be true. But what isn't true is that it will keep on growing and growing and growing and never stop. It will stop. It will peak, and it will feel like the world is ending around me, but then it will start to wane. I will start to feel more in control and more myself and more calm. This will happen. I just need to ride this one out.'

'This feeling is really, really rough, and it definitely seems like I'm in physical and immediate danger. But you know what? This isn't true at all. I'm safe. I'm not in any danger right now. I can find a safe place to sit and wait this out. I will be absolutely fine.'

'All feelings are temporary. These feelings are particularly strong and loud and terrifying, but even they won't last forever. Eventually they will burn out and I will feel better. I just have to survive until then.'

'I can learn to operate and succeed in spite of this anxiety. Anxiety may be a part of my life, but it doesn't have to be the biggest part. It doesn't have to stop me from doing things.'

'I'm not the only person suffering with this, and I'm not alone in working through this. When I'm out in the world and I feel like everybody else is doing great and I'm the only one feeling like the sky is falling, that's false.'

'When anxiety stops me from doing the things that I want to do, it's okay to feel sad and hopeless and angry about that. It's disappointing. Denying this won't help and if I want to get pissed off then that's my right. But this won't be the story forever. A big part of recovery will be working to limit these instances, and when I'm doing better and I'm able to do more, I can celebrate instead of mourn.'

'I've handled days like this in the past, and I've got through them. I may have struggled and flailed and made mistakes, but I survived them. I will survive them again. And I will learn from them, too. That's just how this thing goes.'

'I can honour and be respectful of my feelings while also refusing to let my reality be dictated by them.'

Doctors

Trigger warning: mentions of inappropriate conduct by a doctor.

The first time I opened up to a doctor I was at university. I was nineteen years old and terrified. I told the doctor that I was finding things unbearably difficult. She looked at me without speaking for a few seconds, and then told me that I was probably just hormonal and should try to improve my diet. She suggested I get to bed earlier, and asked if there was anything else she could help me with. I left feeling more defeated than ever, and it took another two months for me to go back. Two months where I felt worse than I had done before, convinced now that I'd just made the whole thing up in my head. But I did go back. I asked to see another doctor, and I was firmer this time (despite feeling terrified to the point of nausea). I explained that I wasn't just sad, I wasn't hormonal, I wasn't just having a bad time, I wasn't just a bit worried about my assignments. I was depressed and I was getting more and more anxious by the day. And this doctor listened, and he told me that he believed me, and that together we would get this sorted. He told me what resources were available through the university, and he explained the different kinds of medication options that we could try. I left that appointment feeling lighter than I'd felt in months. And no, I wasn't cured. And it wasn't the last time I'd see a doctor. And it didn't mean I'd never again see a doctor who treated me with scepticism, or who diminished or doubted what I was going through. But it was the start. Everything that's come after began then, in that little room, with a trained professional who heard and believed me.

The worst doctors stick with you, but so do the good ones. When I was in my last year of university I was lucky enough to get an appointment with a woman who not only believed everything I was saying, but who was also really kind and proactive about helping me to access support. She explained how difficult the system was to navigate, especially as a young woman, and sympathised with me. She took time to explain how different types of medication worked, and the hoops I'd have to jump through during the prescription process. She booked me in for another appointment a few weeks after that, so I could let her know how I was doing, and told me to call if ever things got too bad. She was just doing her job, of course, but at the time it felt like divine intervention. No medical professional had ever been this kind or this engaged with me and my mental health. Which is fucked up in the grand scheme of things, but whatever. I'm grateful for her.

Since university I've spoken to a lot of GPs about my depression and anxiety. Like, A LOT. So many. A smorgasbord of general practitioners. Some of them have listened, some of them haven't, and some of them have been so horrendous that

I still can't think about them without my palms getting sweaty (knees weak, arms spaghetti). I've got lucky a few times, and sat in front of an empathetic, understanding doctor and explained the way I've felt and been listened to and then received the help or support that I needed. But I've also sat across from a doctor and cried until I couldn't breathe and been told that I was just young and would grow out of it. I've been told that I just need a boyfriend. I've been asked to undress to prove to a doctor that I had self-harm scars.

So I'm writing this, a handy little guide for seeing a doctor, and giving yourself the best chance of getting through to them, and ending up with a result that helps you move ahead with your recovery.

Preparing for a doctor's appointment

So you need to get that appointment booked. That's the first step. You can't just turn up at the surgery in a faux-fur coat and cowboy boots and put your foot up on the receptionist's desk and be like, 'Yes, hello my good bitch, I am here to see your finest practitioner of medical medicine.' Turns out they don't respond well to that. So instead you'll have to make an appointment over the phone or online, like a civilised person might do, and then you have to turn up and wait like everybody else. And sure, you'll end up waiting a lot longer than you were meant to, and you'll be forced to pretend to read a *Closer* magazine from 2009 while Jackie from round the corner describes her rashes in detail to you and anyone else who'll listen. But you'll grit your teeth and get through it. LET JACKIE LIVE HER TRUTH, AND BE PATIENT WITH THE PROCESS.

Download a podcast, make a soothing playlist, bring a book. Maybe even this book. Or maybe not. Maybe you'll take *Moby Dick* instead. That's fine. Just make sure you bring something to do for the waiting-room portion of the process. Time works differently in waiting rooms. A single minute can last up to 40 per cent longer in a waiting room, so be prepared for that.

But how to prepare for the actual appointment itself?

1. Plan what you're going to say. (See 'Templates for talking to a doctor', pages 20–22.) Because while YOU know that you're depressed, or anxious, or mentally unwell in whatever way, the doctor is brand spanking new to the situation. They didn't see the prequel. They're coming in halfway through the action and they need a synopsis. That's okay, though, because we're going to work together to give them one that is concise, to the point, and that hopefully gets you a good result. And I know it's scary to sit down and make a list of what's wrong and what hurts, but it'll help you keep your cool when you're in there, sitting across from a doctor who's just asked, 'How can I help?' This moment has toppled me a few times, I've made appointments and then freaked out the minute I was asked why I was there. I've panicked and pretended that I'd come to see them about some physical ailment. I made up a lot of aches and pains, and it took me years before I was able to just come out with it and say, 'Hey, I'm really not doing well mentally. I'm here because I'm depressed and need some help.'

2. Do your research. Being confident in your communication and preparation will help your chances of being taken seriously by your doctor and not given the runaround or fobbed off with some bullshit answer or solution (something which has happened to me many, many times). So get on to Google, get stuck into those resources, and make a note of anything you think might

be important. Knowing what your options are will help show the doctor that you're serious and you need them to be too. Be ready to ask confidently for medication or the referral that you think you need.

3. Prepare for the doctor to not give you the answer you want. Prepare for them to disagree with your analysis and suggest things that you don't want to hear. They might be doing this because they're obligated by the rules to offer you the more basic, entry-level treatments before they're allowed to give you the referral that might eventually lead to a proper and full diagnosis. For example, several doctors have told me they needed me to try a certain number of SSRIs before they were able to move on to the other kinds of antidepressants. And this is a frustrating process. I've sat and I've cried in front of several doctors and begged them to let me try something different. But now, on the other side of things, I'm glad I stuck with the process, and I'm in a better place because of it. I just had to learn to work the system and be patient with it, and expect that often it wouldn't work out just how I wanted, but that my perseverance would pay off. Mental health services are stretched thin. They're underfunded and understaffed and we're nowhere close to where we should be. This means it'll really pay off to have some patience and tenacity on your end, and an understanding of what to expect and what to ask for. The waiting lists are long and private treatment is expensive, but there are beacons of hope within the system and many genuinely good people and services.

4. Your doctor may be a total arsehole. I hate that I have to write this. I wish all of the doctors in the world were good and supportive and ready to act proactively and empathetically to help us manage our mental illnesses. But they're not. Some of them are turds dressed up in little corduroy trousers and

cardigans. And sure they're really CLEVER and SMART and they know how many bones are in the human body. Whoopty-fucking-doo for those guys. But guess what? Those smarts mean nothing to us when they aren't paired with empathy and a genuine desire to treat and understand their mentally ill and vulnerable patients. So if your doctor is shitty (or even just not a good fit for you), do what you need to get a new one. No explanation or excuse needed. You're not being difficult. You're not being dramatic. You're solving a problem that you shouldn't have run up against in the first place. You're being assertive about your mental health, which is brilliant and commendable always.

5. Know your symptoms. If you can, know their real medical names. Instead of saying 'shouty monster brain', tell your doctor that you've been experiencing frequent anxiety. Instead of saying you've been 'chomping on that old sad candy', explain that you've been having severe depressive episodes for as long as you can remember. Instead of saying you've had a 'case of the twizzly floaties', say that you've been highly dissociative lately and it's interfering with every aspect of your life and making it almost impossible to cope some days. Speaking your doctor's language makes communicating the whole picture a hell of a lot easier. It bridges the gap and lets them know exactly what your problems are, which in turn makes it easier for them to prescribe the right medication or suggest the right treatment options.

6. Understand that even the best and most receptive GPs can't be experts in every single area of mental illness. The human brain is such a complex ham that you'll probably need to shop around a bit for the right doctor or specialist. Your local doctor can help prescribe entry-level antidepressants, antipsychotics, beta blockers for anxiety – whatever – but they're not going to be

able to give you a comprehensive diagnosis and a breakdown of all the cutting-edge treatments and therapies available. For this reason, it's helpful to treat them as a portal to more specialised and tailored resources. Let them do their job and give you a rough idea of where to go next, but don't feel disheartened or defeated if they aren't able to give you any final answers. You'll get there eventually, I promise you that. You just need to stick with the system and see this through.

7. If you don't really vibe with your current doctor or haven't felt properly listened to in the past, request someone different. Maybe ask to see a female doctor if you've only seen men so far, or vice versa. This might make the process take longer, and she or he may well be a dickhead as well, but it's worth trying. It's important that you find a good fit, and at the very least feel comfortable enough to open up fully. A doctor who doesn't make you feel comfortable or has questionable opinions about mental health in general isn't going to help you get better.

8. For your first visit, see if you can request a double appointment. This way you're less likely to feel rushed or under pressure to hurry up and get to the point. Because it's hard to just 'spit it out' when the problem is something you've been ashamed of or afraid to talk about for your entire life. The words will feel strange and clunky and embarrassing, and you might need longer than usual to say what you need to say. This is okay! You're not wasting anyone's time or being selfish. You're just giving yourself the best chance possible of being understood and getting the help you need.

Templates for talking to a doctor

Here are some templates for ways to communicate with your doctor when you're ill and you need help.

'I've been depressed for a long time, it's really impacting my quality of life and I need some support because I can feel it getting worse. I've made a note of when the worst depressive episodes occur. I've tried X, Y and Z to try to feel better, but nothing's made a significant difference so far.'

'I'm here to talk about anxiety. It's something that I've suffered with quite severely for a long time, but have only recently accepted that I need medical help with it. I'd like to know what my options are in terms of treatment, medication and daily management.'

'I've received some support in the past for depression, but I'd like to try antidepressants, perhaps in conjunction with other treatments. Right now my quality of life is suffering and it's holding me back. I need help with this.'

'I think I might be suffering with bipolar disorder/OCD/schizophrenia/borderline personality disorder. I'm not sure, but I have X, Y and Z symptoms and I'd like to see a specialist or a therapist who can help me to explore this. What help is available for me and what do you recommend I do in the meantime to help treat or manage what's happening?'

You can say things however makes most sense to you, but try to stick to the essential formula of:

1. Stating the name of the problem (or problems) that you've been experiencing.

2. Stating the severity of the problem and its impact on your day-to-day life (try to cover both its effect on your social life and your work/school life).
3. Stating the frequency of the episode or episodes.
4. Asking what's available right now and what other resources you might be able to get access to in the long term.

Also feel free to take along a notepad or a piece of paper with some important facts or dates written down (e.g. how many spells of serious depression you've had in the past year, the first time you can remember feeling depressed or suicidal or unmanageably anxious, how many anxiety attacks you've had in the last month or so, etc.). Basically anything that gives them as detailed an idea as possible of the severity of what you're going through so they can send you in the right general direction for help. And don't worry if you're still really flipping nervous. I still get nervous and eager to downplay everything the minute a doctor asks me what the matter is, but I'm failing myself and my recovery whenever I do this.

If you do the above and your doctor is dismissive or inappropriate or tries to suggest that what you're going through is normal and doesn't require any help – end the appointment there. It's tempting to want to try to persuade them otherwise, or force them to see how unhelpful they're being and get them onside, but mostly this is just an exhausting waste of your precious and delicious time. A simple 'I think I'd be better seeing a doctor who can help me with my mental health' can work, or 'I came here for mental health treatment; is there another doctor at the practice who will be able to help me with that?' Or just nod and say thank you, leave the room, then stop at reception and book the soonest appointment you can with a different doctor, and get out of there. Because it's a horrible and terrible truth that some doctors are still doubtful and on the fence about believing patients about their mental health. Fuck them all sky high. Sure, I hope they do better in future, but also, whatever. There are more doctors out there and you don't have to put up with a disbelieving or patronising one just because they insist they know better than you.

Diagnosis

There's lots to say about getting a mental illness diagnosis.

Firstly: it's never easy. Secondly: I'm really sorry it's never easy.

As is the case with a lot of things relating to mental illness, there's the way things should be, and then there's the way things really are.

With getting a proper diagnosis, here's the way things should be:

Fairly straightforward. In an ideal world it would be easy to go to a doctor and have them listen, understand, believe you, then refer you on until you meet with someone who understands your situation and can give you a good idea of what you're up against and how best to tackle it. It should be free, it should be confidential and without shame, and it should be supportive from beginning to end. It should also be fairly quick. It should take a reasonable amount of time – you should be able to know when you're going to have your next appointment, and not have to sit for ages on endless waiting lists while doctor after doctor apologises and tells you that there's nothing they can do for you right now.

And then there's the way things really are: NOT LIKE THAT AT ALL MOST OF THE TIME.

Again: VERY SORRY.

It's not my fault, but nonetheless, I feel I should apologise.

Getting a diagnosis is difficult. There's no telling how receptive your doctor will be when you're finally able to get an appointment. You may have to jump through a dozen hoops to get a single referral, and then expect to wait months and months for anything to happen. To actually get a diagnosis will require you to see several doctors. It will probably take years and a lot of frustrating appointments with experts and therapists and specialists of all description. Often you'll be pursuing treatment with only a vague idea of what's actually the matter with you. Sometimes a doctor will just pop you into a broad category (mood disorder, anxiety issues, personality problems) and treat your symptoms without engaging any more thoughtfully or critically than that. And so you need to persevere and work with the system (however flawed), because having a proper diagnosis can often be the only way to get the referrals and the prescriptions that you need to help you feel better. The system is closed, and it takes skill and insider knowledge to navigate, so try to seek out other people who have taken a similar route to you, and who may be able to tell you more about what to expect.

With all of this difficulty and work to get the diagnosis, it can feel like a huge victory when it actually happens. When a doctor looks at you and says, 'This is your problem. This is why it hurts,' it can feel like you've reached the peak, like the worst is over, and with a diagnosis you can finally start getting better and better and better until eventually you're cured.

Unfortunately, this isn't exactly how it happens with a diagnosis. I know, I know. I was horrified too. Couldn't believe it. Shocked. Appalled. On the phone to the manager as we speak.

A diagnosis isn't always the key that unlocks every aspect of recovery. There will still be questions, and there will still be problems that don't have clear or easy solutions.

There's the issue of overidentification, of ascribing every part of your personality to your illness, and being unable to differentiate clearly what feels like You and what feels like Your Disorder or Your Illness. And often there's no easy fix with this. My teenage years were spent learning how to hide my illness and survive it, and now I'm not sure what things I do because of my illness and what things I do because it's within my character to do them. Is there a difference? I'm not always sure.

Overidentification can also mean that we take shortcuts and let ourselves get away with things that we know aren't okay, or in line with who we want to be and how we want to behave. It can act as a free pass to be miserable and unwilling to try. It lets us off the hook, in part. We can hold it up as proof that this is just who we are. No use fighting it. Science agrees we're miserable and self-destructive, so it would be rude not to lean into it and stop trying, right? At the beginning it can definitely be easier to use your diagnosis as a means to shrug off responsibility than it is to use it as a guide to map your recovery, and find new ways to cope and methods of accountability.

So I can't tell you to what extent you should identify with your illness, or what would be healthy for you personally. But if it's problematic, then the signs will be there. If you experience a resurgence or a relapse after you're diagnosed, and it doesn't show signs of abating, that's a red flag. If you find yourself using your diagnosis as a kind of 'get out of accountability free' card, that's another. If you use it to justify objectively bad or self-destructive behaviour that you know deep down you don't totally agree with, you need to look closer at what's happening.

True accountability means looking at the whole picture. It means saying that, yes, maybe you did do something shitty because of your illness, and that, yes, that is understandable, but that, no, it is not an excuse or permission to do it again. And it doesn't mean that the people you've hurt are obligated to forgive any of the shitty things you did while you were ill. So choose instead to self-examine, to let your diagnosis be only one factor, and never a pardon or a way to avoid taking responsibility for damage done.

In the past I've felt an odd kind of attachment to my symptoms and my diagnosis. It was who I'd been for so long that I worried I wasn't really anyone outside of it. Not to mention that it was so much easier than trying. I would fold back in on myself after any attempt at living better went west and declare that I was simply too ill to get better. Recovery wasn't for me. Functioning out in society wasn't for me. I couldn't do it, and I had the diagnosis to prove it. It took a lot more hard work and many more visits to the doctor before I was able to leave this idea behind and move beyond it.

But it's not all bad. Diagnosis has also helped me to find my people, the people who get it, and won't hound me with their misunderstandings about what I'm going through. It exhausts me, having to wade through other people's ill-informed ideas about mental health, and so talking to people who know intuitively is pure relief.

Having a diagnosis also gives me a better understanding of why I feel the way I do, or why I have certain impulses that I haven't been able to easily or logically explain. It's a part of the picture, but it's never the whole thing.

Medication

In this section I'm going to talk about medication. I'm going to talk from experience, and I'm going to tell you everything I've learned from my research and from talking to other people who have taken, or are currently taking, medication as part of their mental health treatment. It's important to bear in mind that my experience with one medication may vary wildly from another person's experience with the same medication. What's sent me reeling into groggy despair has brought someone else back from the brink, and helped them climb into recovery. So please don't ever think just because it's not worked for me, or someone else, that it's not for you. If you go in with that attitude, then you're bound to fail. I know this because I did this. So have your facts straight, know what's up and be ready to communicate any concerns or questions to your doctor. But also know that we all react differently to different medications and the best way to figure it out is to be open-minded and try.

The first SSRI I was prescribed was mostly okay. It would make me yawn constantly and randomly erupt into giggles, but apart from that, it did a pretty decent job of stabilising my mood and getting me out of bed most mornings. It didn't rock my world, though, and so after about six months I went back to my doctor and asked to try something new. I got something new, and it sucked. I hated it and I stopped taking it almost immediately. And very possibly I went into it with the wrong attitude – it wasn't what I'd wanted to try and a few of my friends had told me about their own horrible experiences with it, and so I was feeling frustrated and ready to quit before I'd even started. I took a few, and then I stopped.

I told my doctor I had a bad feeling, it wasn't helping, and that I didn't want to take a single one ever again. Extremely normal and rational decision, I think we'll all agree. But honestly, fuck it. Fuck putting myself in a position where I felt strongly that I wasn't being helped, even if a lot of that feeling was rooted in assumption and paranoia. After that debacle I learned not to psych myself out and over-research, but for that medication in that moment, the damage was already done. Sometimes it goes like that. Sometimes you've just got to do what you need to do to feel better, and for me, ditching that medication and moving on to something else was a decision I needed to make. And the next medication I tried was a lot better and made a real difference to my recovery and kept me alive through some really bad times. So you can all get off my jock.

Anyway, let's get down to business.

What are our different types of antidepressant?

SSRIs (selective serotonin reuptake inhibitors)

SSRIs are probably where you'll start your magical medication journey. My first antidepressant was citalopram, an SSRI that is often prescribed to young depressives who are new to treatment. SSRIs typically have fewer side effects than other types of antidepressant, so doctors will be keen to exhaust this option before trying one of the other kinds. They can also ease the symptoms of other mental illnesses, including anxiety, eating disorders and phobias, to name a few. The science of it goes something like this: serotonin is a juicy little brain chemical that takes messages around your brain. The idea is that serotonin influences mood and emotion in a positive way, so the SSRI works by very sneakily stopping it from being reabsorbed into your brain sponge, and allowing it to do more good. It's not a total magical cure-all – of course not. Depression and anxiety are rooted in more than low serotonin levels, but the point of introducing SSRIs into your recovery is that more serotonin in your system can help lift and steady your mood and make you more receptive to other kinds of therapy and treatment.

Some examples of SSRIs that you might be prescribed are as follows:

- Citalopram / Cipramil
- Dapoxetine / Priligy
- Escitalopram / Cipralex / Lexapro
- Fluoxetine / Prozac / Oxactin
- Fluvoxamine / Faverin
- Paroxetine / Seroxat
- Sertraline / Lustral

Each antidepressant might be known by several different names. There are brand names, which are given to the drug by the manufacturer, and generic names, which are given by whichever companies go on to sell it after the original patent runs out.

Bit confusing, sure, so remember to ask your doctor if you're confused. But anyway, those are your SSRIs in a nutshell.

SNRIs (serotonin-noradrenaline reuptake inhibitors)

These bad boys aren't all that different to SSRIs. They were actually designed to work even better than SSRIs at treating depression. No idea if they actually do. Overall it seems that it's a mixed bag. Some people respond better to SSRIs and some people respond better to SNRIs. Some people like marmalade. Some people take off all their clothes to use the toilet. Anyway.

Here are some examples of SNRIs that you might be prescribed by a doctor.

- Desvenlafaxine / Pristiq
- Duloxetine / Cymbalta
- Levomilnacipran / Fetzima
- Milnacipran / Ixel / Savella
- Venlafaxine / Effexor

NASSAs (noradrenaline and specific serotonergic antidepressants)

These actually have nothing to do with space. Very confusing, I know. Anyway, these are often prescribed once the SSRI and SNRI options have been exhausted. Though they can cause very similar physical side effects, their sexual side effects aren't usually as bad or disruptive as those reported with other antidepressant types.

TCAs (tricyclic antidepressants)

Like NASSAs, these typically won't be the first antidepressants that your doctor prescribes. They're known to cause more unpleasant side effects than other medications, and it's easier to overdose on them than others. But they can help with symptoms of depression, and might be recommended for treating other conditions like OCD.

So, there's a brief overview for you – a very basic introduction to the four different types of antidepressant. Chances are you'll only ever take one or two SSRIs. You may start taking one and then never stop, or you may try a long list before finding something that really works or deciding that they aren't for you. For some, it's a straightforward step in recovery; for others, it's not. Because there are many potential side effects to these medications, and there's no way of telling how your body will react until you give them a try. Common side effects can be physical, like getting the shakes or feeling nauseous or having trouble sleeping. Sometimes these things can be alleviated or offset by slight adjustments on your part, such as always taking your medication with food, or at the same time every day. Sometimes a medication can improve one aspect of your mental health, while having an exacerbating effect on another. I've had medications that have relieved almost all physical symptoms of anxiety but have made me almost catatonically depressed and unable to eat. Others have made me more functional and happy, but also gave me insomnia and night terrors and uncontrollable bouts of giggling. Some antidepressants are highly likely to decrease libido or affect your ability to achieve orgasm. There's really no way to know for sure what effect they'll have without giving them a go. And that's really fucking inconvenient, in my honest opinion, but there we have it. We try them, we see how they feel for a minimum of six to eight weeks (unless you really, really feel like they're not for you and are causing dangerous or unbearable symptoms) and then, if they aren't right, we try something else – whether that's another medication or no medication at all. It's chill. I'm chilling. Relaxing. Having a lime soda by the pool.

And you can find out SO much information online – from medical and scientific accounts of what the medication is actually doing inside your body, to forums where people talk candidly about how they've found them, what effect they've had, and how adjusting their dosage may have affected their mood. And this is great! It's great to know that there are these communities and spaces online that are full of people in the same boat as you and that you aren't alone. The only thing I will warn against is going too far down the rabbit hole of researching negative side effects. You'll come up with thousands of accounts of times when each particular medication didn't work and then convince yourself that this will definitely, definitely not work for you. There's this little thing called confirmation bias, which essentially means that when researching something like this, you'll tend to seek out evidence that will confirm what you're already suspicious of or kind of believe to be true (in this case: that a new medication will either be perfect for you or totally catastrophic).

The real secret with taking medications is to try to relax as much as possible and give the pills some time to either work or not work. Stay in tune with your body, flag any side effects and keep an eye on them, but don't be waiting for a certain disastrous side effect to hit.

Things to remember about medication

♣ Never take additional medications without checking with your doctor that it's safe to do so. The consequences could be fatal. Drug interactions can be incredibly dangerous and unpredictable, and without proper research you're not going to have any real idea of what'll happen when you mix and match your pills. Even if all that happens is you get super sweaty and paranoid, that's unpleasantness that you could do without.

♣ Some medications are prescribed 'off-label', which just means that they're being used for something other than their stated or usual purpose. This is why you may be prescribed beta blockers for anxiety, or thyroid pills for depression. When you're new to taking medication this can be a little confusing or unnerving, so don't hesitate to ask your doctor anything you're wondering or worrying about.

♣ When you're prescribed a new medication you're allowed to take the time to ask your doctor what the medication is for, what effects it might have, whether it's helped other patients under their care, and how long they would recommend that you give it before deciding whether or not you think it's helping and would like to continue it.

♣ A combination of medications may be more effective for you than one pill alone. Talk to your doctor about this and keep in mind that this is a totally normal thing that lots of people do. Needing more than one type of medication doesn't mean you're extra fucked up. Other illnesses often require a mixture of treatments and medications, and it may be no different for your illness.

♣ Don't go cold turkey on your antidepressants if you can help it. Withdrawal from medication can be severely unpleasant, and sometimes really dangerous. If you do decide to come off your medication quickly, be prepared for major fluctuations in mood, severe depressive episodes, trouble sleeping or vivid and unpleasant dreams, serious discomfort plus other physical symptoms such as feeling as though your brain is jolting or skipping (brain zaps), flu-like symptoms or vertigo, tinnitus or stomach cramps, sweating and nausea. Withdrawal can also often cause a resurgence in your original symptoms, so please have a plan in place for that if you're determined to ghost on all of your medication at once. Tell the people close to you what you're likely to feel and give them some idea of the things that they can do to help alleviate these feelings. It will pass and you will get through it, but it won't be an easy ride, and may be severely disruptive to your life. Not cool or fun at all, but temporary.

♣ It's up to you whether or not you think you can endure the side effects of your antidepressants. You get the final say. Often these side effects can be bearable when the overall effect of the medication is beneficial, and it'll seem like a great trade-off. But they can also disrupt your life beyond what you find acceptable. The point is: it's up to you. Nobody else's opinion even begins to matter as much as yours. If your mood has improved but you've lost your libido, it's entirely your call if you want to try something else. If having your sex drive and your sex life intact is important to your quality of life, then tell your doctor that you'll need to find a medication that doesn't affect that. There's no shame at all in it. You don't have to be grateful for any improvement at all. You're not Oliver Twist with his little bowl, begging for an extra gruel sandwich.

♣ It's important to keep an eye on potential side effects even after the initial six- to eight-week trial period is over. Sometimes side effects can appear seemingly out of nowhere or develop a few months into treatment. Try keeping a journal where you write down how your medications make you feel, and if something unpleasant starts to develop, try to discuss this with a professional as soon as possible.

♣ Your needs are likely to vary as you get older. When I first started taking medication I was fine with sacrificing my sex drive and letting my appetite go haywire because the mood-stabilising effect that the SSRIs had was keeping me alive and functional. Now that I have more than five years of experience taking antidepressants and have a better baseline of coping skills, as well as a strong support network, I can demand a little more of my medication. I'm no longer willing to totally sacrifice my sex drive and a reliable appetite unless I absolutely have to.

♣ People will always have very strong opinions about antidepressants. A lot of people will tell you these opinions without you even asking, like a vending machine that constantly shoots out chocolate bars for free, except instead of chocolate bars it's just really annoying opinions that nobody asked for. Personally I'm totally happy with my choices, I know what I'm doing and I've done my research – so I'm not interested in debating antidepressants with anybody who isn't my doctor. But there are reasonable and productive conversations to be had, and often well-meaning family or friends will have some questions and some worries that you can answer and assuage.

Reasons why people take antidepressants or antipsychotics

- To make their symptoms more manageable.
- To stabilise their mood.
- To ease or address their anxiety.
- As part of a larger treatment plan to tackle more than one illness.
- To help them sleep.

- To combat intrusive or violent thoughts.
- Because other aspects of their treatments have stalled.
- Because new symptoms have developed.

All of these reasons are valid.

Misconceptions about medication

Misconceptions about medication are all over the place. They're in your phone. They're in the sky. They're in your trouser legs. They're everywhere. They're often perpetuated by people who have never taken a single antidepressant or antipsychotic and who probably think a gummy vitamin is potentially deadly in the wrong hands. But they're also repeated time and time again in movies, in the TV shows that we all watch every day, by our most well-meaning friends and family. And they can be pretty convincing.

When I was a teenager suffering quietly and secretly with depression, I truly believed that all antidepressants were bad news. I thought that they would turn me into a zombie, change my personality irreversibly and squash any creativity right out of me. As an adult with first-hand experience, I know now that this is all nonsense. I also understand that some people don't get on at ALL with antidepressants, and I know that the side effects can be unpredictable and potentially extremely unpleasant. But I know that they can work, and that they can be a lifeline for people who need a boost out of the deepest, darkest depths of depression and into recovery.

They can also be a key part of lifelong recovery, and there's no shame in imagining a life where you may potentially have to take them forever. And I can be honest with myself and with others: some of the medications I've tried did have those dreaded effects on my mood and ability to create. I can also be honest and say that others have helped to steady me enough so that I could create more freely, and enjoy the process more, and even do so in a way that helped other people. So it's a real mixed bag, yes, but it's nothing like you may have been led to believe. Here are some of the nonsense opinions that you've probably heard about taking medication for your mental illness.

♣ 'Antidepressants are addictive.' Antidepressants are not addictive. Some sleeping pills and certain medications prescribed for anxiety can be very addictive, which your doctor should counsel you thoroughly about. But good old antidepressants? No, although stopping them cold turkey can cause physical withdrawal symptoms, which may confuse people. No longer taking the antidepressants won't cause intense cravings for the drug as in addiction cases, but you may develop some very unpleasant short-term symptoms.

♣ 'Antidepressants don't fix the root of the problem.' No, antidepressants will not put on a pair of sensible shoes and go out and find you your dream job, fix your relationships or teach you how to crochet. But what they can do is improve your stability and your mood and your ability to function so that you can do this work yourself. They can be change-enablers. In other words, they can make the worst of the feelings bearable just long enough for you or a mental health professional to identify the situational and root issues and figure out ways of tackling them.

♣ 'I can take antidepressants until I feel better and then I can stop.' This probably won't be the case for a few reasons. One, as mentioned above, you don't ever want to ditch your medication without serious thought or discussion with a doctor. It'll probably scramble you right up. Also, it's not a curative medication. Your depression isn't a rash or a bout of something nasty but impermanent. If you're taking an antidepressant because it fulfils a certain role in treatment – mood stabilisation, reducing obsessive or cyclic thinking, easing severe anxiety – then before you can take it out of the equation you need to think about what will act as a suitable substitute. If you've reached a point in treatment where you (and your doctor) are confident you have the skills to maintain your mental health without antidepressants – that's great. If not, there may still be ground to cover.

♣ 'All antidepressants have terrible side effects.' As much as I've disliked some of the antidepressants I've tried, the worst side effects have been a weird mouth-taste, bad dreams and a total loss of libido. At no point did they change my personality or put me in any immediate or critical danger. But they can cause feelings of emptiness or suicidal thoughts. If this happens, or if you feel that the side effects aren't worth it, then talk to your doctor and discuss options for switching medications or coming off them entirely. You may find it an unacceptable side effect to put on weight, or for your sex life to change. No judgements here. But just remember that none of that is guaranteed to happen, and you simply won't know unless you try.

♣ 'I'll know right away if they're working.' Your doctor will normally recommend you wait six to eight weeks before you form a firm opinion on whether or not they're doing their intended job – though some people seem to be more sensitive to these changes and can confidently call it within the first month. If you can stick it out until then and they aren't putting you in danger, then try to. When I first started taking citalopram, the first few weeks were rubbish. I was yawning uncontrollably, couldn't get to sleep for hours, felt groggy and struggled to wake up in the mornings, and went right off all food except bread and soup. But after around six weeks, these side effects all waned, and actually I ended up sleeping earlier and waking up feeling fresher than I had before I'd even started taking them. Not all side effects are permanent, and things often do settle down and even out the longer you take a certain medication for.

♣ 'I have to take them if I want to get better.' This is absolutely not the case. You may be encouraged to try them by your doctor and other people in your support network, but this may only be so you can get a good idea of what does or doesn't work. People treat mental illnesses without any medication, and this could be the case for you. What's important is that you keep an open mind and stay informed and supported by people who can help. If medication doesn't work for you, it's absolutely not the end of the road for treatment.

Self-care

It can be helpful to separate self-care into a few basic categories:
- Physical self-care: keeping your body safe; making sure it's fed and cleaned and hydrated.
- Social self-care: spending time with people who are caring; being in public.
- Practical self-care: taking care of bills, appointments and general admin.
- Mental self-care: making sure your brain doesn't turn to goo by reading, playing games, feeling inspired and engaged.
- Emotional self-care: acknowledging how you feel; self-soothing; avoiding situations that make you feel bad.

- Spiritual self-care: if you're religious this might mean maintaining your faith and finding your community, or just connecting with something bigger than yourself.
- Sensory self-care: engaging your various senses in a soothing and beneficial way. This technically might fall under the category of physical self-care, but it's less about necessity and maintenance and more about indulgence and joy, which is why I have given it a section all to itself later on. Whatever the act of self-care is, it just needs to result in an improved state of mind without damaging you long term.

What in the entire heck even is self-care?

Simply put: self-care is taking deliberate action to develop, improve, maintain and protect your overall health, wellness and safety both now and in the future. Sounds pretty rock 'n' roll, right? Effective self-care looks different to everyone, and so it's very important not to approach it as a one-size-fits-all clog. It's not that kind of clog. It's a different kind of clog. And your clog is out there! It is! It's clomping happily about waiting for you to find it and slip it on and go clomping around together as one. It might just take a bit of seeking and discovering to get there.

Self-care at its most effective is often a very different animal than buying yourself a brand new pair of jeans and making yourself an aubergine foot scrub. Self-care is every attempt to keep on top of the aspects of health, hygiene and self-improvement that your depressed brain will encourage you to forget and neglect. It doesn't really mean that you should ignrore all your text messages for ten days and drink wine in the bath for breakfast while calling it self-care.

So what else can I tell you about self-care? What is it? Where does it live? What does it even taste like? What helpful tips can I give you for self-caring your way to a better tomorrow?

♣ Make a self-care plan. The plan itself can be as basic or as complex as you like. It's all about figuring out what works for you. It can be as simple as a list of movies that you like, a squirrelled-away fiver to treat yourself to something delicious, a playlist at the ready to play you to sleep on a particularly anxious night, a group chat with people who you know love and support you and have nothing but good words of encouragement when you're feeling low. It can just be a collection of pictures of cats, or a bookmarked folder of relaxing websites, reassuring words, any number of wonderful things like that. For more information about how to make your own more detailed self-care plan, take a look at pages 157–58.

♣ Accept that you won't always be able to keep up with your self-care. Sometimes you'll be too down in the dumps and too mentally unwell and in too much immediate mental anguish to even get out of bed. You might Google self-care tips and if you could muster up the energy you would LAUGH HARD AND LOUD at all the suggestions to do yoga or eat some berries or get out of the house for a brisk refreshing walk to an organic food market. Because a lot of the times these tips are written by well-meaning people who have no real idea of how bad depression can get for some of us.

♣ An act of self-care can be as small and seemingly insignificant as saying no to something that you don't want to do but would usually have felt pressured into agreeing to. It can be a big overhaul of your life that might take place over a few months. It can be the everyday choice to err on the side of joy and safety. Self-care will look different on good days than it will on days where everything seems to have gone to shit. It can be getting an early night and calling a friend for a catch-up, or it can be calling a crisis hotline because you've relapsed and you feel like self-destructing. Let it be this flexible thing, a companion for the whole rest of your recovery and life.

What self-care should do

Your self-care should:
- Improve your immediate situation as much as possible.
- Attend to your physical and/or mental distress.
- Allow for joy and pleasure without any guilt or self-punishment.
- Involve thoughts of what's ahead and not damage or sabotage your future self for the sake of instant gratification.
- Build on itself, growing into something strong and powerful and self-sustaining.
- Be enjoyable as often as it is challenging.
- Be non-judgemental and not position some actions as silly or less valid than others. If it helps you and it isn't harmful, then it's good and valid.
- Encourage you to challenge and push yourself as often as it allows you to rest and to slow down. The action you take will depend on how you're feeling and what you feel capable of in that moment.

Sensory self-care

♣ Take a bath. Don't rush. Light some candles or some incense. There's no hurry with any of it. Maybe add some bubbles, go nuts. Don't add nuts, though, that's a stupid idea. Feel the water with your hand. Make sure it's just the right temperature. Turn down the lights. Sink into the water. Maybe use a scrub and some foaming, bubbling, brightly coloured lotion that your grandma got you for Christmas. Put on the radio or an album that you love, or haul in a chair and prop your tablet or laptop on it so you can watch some

TV, or a movie, or whatever you fancy. This is your time. There's no hurry. Just try to be mindful. Try to breathe. Try to root yourself in the moment, in this one task of soaking your tired human body in warm, lovely, clean water. Engage as many of your senses as you can. Try not to think about your situation beyond this nice comforting bath. This is about joy. You deserve joy. It doesn't matter what's next.

♣ Eat or drink something delicious. Maybe treat yourself to a smoothie or make yourself your favourite hot drink. If you have some chocolate or a treat stashed away for just this moment, sit down in a comfortable place and eat it. Lean into the moment. It tastes good. It's warm. It's sweet, salty, full of cream. Whatever. You deserve it. A freshly baked cake or biscuit or an entire warm pie can work brilliantly – hold it, smell it, taste it properly. And you don't even have to do the baking part yourself! That's the magic of it! You can buy a bag of cookies from the supermarket and throw them in the microwave and then BAM! You left them in there too long. They exploded. Back to the supermarket you go. You do it right this time. BAM! Delicious. This is the future, baby, and I'm flipping glad we're both here to see it.

♣ Do your entire skincare routine from beginning to end. Take your time with each step. Don't be tempted to rush any of them. You're not doing this to just get your face clean, no sir. You're doing this because you're recognising how important it is to spend some time on yourself. So take your time with this. Wait for the water to be the right temperature before you let it touch your face. Massage your cleanser in for a little longer than usual. Make sure your face is totally clean before patting it dry and putting on your toner. Take your time with it all.

♣ Change your clothes. Put some new underwear on – something comfy and clean. Don't pick any clothes that cling or feel uncomfortable anywhere on your body. Choose comfort over all else. Soft socks and a soft hoodie are your best bet, but whatever works for you. There is no judgement here in the Sensory Self-Care Zone. We trust you to make your own decisions.

♣ Spray what you're wearing with perfume, aftershave or body spray. Alternatively, you can spritz a blanket or a pillow, and then you can lie on it or hug or wrap yourself up in it like a delicious human burrito. Have a lie down with a podcast, an album or a book, or just shut your eyes and enjoy the smell and the sound and nothing else.

♣ Watch a nature documentary. There's something especially soothing about nature documentaries compared to other shows. Maybe it's the colours, or the fact that they have almost nothing to do with the human nonsense that keeps us awake at night, I'm not totally sure, but they're soothing in a way that few other things are. Sitting somewhere comfortable watching a nature documentary and doing your best to focus on nothing else for the hour or two that it's on is a great bit of sensory self-care. I can personally vouch for this. Same goes for a film with subtitles. It essentially tricks you into either learning an entire other language or putting your phone down and focusing on what you're seeing on the screen. *Je suis* yes please, bitch.

♣ Take a walk. Plan your route before you head out if you think that might help to ease anxiety, or just put on your shoes and hit the pavement. Put on a playlist or an album and pound the streets. Stay as close to home as you need to, but try to walk confidently, as fast or as slow as you want, and enjoy the movements of your body. Enjoy being outside if you can, or at the very least feel proud of being able to step out, even if you can only manage it for a short while before feeling too anxious.

♣ Find a space with plenty of room and stretch out your body. Start with your feet and your ankles and work your way up to your head and neck. Take your time with it. Maybe try following a guided video on YouTube. Stretching your body after you've been lying or sitting down for an extended period of time can feel brilliant – and at the very least you'll avoid tightening up totally and having to deal with cramps or stiffness later.

♣ Brush your teeth. Set a timer or play a song that's a couple of minutes long so you're not tempted to give it a half-arsed few scrubs before giving up. Brush deliberately. Teeth, tongue, the roof of your mouth. Floss carefully and then count to ten or twenty while you rinse with mouthwash and then cold water. Let the whole process take as long as it takes. A clean mouth feels good. A clean mouth feels better than a furry one. Enjoy your clean mouth. You deserve it.

♣ Wash your hair in a nice hot (or cool) shower. As with the other things on this list, I want you to take your time. Use shampoo and conditioner and then whatever other products you have that'll make it do the shiny, squeaky-clean-ish thing that makes life a little easier to bear. And then comb it out properly, and blow-dry it if you still have the energy

♣ Use a pumice stone or some other kind of skin-filing device to buff all the dry and unwanted skin off your feet. If you personally love all of the skin on your feet, then please feel free to disregard this advice. Celebrate your foot skin. If you do fancy having smoother feet, then take your time with the buffing. There's no rush with sensory self-care. It's about the journey. And when you're done, rub some foot cream or just regular body moisturiser into both the tops and soles of your feet. Make your trotters all soft and happy.

♣ Dim the lights and light a scented candle or two. Bake a batch of cookies or a loaf of bread. Burn a few sticks of incense or use an essential-oil diffuser or mister – basically anything that makes the room smell delicious and inviting and soothing. Good and calming smells include lavender and sandalwood.

♣ Brush your hair while you watch an episode of your favourite TV show, or sit in a sunlit room, or out in the garden. Maybe comb in some oil or serum or leave-in conditioner. If you can get someone else to brush your hair, even better.

♣ Have an early night. Commit to being comfortable in bed by at least an hour before your usual bedtime. Put on your comfiest pyjamas, create a vortex of comfortable blankets – and then nest. Maybe throw on a movie or a TV show or an audiobook to fall asleep to if that's your particular jam. Switch on a nightlight. Make this the bedtime of dreams. Literally.

♣ Buy yourself some flowers every few months. This can be a (fairly) inexpensive way to treat yourself to something that you probably don't get all that often. If you do get it all that often, then cool. You're a famous celebrity. Whatever. If not, this is your time. Go to the market, or order some online. Choose something beautiful and fragrant and put them by a window in your room and just enjoy them for the sake of enjoying them. You are a person in the world and you deserve to be near beautiful things.

♣ Go and sit in a warm and sweet-smelling café for a few hours. Buy yourself your favourite cake and hot drink and stay there for as long as you like. Bring a book, bring headphones, bring a notebook and pens. Bring yourself, and a willingness to sit and breathe and be there.

Boring self-care

♣ Get yourself a bottle or glass of cold water. Sit and drink the whole thing. Chances are you're not drinking enough water, and since dehydration can mess with your physical and mental well-being, you need to address this sooner rather than later. A top tip for if you're ever feeling a bit crappy and sluggish is to drink a nice big glass of water.

♣ Have a little snack (a snacklette, as it's known within the scientific community). A piece of fruit, a handful of nuts or an energy bar is a good, sensible, energy-boosting snack, but honestly there are no rules. Have whatever your heart desires. Snack it up real good.

♣ Put a wash on. Grab all the dirty clothes you can carry and throw them into the machine. Not only is it one fairly big chore down, it also obligates future-you to get up and deal with your wet clothes later on. Boring and tiring, yes, but also a little energiser for when you're feeling utterly hopeless and awful and like you're dissolving into thin air.

♣ Pick either a single task or a section of your room to tidy. It can be as simple as dusting and organising a couple of your bookshelves, or folding and hanging up all of your clean clothes. You could divide your room into four sections and tackle EVERYTHING in one area at a time. Dust, hoover, put away, whatever needs doing. When the section or task is complete, you're free to continue or go back to bed.

♣ Get all of the bowls, plates, cups, cutlery and glasses (basically anything that doesn't live in your room and needs to be returned to the kitchen) and then take them to the kitchen. Put them in the sink or the dishwasher and get them clean. When they're washed up, put them away. It'll stop your bedroom from feeling quite so much like a garbage dump and make it a slightly safer and more relaxing place for you to exist in.

♣ Organise your medication. Fish all empty packets out of your drawers, bags and pockets and throw them away. Then, when you've got all of your existing meds in one place, you can see how long this haul will last you. When you've done this you can make a doctor's appointment, or set a reminder on your phone or calendar to remind you before they run out to get more from the pharmacy. Future-you will thank you when you avoid those dreaded withdrawals and last-minute tearful calls to the doctor.

♣ Change your bedding. This can be quite a physically draining task so you might want to ask for help from a friend or sibling or partner or a large and dexterous lizard. Giving yourself the gift of clean sheets, if you can manage it, is one of the truest acts of self-care there is, in my humble and totally correct opinion.

♣ Take some vitamins. I have no idea if vitamins work or even what planet they come from, but I'm pretty sure that they're not harmful so long as you don't take more than the manufacturers recommend. So eat a vitamin and consider it a win. Or eat some vitamin-packed foods if you can. Fruits and vegetables probably have some of those suckers inside them, so grab a kiwi with your noodle pot and get stuck in.

♣ Sort out your make-up or toiletry bag. This can be as simple as checking that the lids are firmly on things, seeing whether anything needs throwing out or replacing, cleaning some sponges and then putting things back. Or you can go absolutely Jon Hamm about it and turn your make-up bag inside out and give it a good scrub with some hot water and soap, sharpen all the pencils and make sure they have their lids on, soak all the sponges in hot soapy water and then set them out to dry properly, give your brushes a thorough clean – the whole shebang.

♣ Reply to the text messages and emails that you've been ignoring. I'm willing to bet that there are a few. Let your friends know that you're alive and tell your grandma thank you for the letter she sent. Fire off as many texts as you can handle and then put the phone on charge, along with your laptop and maybe any portable chargers you have lying around (just for good measure).

♣ Take out the bins and change the bin bag. This also goes for the little plastic bags of rubbish lying around your room, in the bathroom, on the side in the kitchen. Put them all in the bin bag and get them out of your house. Banish them out onto the street. Put them out into the world and request that they never return to darken your door again.

♣ Take a moment to think about your mental health. Take stock of where you are today. Consider your levels of anxiety, depression, paranoia, psychosis. If you use a journal or other mental health tracker, get that out and fill it in. Has the last week been extra difficult? Have you made enough time for self-care? Have you been managing to take your medication on time? Have there been more triggers than usual?

♣ Book a doctor's appointment or an emergency therapy appointment. If you're doing badly and are up against new obstacles or worries, get to a professional as soon as possible. If you can't face making the appointment yourself, tell a close friend or family member that you could really do with help making the call. And please remember that this is nothing to be ashamed of – being a person who advocates for themselves and does all of their own nonsense all of the time is a ridiculous ask. Sometimes the bigger victory is reaching out and asking for help.

♣ Do a food shop. At the bare minimum, make sure you're sorted for meals and ingredients for the next two or three days. Make a short list of things that you're confident you can make, and what ingredients you'll need to pick up. Maybe that's a vegetarian chilli, a pasta bake, a risotto, or a few ready meals. No judgements from me. I live in a book, babe. You're winning. But also buy something full of 'nutrition' and 'health' to snack on as well, just so you can keep your energy up on days when you're not so up to cooking. A bag of apples. Some nuts. Raisins. Whatever. You're driving this depression-survival train. Toot toot, motherfucker. Toot toot.

♣ If you're able to keep food in your room, then fill a sealable container with a selection of non-perishable snack foods. Think granola or energy bars, chocolate, dried fruits, crisps, nuts, seeds. Anything that doesn't go off for at least one calendar year is the ticket. That means no soft cheeses or luncheon meats. Zero. Zilch. Not even an emergency brie or an SOS ham.

♣ Do some basic grooming. Brush your hair. Clip your toenails. Clean the insides of your ears. Pluck your eyebrows. Shave the areas of your body that you like to shave. If that's none? Cool. You saved some time. Scrub under your fingernails. Take care of the things that might not be particularly indulgent, but are important for keeping up appearances. Treat yourself well. Care for yourself. Show yourself slow and deliberate gentle attention. Demonstrate that you're worth this kind of attention. Because you are. You really, really are.

♣ Try something new to improve your sleep. Sleep is actually pretty bloody important – something that I may have mentioned either before or after this. Who knows what order the chapters are in? I'm not a wizard. Anyway. Sleep = good. No sleep = real bad. So try something that you've not tried before. That could mean ditching all caffeinated drinks after 2 p.m., or throwing some essential oils in a vaporising machine and doing some deep breathing. It could be trying ASMR or using a meditation app. It might work or it might not. There's no knowing until you try. But even just the act of trying these things shows a willingness to look after yourself, which long term will make all the difference in the world to how you treat yourself.

♣ Set an alarm on your phone or laptop for your meds. Do this right now. Not later. Not tomorrow. Not in several millennia. Right now. I don't care that you can't be bothered or that 'you mostly remember to take them already'. The human brain is a flawed machine, and you might not know the havoc that forgetting your meds or taking them at different times of the day could be causing your brain or your body. Maybe it does no harm at all, but this is not a risk that you're taking on my watch. It's one of those boring cornerstones of recovery and wellness. So set your goddamn alarm. Right now.

♣ Set reminders for other things, too, while you're at it. Depression fog or general lethargy can trick the best and brightest of people into missing appointments and birthdays and meals and showers. This means, of course, that it can doubly screw the more spaghetti-brained of sufferers. Hi. That's me. I'm the lovable dumbass who keeps leaving her phone in the wardrobe. So set reminders. Have a calendar that you fill in religiously. Carry a notepad and pen around with you for the things you don't want to forget about.

Really stupid things that people think and say about mental illness

None of us here are in any doubt that there's a culture of shame around mental illness. A lot of mentally healthy people don't understand the first thing about mental illness until they're confronted with it. Some people will try very hard to learn, and many will be able to grasp pretty well what we're going through. Some usually very mentally well people might go through a bout or two of depression in their lives, so they're able to empathise somewhat. But some people will never understand, and they'll never want to understand, and they'll put their fingers in their ears and sing a song of ignorance for the rest of their lives. These people are not people that we need on our team, and they're people we will eventually learn to ignore and not care about. But before this happens they're people who can do incredible amounts of damage. Which is a real pain in the tit. Sometimes it's people we love, or people we get on very well with usually, who turn out to have devastatingly ignorant ideas about mental health. These are the ones that do the most damage. Hearing from a parent or a sibling or a close friend that we're just overreacting, or attention-seeking, or being weak causes a kind of shame that aches for a long, long, long time. Especially if we've just opened up to them or asked them for help. It stings and it hurts and it can set us back a long way in recovery.

Whenever I'm overwhelmed by feelings of shame about the way I am, I think about dinosaurs, who were all huge, freaky-looking lizards. They didn't care about anything. If I went back in time to the dinosaur days, would any of them care that I sometimes feel really depressed and anxious? No. They would eat me immediately. And I think that's just so beautiful.

Anyway, here are some things that you're going to hear that are actually entirely bullshit.

♣ 'It could be worse! Be grateful for what you have.' Anyone who says this is wildly uninformed and also just ate some really bad pickles. If you're hurt, you're deserving of healing. If you're having a hard time, you deserve that time to end. Your pain requires confronting and unpacking and banishing through determination, empathy and positive support. What is does not need is some idiot who's never suffered a day of depression in their life telling you that you're just being ungrateful. What these people really mean when they tell you to be grateful it's not worse is that they don't really understand how things work and just want you to be quiet.

♣ 'Just look on the bright side!' I don't even want to explain how annoying this one is, but I will anyway. Fuelled by rage and irritation, I persist. It's annoying and infuriating because it totally misses the whole bloody point of what depression is – an illness that severely impairs your ability to look anywhere but right into its deep and gloomy peepers. What exactly is the bright side when you're deeply, deeply depressed and severely ill? Where's that light? The answer is that there sometimes is no light – YOU UTTER MELON. The light is way down the line. The light is weeks of patient endurance, medication, therapy, sleep. The bright side is not there when we're depressed, so don't tell us to do the impossible. Instead, we need our people to remind us that there's a future where life isn't like this. If you're in any doubt about what you should say, consider whether you'd say it to someone with a serious painful physical injury. If not, then don't say it to us. Don't tell us to ignore the agonising pain and think of something else. Positive thinking doesn't un-sprain an ankle or un-poison our food, and it sure as shit won't unscramble our noggins and make us feel great again. It's a useless, idiotic thing to say and you're absolutely allowed to discard this advice immediately if you're the depressed person who's just been forced to listen to it. Put that advice into the bin, my misguided amigos, and do better.

♣ 'Everyone feels like this sometimes.' I guess this is meant to be reassuring, though it's very clearly not. Everybody does feel sad sometimes, that part is true. Everybody has bad days, bad moods, bad bad Leroy Browns. No lie there. Everybody experiences emotions. Again – totally true. But what not everybody feels is mentally ill. Because not everybody is mentally ill. Some people will go their whole lives and not ever experience a real depressive episode, or have an anxiety attack, or be traumatised by an event or relationship. When they say, 'Everyone feels like this,' they admit to thinking that depression is sadness, and anxiety is worry, and a personality disorder is just feeling a bit funny sometimes. These are all things which are at the heart of so much of the nonsense we're forced to listen to.

♣ 'If you can't do it for yourself – do it for the people who love you.' This makes me want to smash an entire bag of biscuits into crumbs, it's truly that stupid. And then use those crumbs to form the base of a delicious cheesecake which I will later eat in a warm, toasty bubble bath. Honestly, it's so weird and I wish that everyone who ever even thought about saying it would choke on a small toffee and then not get around to saying it. Like I don't mean they would DIE from the small toffee – I'm not a monster – but it would definitely shake them up enough that they would completely forget all about ever wanting to say that stupid thing that they were about to say.

♣ 'You'd feel better if you tried yoga/meditation/exercise/putting gummy vitamins up your butt.' Look: I know I just told you to do all of these things, and maybe that was deeply annoying for you. But reading it in a book is far different from having someone get right up in your business with it. For starters, you can't simply close a person and put them back on the shelf. They do not like that. Unsolicited advice from people who've never suffered from a mental illness is fucking infuriating, whoever that person is. It ignores that we've definitely already heard this advice a million times before and paints us as dim-witted idiots who are too stupid to know what's good for us. We know that exercise can help alleviate depression. We're not newborn deer. We've got Google, too. And no doubt we've tried these things, and either they've worked from time to time or they haven't. But they're not always accessible for a lot of reasons.

♣ 'Life isn't fair. Get over it.' This is just a dick move, whether it's in reference to mental illness or a kid losing their favourite toy in the park. The universe may be a big, beige, indifferent entity, but it doesn't give you the right to be a prick down here on Earth under the guise of 'life's a bitch and then you die!' You're a bitch. Shut up. When someone's in pain and your reaction is to shrug and make a comment like this, that makes you a shallow, spineless ghoul. We aren't the problem. Compassionless, mean-spirited commentators are the problem. We're just doing what we can to survive. These people can go and stand very far away, in my professional opinion.

♣ 'You look fine to me.' Heads up: this is not a compliment. It's an embarrassing and stupid move to try to invalidate someone's very real illness just because it doesn't present in the way that some ignorant wally expects it to. It happens with mental illnesses and invisible physical illnesses all the time. And all the time it totally bloody sucks. People can be extremely unwell and not look sick to the average observer. They can put make-up on and shave and shine their shoes before leaving the house and still suffer from a terrible debilitating condition. Your illness isn't suddenly less serious just because some dickhead makes a snide comment about how normal or functional you seem. They don't know you. You know you. So trust you.

♣ 'I would never take antidepressants myself. They turn you into a total zombie.' I blame TV dramas for this one. There's always some brilliantly talented but troubled artist who tries antidepressants and becomes an unrecognisable square with zero personality and zero joy in life. It's ridiculous. What's most likely to happen with antidepressants is you try some, they either agree with you or they don't and then you either keep taking them or you stop. As we've covered earlier, most of the time people experience no worse than a loss of sex drive, trouble sleeping and a change in appetite. But of course some people don't get on with them at all, and that's totally valid when it happens. Having people (both friends and professionals) around you who are supportive, know the facts, and vow to be non-judgemental is a game-changer when it comes to trying antidepressants.

♣ 'I thought you had to be [insert random metric] to be considered [insert mental or physical illness here].' Honestly, what are people thinking with this one? Are they okay? Did they spill some hot soup on their trousers and are now taking it out on us? Quick tip for anyone who isn't mentally ill who thinks they should make a comment like this: don't you do it. All this tells us is that you either don't know any mentally ill people, or the ones you do know don't trust you enough to confide in you. Either way it's not a very promising sign. Mental and physical illnesses present differently in everyone. Some people who suffer with depression don't miss a day of work, others aren't able to work at all. This doesn't represent a weakness on one side and heroism on the other. We're all just different.

Listen, if you aren't going through it, then get over your broken sense of right and wrong and help those of us who are. Stop heaping on the shame and turning your back on the problem. Stop repeating the same shit that either kills people or drives them to bury their feelings and their pain and live in shame. Stop asking us to try harder when you won't even open a book and learn about what it is we're going through. Stop. Pause. Make right all the times you got this so, so wrong.

Everything I know about good days

- Good days don't have to start out good. In fact, they can start out truly flipping terribly.
- Good days don't have to involve huge and explosive victories. They just have to be days where you push through something hard, learn or relearn something, or figure something out with your own glorious brain (even when that brain feels a little foggy and scrambled).
- You're owed good days. You're as good a person as any person on Earth and probably better than a lot of them. A lot of them are real dicks.
- You'll have more and more good days as you go through your recovery. There will always be bad days too, of course, but the good days will visit more often as you get better, and you'll learn more ways to live in them more permanently.

- You're allowed to just enjoy your good days. It's tempting to want to use them up for everything they're worth, to squeeze every bit of potential out of them like toothpaste from the tube, to catch up on everything you've fallen behind on. But you're also allowed to just sit with the good mood, take the day moment to moment, bask in it like a happy snake in the sun. In the warm, bright sun.

Everything I know about bad days

- Bad days do what they like. They're naughty teenagers that act out just because they want to. Sometimes they'll follow logically from bad news or a bad thing happening, but sometimes they'll just rear up out of the abyss.
- Bad days are not forever. They may stick together and last for a week, but there will be an end. This is guaranteed.
- You'll survive bad days however you can. Use any skills that you've learned, and do your basic best to keep yourself fed and hydrated and safe, but aside from that, just ride them out and wait for them to end (they always end).
- You're not weak for not being able to go about your life as usual on a very bad day. You're allowed to call in sick, or ask your friends if it's okay to reschedule. You're allowed to half-arse some stuff and ignore other stuff altogether. Bad days are exhausting.

Preparing for bad days

♣ Know what your triggers are. In other words, know what situations, pressures, people or feelings are most likely to send you slipping into a very bad or unpleasant place. Common triggers include an argument or falling out, a violent scene in a book, movie or TV show, a big change in routine, drinking too much, hearing upsetting news, any kind of contact from an abuser. These are the obvious ones, but triggers can be literally anything – loud noises, a perceived rejection or slight, a certain song or sound, criticism. Triggers are personal, and it's important to know what yours are so you can plan for them. Sometimes you can prepare for triggers by checking warnings on movies, books or TV shows, or by letting your friends and family know what to avoid when taking you places or starting conversations. And you can work with your doctor or therapist to help lessen and overcome certain triggers. But life is big and busy and has a habit of throwing exactly what you don't want right in your face. When this happens it's good to have a contingency plan.

♣ Tell trusted friends and family what to expect from you when you're feeling depressed and make sure they know that even when you're doing well and 'recovering' there will still be bad days. Communicating with them on the better days about the future is a way to ensure that when the bad days come back around, they're more prepared to deal with them. Having to hold their hands through it won't be an option when you're feeling terrible and depressed, so talk to them when you're on the up, get them well educated and well prepared for how you're likely to feel and act. Give them a list of the kinds of things that they can do to help when you're in a slump or having a bad day. Hand them this book and ask them to read it cover to cover.

♣ Have a care package stashed away for when the worst of it hits. Yes, I KNOW, I know – it's embarrassing and corny and twee and very likely not the kind of thing that you'd normally consider doing for yourself. And if it's too out of your comfort bucket, pick someone who loves you and subtly blackmail them into making you one. I'm kidding, of course: this is actually very much exactly the type of thing that loving friends and family are here for. You could even offer to make one for a friend who'll make one for you. That way you have a tangible thing to turn to when you're feeling in need of comfort, and you'll be helping a friend at the same time.

♣ Make sure that someone at your work or school knows that you might have days where you'll be too ill to make it in. Finding a sympathetic person in your place of work can be tricky, and if you don't feel safe opening up about your illness, then please follow that instinct. If you can provide a doctor's note, it puts you in a far stronger position, regardless of whether your workplace is sympathetic or not. Having medical proof and a complete record of your illness will help you out a lot down the line, so prioritise it if you can. But even just someone you can confide in or who knows broadly that you're not always going to be able to perform at 100 per cent can be a lifeline.

♣ Have a clean set of bedding stashed away for the times when you're not going to be able to do any laundry. Have a set of basic unworn underwear and socks stashed somewhere too, and maybe some cheap T-shirts that stay in their packet unless absolutely required. Some days you just have to fake being a high-functioning human. Take these delicious shortcuts and don't ever look back.

♣ Make a folder or scrapbook (this can be a tangible one or on your computer or tablet) of easy, cheap and nourishing recipes so that you're not stuck for something to make on those days when you really can't face standing in the kitchen for longer than half an hour. There are great ideas online. Alternatively, collect the names and numbers of takeaway restaurants in your area that deliver.

Disclaimer: This list makes it sound all practical and effective, like you're planning for an alien invasion and everyone's strapping on their tinfoil hats and filling up their water guns. It's not quite like that, unfortunately. This involves things like finding a quiet place to slow your breathing, or having someone you can text or call who you know will say soothing things. It's having an album on your phone filled with hilarious pictures and forcing yourself to look at them, engage with them, and try to make them the centre of your focus. It's a comedy playlist or a meditation mix. It's a cold glass of water and a soothing song. Tinfoil hats entirely optional. It's important to remember also that this is nothing to be ashamed or embarrassed about – this is how SO many of our human brains are put together, all squashy and scared and needing a bit of extra protection. It's normal – it's just really annoying. It's just human brain-atomy. Which is a word I made up. With my squashy, weird, lovely brain. It did that.

On bad days

On bad days you just have to survive.

On bad days you are allowed to cry for hours, or sleep until the afternoon, or feel as though the sky is falling.

On bad days the sky does not fall.

On bad days the sky stays put, perfectly untroubled and unchanged by how you feel down here on the surface of this strange world.

On bad days you will feel like you're not meant to be here.

On bad days you will think about the ways it hurts. You'll go inside the hurt and see nothing but endless dark endlessness. You'll remember every single mistake you've ever made. You'll think about the world without you in it. You'll imagine that the world would be better like this.

On bad days this will be wrong. On good days, too. On all days, it will be wrong. You are always welcome here. You are here to be here. You are here for a reason. Perhaps that reason is just to make it through and find your peace. Who knows. But there is a reason.

On bad days you just have to make it from one end to the other. You don't have to achieve any more than that. You just have to hold it together as best as you can. You can escape from work or school or university, you can make a dozen excuses if you need to, you can cry in the bathroom and fall apart on the drive home later.

On bad days you just have to live minute to minute, and trust those minutes to make themselves into hours, of which there are only ever twenty-four in a single day – however truly, truly terrible that day is.

On bad days every single bit of progress you've made in recovery still counts.

On bad days you just have to survive.

On bad days you do survive.

On bad days that's enough.

How to better manage your distress and anxiety

When we start feeling overwhelming or intense emotions – perhaps after a stressful or upsetting encounter or event – it's very easy to feel as though you *are* those emotions, like they're taking you over, filling you up and controlling you. Like if an evil parasite crawled into your ear and grabbed your brain controls and started going totally bonkers and making you get bad haircuts and cry until you're dehydrated. Succumbing to seriously overwhelming emotions is easy and understandable. Look at me here, understanding. And lashing out at the people who've upset us – or who we perceive to be the cause of the feeling – is also understandable, but it's also pretty unfair to them and will do no good for your current or future emotional state. Feeding this particular monster will just drain you dry like a lemon drizzle cake that's been lying out in the hot sun.

Stopping your anxiety mid-attack would be like stopping mid-nightmare to wake up and have a cup of tea before choosing a nicer dream to go back to. It's just not realistic, pals. But there are things that we can do to ease it ever so slightly, bring it to an end as soon as possible, and potentially reduce any harm to ourselves or worry to others.

♣ Try to identify what it is that's making you feel the most stressed. Give it an exact and non-exaggerated name. If it's money worries, call it that. If you're stressed about your job, identify it as such. Try to avoid broad and catastrophic responses like, 'I'm stressed because my life is falling apart and everything's absolutely terrible.' This isn't very helpful. So be specific about all of the things. Cut them down to size and don't let them loom over you like great and unknown monsters. They're not monsters. They're problems of a certain and exact size with solutions of a certain and exact size.

♣ Ground yourself by engaging your senses. Lavender oil helps me to de-stress just a little, but you might get the same effect from smelling a freshly baked loaf of banana bread or some clean laundry. Experiment. Figure out what works for you. You can also try taking a deep breath, looking around you and identifying by name five things that you can see, four things you can touch, three things you can hear, two things you can smell and one thing you can taste. Take another deep breath now. There are many more grounding exercises you can get your lovely human hands on – a quick internet search should do the trick.

♣ Take action. Do something with the intention of alleviating the stresses that you've identified. That might be something pretty big, like actively looking for a new job, or a new flat, or having a difficult conversation with somebody about the way that they're treating you. It may be sending an email, or a text, or reaching out to somebody to say sorry for something and try to make amends in a tense situation. It can be calling to book a doctor's appointment (or asking someone to call for you). It can be downloading an ebook or taking an online course about how to better manage your finances. Taking direct action, even when the action itself seems very small, can help you to feel more in control of what's troubling or distressing you.

♣ Set aside a certain amount of time to worry. Fifteen or twenty minutes where you have full permission to freak out and to sink into fear and exaggeration and terror. Let the worry loose. Think about everything you're worrying about right now. And then when the time's up, gather yourself up and commit to carrying on with your day.

♣ Ask for help. It's the most obvious advice but because people are stubborn morons, they resist taking it. So suck it up and get asking. Your friends, your family, your partner – they aren't bullshitting you when they say they want to help you get through the really hard times. Call or text them and tell them that the hard time is happening now, and that you might need some support. Ask for advice, or for someone to help you prepare for something. Ask for someone to spend time with you, or keep you company, or walk you somewhere, or reassure you that everything will turn out okay. These are things we can do for each other and these are things we need to be open to asking for. Being open to receiving without apologising for needing is a thing worth fighting for.

♣ Fake it until you make it. Act as though you have this situation totally under your control. Behave as though you're confident and in control and, whatever's coming, you have no doubt that you can handle it. Act as though you can see into the future, and you already know that this all turns out okay. Act as if you've seen this movie before, and you know the ending by heart. The ending is you doing well and feeling better, stronger and more in control. The ending is you being surrounded by people who love and care for you just as you are. That's how this ends, so you can relax. All you need to do is make this current moment work. Right here, right now, you just have to keep going. Faced with something totally new that seems terrifying and overwhelming and completely out of your control? No problem. You're going to figure it out, take steps, make moves, ask for help, learn what you need to learn and then learn some more. This is something that you know, something you can be utterly certain of. So give yourself permission to pretend you know what the fuck's going on. Future-you knows. Future-you is totally okay.

♣ Take a piece of paper and write down exactly what you're worried about. Then underneath that write down some pragmatic and straightforward ideas for dealing with these worries. Rewording and removing the 'worry language' is a way to cut the issue down to size. Similarly, a worry journal (a notebook you keep solely for you to scribble your fears into) can help you to purge the worst of the distress and feel a little better.

♣ Identify the emotion or emotions that you're feeling. Give them their real names. Make a list if you think it might help. When I'm really distressed or upset, I find myself only able to identify with my most extreme emotion. Whereas at any given time, I'm actually feeling lots of things. So even when I'm anxious and that's the only thing I THINK I'm feeling, it's not. So look deeper, and name some of the other feelings you find.

♣ For slow-burning and less immediate anxiety I recommend as much distraction as you can pack into your free time. There are suggestions on pages 156–57 for good distraction techniques, but really any harmless (or mostly harmless) act that takes your mind off that itchy, nagging, annoying anxious feeling will work.

♣ Retreat. This doesn't mean totally flee and hide and never speak to anyone ever again. But remove yourself from the situation that is causing the panic for just long enough that you can get things more under control. If it's a situation that requires you to return at some point – perhaps the attack happened during work or school hours or a social occasion that you know you really shouldn't miss – then take yourself away to somewhere quieter and safer when you feel the attack building.

♣ Dunk your face in cold water. Hold it there for a few seconds, then stand up and breathe. Then do it again. Do this until it helps, or maybe until you decide that it's not helping and this advice is terrible. Try for a minimum of five dunks before jacking it all in, though. Making physical changes to your body can help you to trick yourself into feeling less anxious.

♣ Do some physical exercise. Whether that's a quick run or a sprint up and down the garden or some vigorous dancing to an eighties synth-pop medley in your bedroom while wearing Spandex – it doesn't matter. Getting your heart rate up through physical activity can help keep the anxiety down. This is called Science, something I've only recently heard of. Honestly, I'm not totally sure about it, but that's an issue for another time. Even aside from the physical effect, it's just a nice gesture from you to yourself to set aside ten or twenty or thirty minutes to do nothing but run or swim or walk or cycle. It gives you an opportunity to think through anything that's troubling you or just distract you enough from the feeling to curb the worst of the symptoms.

♣ Breathe through it. I cover breathing techniques in more detail on pages 265–67 and, as crazy as it seems (even still to me sometimes), controlling your breathing and practising breathing exercises can make a huge difference to how you feel both physically and mentally. There are some very simple and effective breathing techniques for countering hyperventilation and anxiety. By changing your breathing rate during a panic or anxiety attack, you can elicit a parasympathetic (long word that just means it's to do with your nervous system) response within your body, causing it to relax and for the attack to ease.

♣ Try to talk about it aloud – either in person or over the phone to a trusted person. Or, if you can't manage that, then try talking to yourself. This feels extremely odd and embarrassing at first, but it can help – and you can always pretend to be on the phone when you do this if you're worried about people staring. Vocalising what's going on can help you to figure out a solution.

♣ As your thoughts get more urgent, try commanding them to stop. Tell them to stop out loud if you can. Force yourself to correct the erroneous and panicky thoughts with accurate and calm thoughts. 'No, I'm not in any danger. My body is responding as though I am and I just need to ride this out. I'm okay. I'm here, I'm safe and I will be through this very soon.' Say it through tears. Say it with a shaky voice and a sweaty brow. It doesn't matter. Remind yourself vocally that you're going to be all right and nothing bad is going to happen.

How to practise basic mindfulness

Depression and anxiety, and the years I had to spend hiding them and dealing with them on my own, did a number on my ability to think calmly at the drop of a hat, and so now I'm doing the hard work to get back to a place where I feel good.

Mindfulness is, at its essence, learning to live and exist in the current moment. It can be applied to almost any action or situation. You can walk, eat, read a book and chop an onion mindfully. Living mindfully means removing fear and worry and expectation of the future from your daily routine. You root yourself firmly in the present, firmly within the possibility of right now and right now alone. The future and the past exist without judgement, and you recognise that you don't have power over them. In fact, you don't have power over anything except the current moment and your current action. What this comes to mean, instead of powerlessness, is freedom. These changes happen slowly, and they happen deliberately. Like getting any kind of training to stick, you'll need repetition and effort. Personally, I think this is a scam. I like instant gratification. But the universe has other ideas for me, and until I can become ruler of all creation, I'll have to play ball.

♣ Basic mindfulness can be as simple as saying, 'I am here. I'm nowhere else but right here.' You can do this as you clean the dishes or walk your nine ferrets in the park or wash your hair in the morning or drive home from work at the end of the day. The effect of mindfulness isn't to limit your dreams or keep you locked into whatever heinous situation you're in right now; it just means accepting that this is the situation right now. This is your plate. If you hate lasagne but you have the lasagne, the lasagne is your current situation. Insisting that it's fish and chips doesn't change anything. It actually makes change more difficult.

♣ Start with your breathing. It's the most accessible thing to you. You don't even have to get up from where you're currently lying or sitting. Wherever you are right now, reading this, try a simple breathing exercise. Breathe in, and recognise that as your in-breath. Breathe out, and now recognise that as your out-breath. Keep doing this until you feel more relaxed.

♣ Before going to sleep, lie quietly. Attempt to empty your mind, but don't get cross with yourself when you can't completely purge your head of all thought or noise. When other thoughts creep in, calmly and non-judgementally let them go. Don't engage with them. Let them arrive and then let them leave. Do this until you fall asleep or until you feel a little calmer. And it doesn't matter if the thoughts keep coming. You can bet that they'll keep coming. The purpose of this exercise is to change the way you react to the movings of your mind, not to shut down operations entirely.

♣ Remember that you can practise mindfulness at pretty much any given moment. You can mindfully walk, mindfully bathe, mindfully make a chicken salad sandwich. So don't overthink it. Don't insist that you're not prepared for your mindfulness exercise, that you'll have to do it later. It requires nothing of you besides a little willingness and a moment to identify where you are, how you feel, and what you're doing.

♣ Remember that mindfulness is not about winning. It's not about out-achieving anyone. There's not even really any point to it besides helping you to feel better and calmer. It's entirely for its own sake. There are no prizes or awards to be won beyond your own improved sense of peace. A classic scam. Those bastards.

How to get shit done

Getting shit done is the answer to so many of your problems. Unfortunately, getting shit done when you don't even want to exist seems pretty fucking impossible. But it's NOT impossible. It's doable and haveable and conquerable. You can do. You can have. You can conquer.

You can live a good human life that doesn't feel fraught and small and meaningless.

But you have to do things to get there. Don't look at me like that. You knew what I was going to say. Now, I'm not saying you have to do them well, or with a smile. You can do them with a terrified, anxious grimace on your face. You can do them begrudgingly. You can break them up with four-hour spells of crying and lying face down on the floor. I truly don't care. It doesn't matter. You just have to do them. And here's how.

1. First you need to be honest with yourself: you may be a person who avoids stuff that needs doing. You may be well practised

and well capable of pretending that things that need doing do not need doing at all. You may have a long history of putting things off, swallowing the terror and pretending that all is well. This may be something you do and you have done it for a long time. And so the fuck what? Me too. It's not a life sentence, it's not the end of the world. It's just a fact. So go into this with that knowledge and be willing to work on it.

2. Set your timer for twenty minutes per task. It's great when you're feeling like shit to know that when the twenty minutes is up you have full permission to stop and rest. It's just twenty minutes of action. Unthinking, repetitive action. Fill out those forms. Hoover. Throw away all empty cans. Put empty bottles by the back door. Reply to five emails. Text all casual friends back, tell them that you're fine. Text someone you love and trust and tell them that you're not fine. Ask them for one specific piece of help.

3. Don't ask too much of your to-do list. If you overload it with a random and terrifying mix of long-term and short-term goals, you're going to get dizzy and have to lie down for forty-nine straight hours. Same goes for throwing the quick and easy tasks in with the time-consuming and difficult ones. Keep it reasonable, keep it short, keep it achievable, keep it to things you can and will do that day or week.

4. Make yourself accountable to someone. Tell your mum, or your best friend. Let them know the main thing you want to achieve that day and get them to check in with you later. It's nuts how much easier it is to get something done when there are other people in the mix. It's harder to lie and say, 'I didn't even want to do that anyway,' and bury yourself in denial and inaction and fear. Get them to gently remind you, or ask how

it's going, or even give you a hand with getting it done. And also choose someone who'll be non-judgemental if you try to get the thing done but end up falling a little short, or having to ditch it entirely. Choose someone who'll be able to cheerily say, 'Well, who cares? You tried. That's enough. We'll give it another go tomorrow.'

5. Boil the kettle for a cup of tea (or another type of hot drink, or a hot-water bottle or to use to steam your face – whatever). While it's boiling, do as many other chores as you can. Wash up some dishes (or even just fill up the sink and soak them). Put a load of clothes into the washing machine. Wipe down a surface. Take the rubbish outside.

6. Do one task at a time. Set your timer for a minimum of twenty minutes and focus entirely on the job at hand. It doesn't have to be the hardest task on your to-do list, or the most time-consuming. It just has to be something – anything – that needs doing. So put your phone to the side, somewhere where you'll hear the alarm but won't be able to absentmindedly pick it up and start scrolling through Instagram. And then get to it.

7. Change the way you talk to yourself about your chores and your goals. Instead of treating them like great big looming necessities, try looking at them as small challenges to be completed and ticked off and then used as little stepping stones through the strange and confusing land of human existence. Instead of sitting there and thinking, 'Oh my God I have SO much to do. I NEED to make a start or else everything's going to go to shit,' try to start thinking in looser, more accessible terms. For example, why not work out a timescale that takes into account whatever you're struggling with that day. Treat the accomplishment of said task as a lovely achievement. Think

about how you will feel when it's finished: proud, unstressed, less burdened, way more calm and at peace.

8. When you hit a wall with one thing, put it on pause and do something else instead. If you need to organise your entire wardrobe or desk and your chest is tightening just looking at it – then stop. Look around. Focus on another task that involves a lot less time and engagement. Do that thing instead. Put a wash on. Make the bed. Hang up all your clean clothes. Then, when you're ready to come back to the anxiety-inducing task, try tackling it differently. Take half a drawer at a time. Fold everything. Throw away all of your rubbish. Start making piles of things that will need to be put together as you go. Take as many short breaks as you need. Throw on an album or a podcast or a TV show to listen to if that makes it more bearable. Because it really doesn't matter HOW you get the thing done, just as long as the thing gradually gets done. That's the secret of productivity for most people on Earth. Nobody's there watching and grading and judging you. It's just you and you. There's no competition. Getting shit in order is for your benefit, not to impress some invisible jury.

9. Break each task down into single steps. If you're feeling dreadful but know that you really should put a wash on so you can have some clean clothes to wear, make it as easy as possible for yourself. Consider what needs doing in small and manageable points. Firstly, all you need to do is stand up. Then you need to get the dirty clothes together in one place – preferably into some kind of big container or bag. Next you just need to carry your clothes to the room where the washing machine is. Now you put the clothes into the aforementioned machine. After that you put a washing tab in the machine, or some detergent in the special drawer. Then

close the machine. Press whatever buttons need pressing. Choose the right setting. Click GO. Then you're done. Maybe set a reminder on your phone so you don't forget to take the load out – or not. Maybe you're a risk taker. That's very sexy. Would you like to go get milkshakes later?

10. Consider what's holding you back. It's easy to chalk your inaction or avoidance up to laziness or depression or a total lack of motivation, but often there are way more complex reasons for your reluctance. Do you have an associated fear? Are you mistaking physical tiredness for despair and inability to act? Or maybe it's the other way around? Are you stressing yourself out thinking about other people seeing you trying to do something (like taking your bike to get repaired, or going to the post office to collect a parcel, or going to the gym to work out)? Knowing what it is that's holding you back or making a task unbearably difficult when it should just be boring is pretty game-changing. It means you can factor that in to your plans and then learn to work around it – for example, calling ahead to find out how busy somewhere is before setting off, or scheduling an appointment, or asking a friend or family member to do something with you so it's less daunting. It also means you can learn to be more reassuring and kind to yourself about the whole thing.

11. Reward yourself for completing tasks. Life doesn't have to be a rotten, difficult, mindless slog towards maximum productivity and then eventual death. That's nonsense talk. Introduce rewards, self-validation and self-congratulation. Don't listen to anyone who scoffs and acts like a natural part of adulthood is just completing boring difficult chores and then carrying on with life like nothing happened. Fuck that idea into deep space and beyond. Giving yourself something good to work towards

isn't weak or childish. Plan an evening of movies and margaritas and snacks for accomplishing everything on your weekly to-do list. Give yourself a set break after three hours of solid cleaning and housework. Do whatever you want in that time. Watch an episode of your favourite TV programme. Make and eat a delicious batch of cookies. Go to the gym for a workout or a swim or to sit in the sauna (i.e. the boiling hot panic room that some people seem to find relaxing even though it's literally hell).

12. Tell yourself that you only have to do five minutes of the thing you really don't want to do, be it working out, replying to emails, working on an assignment, making appointments, tidying the kitchen. Chances are you'll end up doing a lot more than five minutes, but even if you don't, you'll feel better for having tried. I promise.

This will pass

Your depression apathy will pass. Your brain fog will pass. Your sobbing spell will pass. Your work anxiety will pass. Your situational anxiety will pass. Your insecurity and heightened fear of abandonment will pass. Your desperate desire to self-sabotage will pass. Your heartbreak will pass. Your urge to self-harm will pass. Your blind fury will pass. Your urge to contact an abusive or toxic person from your past will pass. Your inability to get out of bed will pass. Your feelings of worthlessness will pass. Your sense of wrongness will pass. Your suicidal ideation will pass. Your inability to eat or wash or tidy up will pass. Your hatred of the whole entire world will pass. Your fear of the front door will pass. Your panic when the telephone rings will pass. Your inability to talk or vocalise your feelings will pass.

All of it
will
pass.

You're the aubergine

If an aubergine farmer was growing an aubergine and it wasn't thriving, what do you think the aubergine farmer would do? Would they shout at the aubergine? Would they try to genetically engineer the aubergine to grow better? No. They'd look at the soil and the environment, and they'd change what they needed to change so that the aubergine could thrive and flourish and be mad delicious. And you know what... get this... YOU are the aubergine in this scenario. An incredible plot twist that nobody saw coming.

You are the aubergine.

Things in your environment are out of whack and perhaps you're not getting the treatment and help that you need to be a truly good and happy aubergine, but this can change. Identifying the problems and then implementing changes and taking slow and deliberate action will make you into the better and happier aubergine that you're desperate to be. This metaphor is falling to pieces, but you are not. You are okay.

Take a break

Take a break from trying to pull up all of the old and rotten parts of yourself. Take a break from trying to fix everything that doesn't work just right. Take a break from looking directly at all of your faulty broken bits.

Instead, try planting new and better things in a new and better part of the garden. Focus on that on the days where you feel stuck. Let this new garden grow. Let the dead finish dying and work as hard as possible at growing the good and the new things that you're making every day. This is a victory. This is a way through the worst of it and towards something better.

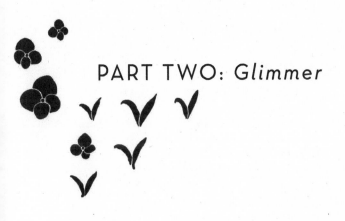

PART TWO: *Glimmer*

PART TWO: Summer

What a good day really looks like

You'll start by opening the curtains, and then maybe the window. The light and the fresh air will offend something deep, deep down inside of you, but you'll ignore it. You'll tidy up your bedroom, first by just throwing away every bit of rubbish you can lay your hands on. Put it in a black bag. Don't worry about what happens after. Don't think about taking the bins out, or the recycling, or that it's gross and disgusting and you don't want to do it. Just put it all in a big bag and consider it a victory. Pick up rubbish, put rubbish in bag. Pick up rubbish, put rubbish in bag. No, do not get in the bag yourself. The bag is not for you. Keep going. Pick up that Coke can that's full of cigarette butts and gum. Put it in the rubbish. Receipt you don't need? In the rubbish. Old food – in the rubbish. And YES – it's tedious and shameful and you don't want to do any of it. You can say that aloud, or yell it. Just so long as you keep going with it. Just so long as you throw everything away.

And when it's thrown away and the windows are open and the sunlight is coming in, you're going to take a shower. Or a bath. Or just cover yourself in washing-up liquid and run through your neighbour's sprinkler. Get clean in any way you can. Clean away however many days it's been since you were last able to do this. Take as long as you can stand and be as thorough as you need to be. Then dry yourself. Cry if you need to cry. Maybe you've been crying this whole time. That's okay. Cry and dry – and when you're dry put on the cleanest clothes you have that aren't pyjamas.

Then it's time to make the bed. If you can change the sheets, that's great. If not, no worries, just straighten the duvet and put any books or magazines or letters or precious amulets that are in the bed on top of the duvet or on the side table or the shelf. Squish the pillows a little. Make them feel special. Then it's time to make some piles. You're going to put all of the dirty clothes into one pile, all of the dirty dishes into another. Do not mix the piles. Mixing the piles is too dangerous to even think about. The clothes are going into the washing machine – or if you wash them elsewhere, they're going in a laundry bag by the front door. No arguments. Do it. The dishes are going into the dishwasher or the sink. If the dishwasher – put the magical tab in and turn that fucker on. If the sink – turn on the tap. You're going to wash the dishes now. You're going to wash them with your hands in the warm water. They will go in dirty and they will come out clean.

You're going to wonder how you got here, how you became a person for whom this is all so, so difficult. I'm not wondering that. I already know. You have depression. You're mentally and physically exhausted by what you've been through – what you're going through right now. It has flattened you and broken you and made you into mulch. And it hasn't done this to you because you're weaker or more faulty than other people, it has done this to you simply because that's just what mental illness does. And this is what you're doing: fighting back. Washing the dishes. Doing the laundry. Even just opening the window.

In doing this you are pushing back against the Worst Fucking Feeling in the World, against the terror and the endless grey abyss, against the whole exhausting agony of it all.

This is you learning the secrets that only those of us with these brain monsters know: that bravery doesn't always look like Mel Gibson in a little skirt running into battle. We know that bravery is in the little resistances, the dishwasher filled up and turned on. The late bill paid. The floor hoovered, the call to the doctor made, the window open.

The light coming in.

Avoidance and its cures

Avoidance is putting everything that needs your attention into a pile on your right, and then looking determinedly to your left. It's humming and pretending that you don't hear your own voice at your right shoulder, asking if you could just *please* come over here for a second and take a look at this mess. It's letting that sickness build inside you while everything that needs doing goes undone. It's a growing, building, awful kind of fear. It's like when you're a kid and you eat some watermelon seeds and someone says, 'Ha ha, those watermelon seeds will grow into a watermelon tree inside your tummy and you will DIE.' Which, on reflection, is a highly fucked-up thing to say to an infant. But it's like if that could actually happen. The seeds are what you first ignored. The roots and the trunk and the branches are the cumulative panic of not doing what you should have done within a reasonable time frame and now it's very, very late.

The solution, of course, is to do what you need to do and do it now and do it with as little fuss as possible.

Which would be easy if you'd only put it off for twenty minutes, or a day, or even a week. BUT SOME OF THIS STUFF IS BACKDATED A SERIOUSLY LONG TIME. The mountain looms and we shrink and try not to think about any of it.

But think about it we must. If apologies need to be made, make them. If messes need cleaning up, clean them up as best you can.

Human life is a fucking TRIP, and messing up and hiding from it is an extremely understandable move. All we can do is tidy up past mistakes, draw lines under them, and learn better for the future. Because we have a future, and it is ours, and all of this tripping and falling and messing up is us preparing for things to get a lot more fucking peaceful.

Let's be real, though – it's not an easy thing to do for a lot of us. And I definitely don't want you to feel ashamed for not being a natural at it. But being more efficient at paying bills, and organising receipts, and remembering to eat, and doing our laundry – all of these things can make us feel more human, and also save us that kind of world-weary panic and heaviness that makes us feel too useless to do anything at all. You're a person on this planet, and being a person on this planet means having lots of little responsibilities always nagging at you, dragging you this way and that. Your options are to either address them, get on top of them, and stop them being quite so anxiety-inducing – or you can choose to run from them. You can shut yourself in the quietest corner of your mind and sing a song. There is a choice. This choice is made harder by the delicious trap that is depressive pointless misery, but it's there.

And I'm not telling you this as someone who's conquered or mastered it all. I'm still trying things. I'm doing better. I'm still here. And so are you, or else you wouldn't be reading this.

We're both still here on Planet Earth. Disgusting, scary, beautiful Earth. We're doing life. And sure, sometimes it feels like we're doing it underwater, or with our hands tied behind our backs. But we're doing it, and that makes all the difference in the world.

But to do better you have to remember that you aren't just your friend. You're also your protector, your champion and your guide through this odd, difficult planet and that odd, difficult brain of yours. And that involves a hell of a lot more than just saying, 'Oh no, babes, it's okay, you can just sleep today. And tomorrow, and the next day, and ALL DAYS FOREVER.' Yeah, that's not what you're going to do any more. You're going to make the call every day to do exactly what you are able to do – perhaps sometimes a little more, but mostly just exactly what you're capable of doing on that particular day.

At first this will be very little. You'll be able to get up, make a cup of tea, sit quietly with it. And your present emotions will be sadness and stress and emptiness and exhaustion. You'll think too much, or else you'll look at a wall and feel nothing. This is where most of us start. This is where many of us live for years and years, stalling at the place between Hellish and Slightly-Less-Hellish. We live in the endless rubble of a life we suddenly have no idea how to go about rebuilding.

But getting up out of bed on a day when you really don't want to is rebuilding. There's no fanfare. There's no parade or huge outward victory. Nobody jumps out of a cake and blows a trumpet in your face. In fact, some people will still look at you as though you're pathetic. And you still feel pathetic a lot of the time. That's fine. That's entirely normal. You're doing an extraordinary thing that people don't realise is extraordinary. This is your burden. You start. You get up. Very Little becomes A Little More Than Very Little. That in turn becomes Something Quite Significant. That grows into A Life That You Personally Never Imagined You Could Live But Here You Are Now, Living It.

And there will still be days when the very idea of going to the gym, or to the library, or even getting up out of bed to get a glass of water will seem repulsive. You'll gag a little, like you just ate a bug (and not even a delicious kind of bug). 'I'm not going,' you'll say. And that's fine. You don't need to threaten or yell or tell yourself off for deciding to take the day off from a certain part of your routine. If you wake up and you know in your bones that you're really not up to going to the gym, you don't go to the gym. It's that simple. Instead, you'll attempt to do something else. You'll adjust the plan. Gym's out, but a walk around the park might be in. Or perhaps a twenty-minute meditation on the sofa. As long as it's more than lying in bed, it can be anything. A compromise will still be a victory. Having a solid baseline of shit that you're going to do, or attempt to do, every day – that's victory, too. And once that starts working (and with enough tweaks elsewhere in your life it will), you'll do more. Like this you'll stop doing nothing and start doing all kinds of things.

You'll care for yourself. You'll care what happens to you.

Like this you'll live a human life.

In defence of selfishness

It's as if at some point some of us just decide that life is meant to be difficult. We're miserable and we're struggling and we hate it, but we also think, 'Yeah, but I deserve this, though, right?' And the answer is, of course, NO, YOU LEMON. You do not deserve this. You're treating yourself carelessly right now. You're being too harsh on yourself, and you're being too easy on other people. Even the people that you don't like very much. It's all unfair and it's all incorrect and it's all just a long, painful way to ruin your own life.

So how do you firmly place yourself slap bang in the centre of your own life? How do you learn to give less to undeserving others and more to yourself? How do you redistribute your energy to finally favour yourself after years of doing it the other way?

With a lot of hard work and patience, that's how. Not super-duper fun, but that's how it goes.

So let's crack open some cold hard facts with the boys.

Firstly: YOU ARE THE MOST IMPORTANT PERSON IN YOUR LIFE.

You are! And this doesn't mean you can't *love* other people more – like if you have a child or a truly significant iguana. That's fine – but YOU ARE STILL THE MOST IMPORTANT PERSON FROM A LOGISTICAL AND PRACTICAL STANDPOINT. And the more you remind yourself of that, the stronger you become – because the better you do, the better all of your people do. The better you feel, the more you can give. When you're depressed and self-defeating and stuck in a bad spot you'll have very little to give to anyone else. And I'm not talking about productivity or your ability to thrive at work and make money for your boss here. Forget that noise for a hot minute. I'm talking about the joy that you're able to share with the people (and the lizards) around you. I'm talking about how generous you can be with your time and your love and your mutual wonderment of the world. When you're happy and mentally taken care of and on your own team you're a better friend, parent, partner. And most importantly, you're a better self.

Secondly: YOU'RE ABSOLUTELY ALLOWED TO DO THINGS FOR YOUR OWN HAPPINESS AND COMFORT. This isn't news for a lot of people. They get that they're meant to be doing a lot of this life malarkey for themselves and their own enjoyment. They're like, 'Duh, what else is new, Book?' But some of us are out here in the world being genuinely unaware that we're allowed to do things purely for our own fulfilment, advancement, happiness and joy. It's entirely brand new information, and so we need to be reminded and we need to find ways to internalise it. So this is me reminding you. Here it is. Take it. Drink it. Blend it with some oatmeal and use it as a face mask. Throw it on a cracker and chomp it all down. Kiss it on the mouth and call it Judy. Whatever you need. Just do better by yourself and remind yourself as often as you can that you're allowed to do things just for the sheer bloody joy of it.

Thirdly: DON'T KEEP PEOPLE AROUND WHO DON'T MAKE YOUR LIFE BETTER. I know this is difficult when you have a really horrid grandma who you can't realistically avoid seeing at Christmas or family wrestling nights. For most of us there are at least a few people who we can't just boot out of our life for very valid reasons. But wherever you can afford to cut away negative and unkind hangers-on, do it. Identify the emotional vampires and stop texting them back. Observe the comings and goings of your precious energy and stop doing totally unreciprocated and unappreciated emotional labour. You'll have to be brave to act on this. It'll be hard, and stressful, and fraught, and you'll doubt your decisions right up until the point that your life starts to get better and easier and less DREADFUL because of someone's absence from it.

Listen: you have the universe's permission to be delighted with yourself. Even if you believe the universe is big, cold and indifferent, you have full permission to be delighted – or if delightedness isn't on the agenda just yet, then you have permission to at least go in its general direction.

Here's a good rule of thumb:

If you love it and it makes you feel good and strong, keep it for as long as you can. Go to it often. Treat it like a very precious thing.

If you hate it and it makes you feel like an old bag of human hair floating through a sewer, consider every available option for not having it in your life any more. Whether it's a job or a person or a small cursed amulet, there will be things you can do and there are steps you can take to get away from it. You may need to ask for help, and it may take planning and a lot of courage. It may involve being tough and brave and determined. It may take time. But no situation is final, and no feeling is forever. In situations where you're unable to immediately leave because of abuse, remember there are people you can talk to, and it is never something you cause or deserve.

In making big changes and creating a better life you *will* burn bridges and you *will* feel very sad about it, even though those bridges were made of old rubbish and pain and led only to horrible people and their horrible ideas. It's okay to feel sad when you put distance between yourself and toxic people. Those toxic people and situations probably made you feel loved and welcomed and safe at some point in time. They very often do! That's how they get you. But the rewards will present themselves in time, when you find yourself tougher and free-er and more able to maintain boundaries in your personal and professional lives. When you're happier and more protected and less afraid. Happiness and stability is what you get in this exchange, but you do have to be patient. Because before shit gets good, it gets bad. Or just stays the same. I don't know. I can't tell the future.

Other people's advice

Other people's advice won't always work for you. It may in fact very rarely work for you. This doesn't mean you're faulty or difficult or untreatable. This also goes for everything in this book. It's just advice; it's as well meaning as it comes, but still, none of it is an absolute certainty and none of it has to be your cup of tea.

The thing to remember when other people counsel you on your illness is: this person does not know you better than you know you. Not even when they're a doctor or your mother or your partner. It's you that lives in your head and your body and it's you that knows exactly how that feels. However well meaning and loving the advice is, if it's not something that sits right with you or you feel deeply that you aren't ready or willing to try it, you don't have to. It's as simple and boring as that. You don't have to. You aren't letting anyone down by saying 'No' or by saying 'Not yet' or even by saying 'Never'.

Trying things is key to recovery, sure. But you're not a guinea pig or a jelly baby in a test tube. You're a whole entire person who is working every day to stay alive and sometimes that alone has to be enough.

If something frightens you right now, exercise your right to say that you aren't ready to discuss it.

If something has frightened you in the past and you've sworn never to do it but now you think you might be ready to try it, exercise your right to change your mind about treatment whenever and however you goddamn please.

Other people want you to get better. Some of the people who want you to get better have a strong and clear understanding of what mental illness is and what it means to be a sufferer. Other people want you to get better with absolutely no idea of what any of it means. Some people just want you to be well and normal and happy in a way that they understand and can make sense of.

And whether this is well meaning or not, it can be a very unsettling and invalidating feeling. Knowing that someone you love and care about is afraid of and unnerved by your illness is a strange kind of betrayal. Mostly because we understand that fear. We felt it when we first realised we were ill and that we weren't going to magically and drastically get better overnight.

When a friend or a family member offers you advice, or brings you research or herbal remedies or books or pamphlets or healing amulets that they dug up from the ruins of an ancient civilisation, what they're trying to do is help you to get better. Which is a kind and well-intentioned thing to do. But however kind and well-intentioned these gestures, none of us are bound by any code or honour system to indulge them. Every idea or theory that other people have about our recovery is *their* theory or idea. You don't have to do things that you don't feel up to or that you don't think will work. This is your treatment and this is your life and your brain and your day-to-day existence on this planet. When it comes to unsolicited and unhelpful advice, it really doesn't matter how much the offerer loves you. It doesn't matter how much they just want you to be well. They're not inside the dome of illness with you. You're here and you're fighting this and your recovery is up to you to steer. They are needed most on the sidelines, cheering you on.

Some brave things

A list of brave things that DEFINITELY are brave but DEFINITELY don't FEEL brave even though (like I said) THEY DEFINITELY ARE.

♣ Accepting that you aren't ready to do something yet. Whether that's applying for a job, moving out, tapering off your medication, taking a certain step forward in your recovery. These things may feel like failures because they aren't an active step forward, but I promise you that it's bravery and maturity to be able to say 'not yet' to the things you want to do but that aren't in your sight just yet. It's not saying never, it's just saying, 'I'm not ready yet, but with time and work, I absolutely will be.'

♣ Standing up for yourself, even if it's terrifying, even if it doesn't yield the results you wanted, even if you feel shaky and anxious and tearful for the whole day afterwards. Asserting yourself and your boundaries and what you expect and deserve from those around you is a brave and necessary step in recovery. However and whenever you do it, it's a win.

♣ Doing something that scares you, even if that something seems very small and mundane, like leaving the house to post a letter, or talking on the phone, or going somewhere new by yourself. Whenever you do – or even just attempt to do – something that has an associated fear, you're fighting back against it. You're inching closer to a fuller and more stable life. You're doing the Life Thing and you deserve to feel proud of that, you wonderful bloody egg.

♣ Asking for help from someone, whether that someone is a doctor, a friend, a family member, a kind voice on the other end of a helpline, whoever. The act of asking for help is always a courageous one. It feels very uncourageous, of course, as do most of the bravest things regarding treatment of your own mental illness. So here I am to remind you of the inherent bravery involved in putting down pride, fear and shame, and reaching out for help when you need it.

♣ Getting up and out of bed on a day where all you want to do is go back to sleep. Even if you get out of bed and do very little. Even if you go to work and do the bare minimum (or somehow even less than that). Even if you wear two different shoes to the shops and buy gum and a box of microwave macaroni cheese. On days where you push through the sickness and the fear and you go outside and do something, that is a win right there.

How to be good online

When Tim Berners-Lee invented the internet several hundred years ago, he did so because he wanted us all to have instant access to every possible dog picture under the sun. And every time you use it to compare yourself to supermodels or YouTubers or whoever, you are making Tim Berners-Lee cry. Why would you do that? Why? Why would you? Why?

The internet is an amazing tool, yes. The best, honestly. It's a place where you can find your community, educate yourself and others, find a passion, find work, fall in love, hone your craft. But it's also a hell toilet. Yup. It's a toilet from hell and we must DEFEAT IT. Because there are so many ways to misuse and abuse and obsess over it, and unless you learn some goddamn self-control it's likely to just fill your belly and head with poison and make you miserable. And then when you've learned some control, you need to come over to my house and teach me some goddamn control because I still can't log off to save my life. And then we'll go and get some milkshakes.

So here's my advice for if you love online but also it makes you cry on the toilet sometimes.

♣ Unfollow everyone who makes you feel shitty about yourself. That goes for any models whose human bodies make you feel like your own non-supermodel body is bad and worthless and wrong.

It goes for any billionaire eyebrow mogul whose life makes your own life look like a MESS. It goes for any distant family member who can't control their damn mouth and LOVES doing racism on the interweb. All of them. Hit that delicious unfollow button for all of the above. Don't even hesitate. Hit! It! Now! Don't! Look! Back!

♣ Look at the people you do follow. If they all kind of look the same... sort yourself out, babes. Get some diversity. Stop depriving yourself. Stop being silly. Follow people whose bodies look different from yours, who do different shit, who don't just post pictures of their coffees next to a cactus next to a pair of sunglasses that cost more than all your sunglasses put together. Make your Instagram feed an inspiring, reassuring, HEALTHY place to be. The internet is full of places that celebrate people who look exactly like you. They're full of places that celebrate people who look totally different from you. The internet is also full of places that celebrate people who are thin and white and conventionally pretty. Figure out which of these places make you feel most welcome and comfortable in your skin right now. Fill all your newsfeeds with these people. Then also figure out what challenges you, what might stand a chance of opening your world up, and then follow a bunch of people who do that. Look – the internet and the media can be lazy and boring and SO predictable in the things it wants us to be. So go beyond it. Take control of it. Curate your online spaces to be beautifully open and diverse and inclusive. You won't regret it, and it'll teach you something every day.

♣ Log off sometimes. Have set days where you don't go on your phone once you're in bed. Set a little digital curfew, like your phone is your badly behaved son and needs some time out to think about what he's done. And it will be hard! It will suck! You'll toss and turn under the duvet wondering what's happening on your Instagram, or if someone's replied to your email or whether Cher's tweeting RIGHT NOW and you're missing it. But you have to be tough with yourself. Make a rule. No phones after eleven on a weeknight, for example, or no social media between the hours of nine and ten in the morning. Whatever fits in with your life and your job and your routine. You can also try it with your friend or partner. Try having date nights where phones are not allowed at the table, or even out of the house with you. It's weird at first, like going outside without a shoe on or with one of your boobs just hanging out of your shirt, blowing in the breeze. But eventually you get used to it and will probably be very glad you did it.

♣ Follow helpful, positive social media accounts. It's great to have an open, honest community of similarly struggling friends, don't get me wrong. It's great to empathise and send support and be free to talk about all the hurt and the pain and the difficulty that comes along with these illnesses. But your feeds shouldn't be only that. There needs to be some helpful, practical, positive advice thrown in there. So sprinkle it in. Find some mental health writers that you like, find some advice columnists or people in recovery. Even one of those cheesy inspiration quote accounts. Also you are obligated to follow cute animal accounts that post delightful videos of otters playing with tennis balls and dogs rolling around in straw. That's absolutely non-negotiable and you must, by law, follow this advice.

♣ Mute harmful or triggering words. A lot of websites or apps have this function now and utilising it can be an absolutely stellar move. Seeing content relating to self-injury or suicide or assault can throw an otherwise good day off, especially early in recovery, so get those words out of your feeds where and when possible. It's nothing to be embarrassed about, either. It doesn't make you weak or pathetic or melty like an ice cream left in the sun. It makes you a human with a difficult past who's just trying to make it through the soup and out into the light. So mute away. Mute to your heart's content.

♣ Pick your battles. I'm mostly talking to myself here because I absolutely LOVE a good barney on the interweb. But it can take its toll, and mostly you're just shouting into a sad little void at sad little people with sad little lives. I get why it's tempting to want to shut down every bigot and every idiot and every arsehole until the cows have come home, but there's only so much you can do before the cows are like, 'Seriously babe, you need to take a break. Go outside. Go for a walk. We're really worried about you, hun.' You don't owe anyone anything. If you want to vent – go ahead. But try not to get sucked into an argument that lasts for more than four or five responses. If in doubt, follow my method: roast, counter-roast, then mute and move on.

♣ If you ARE going to be an absolutely rowdy bitch online (like I am extremely prone to being), try to do so without putting yourself in actual physical danger. There are a lot of people on the internet who are FULLY RIDICULOUS and will go to weird lengths to find out who you are, where you live, where you work, how many fish fingers you had for dinner and what they can do to make you feel afraid. It's scary and it's unfair and it's a totally disproportionate reaction to calling someone a tit online, but there we go. You're not always dealing with rational people, so just be cautious. Don't post the name of your workplace, or your hometown, or where you go to school or university. Just post pictures of your dog. And then forward them to me. Thank you so much.

♣ Know that the harmful websites do exist, and will probably always exist, but that you don't have to visit them. They're out there, sure, websites with all kinds of tips to help you stay sick and get even sicker. But they're not somewhere you need to go any more. You're in control of where you go and what you look at online. And sometimes you'll want to visit them again, and maybe you even will. But that's okay. Because every time you resist, every time you sit on your hands, or click on a funny YouTube video instead – that's a win. You can bank it. You're better than those websites. For every one of them that exists there is a website designed to soothe you, make you calmer, ease your anxiety and teach you ways to better manage your mental illness. So set up a website blocker. Get ahead of the game. Find a plug-in or a program that works for you and install it.

♣ Monitor your usage. If you find yourself lying awake at 2 a.m. most nights staring exhaustedly at your phone or computer but also not being able to put it down for more than a few minutes without picking it back up, there may be a problem. If you get antsy and distressed if you're away from your device for more than three minutes, then it might be time to get tough on your usage and learn how to exercise some restraint. I don't mean to sound like a crotchety hag here, yapping about technology destroying society. Technology is fab. I love it. It's my WIFE for crying out loud. But we can also all get a bit dependent on it. No shame or embarrassment. It's easy to do and totally understandable. But if it's having any negative impact on you and the way you live, then that's as good a reason as any to fix it up a little.

Try to stick to some rules: for example, maybe no phones in bed after a certain time of night, or you can set yourself a window of two or three hours in the day when you're not going to go on social media at all. NOT EVEN ONCE NOT EVEN TO SEE A MEME. Things like this seem stingy and unhelpful and needless but they can make a huge difference to mood, productivity and your ability to communicate with your in-real-life humans.

♣ Remember that you're allowed to take a break from the news. I know it feels like you need to keep up with every single thing that's happening at once in the world so you can stay alert and informed and up to date. But the world is kind of a mess and a lot of the news is soul-crushingly sad and depressing. Which, crazily enough, doesn't help with this whole depression thing one bit. So feel free to switch off. If your Twitter feed is teeming with political hot takes and breaking news, then get a new Twitter account that you use solely for following comedy and cute animal accounts. When your main feed is too much, head over there. Relax. Watch a pig in welly boots trot around a farm. Breathe. You have full permission to take breaks from the world when the world feels too much to bear. Because we're not built to process this amount of terrible and stressful information, and it can hurt us quite a bit to act otherwise.

♣ Download some mental health or productivity apps. If your phone is a space that you spend a lot of time in, then it's well worth making it as safe and non-toxic as any other. That's just the rules, all right, so don't give me any attitude. Luckily for you (and the rest of us), there are plenty of ways to use your phone that still fall under the heading of RESPONSIBLE AND MENTALLY PRODUCTIVE. It's not just a machine with which to take beautiful selfies and drunk text your ex.

♣ Delete old text conversations between you and people who've hurt you or who you've had to cut out because they're toxic, unkind or just aren't a part of your present. Delete old photos of things that make you sad or distressed to look at. Fuck posterity. Fuck creating a record. Fuck wanting to look back at all your worst moments. Delete the shameful evidence. Take a big, deep breath and do it. Cleanse your phone and your laptop of all of their ghosts and spirits and shadows. Hit delete. Do it because it's a step towards moving on from old hurt, and it will make your phone a safer place to be, especially when you're feeling tempted to wallow or indulge an impulse to hurt or punish yourself. Remove the option now and thank yourself later. And also thank me, because I'm a handsome angel from heaven.

♣ Remember that the internet can make us all into arseholes. This is because of something called the disinhibition effect, a fancy scientific way of saying, 'When we're interacting with people remotely we lose the usual inhibitions and manners we'd have in a face-to-face discussion and become raging dickheads.'

♣ Try using your phone for good. Set encouraging and inspiring reminders for yourself throughout the day. Set your phone wallpaper to something cheerful. Use it to send kind and reassuring messages to your loved ones (who will then in turn probably send back more kind and reassuring messages in return, thus creating an infinite kindness loop. Very groovy).

Tips for sleeping better

I've had problems falling asleep ever since I can remember. At age seven I would insist that I had never, ever, EVER been to sleep. I thought this because I could never remember having fallen asleep before. Sure, I could remember waking up, but that seemed like a very minor detail at the time. I had never fallen asleep and that was just the facts. Almost two decades later and I still feel the same way sometimes. Thankfully it's not as bad as it was. I can usually go months without having a sleepless night, and when I do I usually spend it doing something productive, like organising my drawers or alphabetising my DVDs. When I was at my most depressed I didn't. I lay awake and thought about the awful, terrible things that had happened to me, and the awful, terrible things that might happen to me in future. Also I watched a LOT of *Gilmore Girls*.

Me without sleep is a nightmare. I feel scared and vulnerable. All see-through and armour-less. An armadillo without any skin. A vampire who accidentally ate a bite of garlic bread and is FEELING IT. Lack of sleep makes me extra-sensitive to sound and light and it takes me longer than usual to process what's happening around me. When I'm sleep-deprived the positive and strong brain filter that I've been carefully crafting throughout my recovery falls away like candy floss in a puddle of water. Bad thoughts chase after one another unchecked. I don't make good choices. I don't feel like myself. I hate, I seethe, I clunk through the day like a faulty tractor in a field full of rocks.

So sleep is important. Repeat that to yourself. Sleep is *important*. For mood disorders especially, a regular and healthy sleep schedule can underpin your whole recovery. It's one of those boring realities that it takes some of us a lot longer than others to get a real grip on.

Let's talk science. Hold tight while I do a google about sleep. Think about narwhals or something. They're pretty crazy, right? What's that big horn for? Are they roasting marshmallows down there? Jousting? Anyway, I'm back now and I googled it and it turns out science doesn't know jack shit about why we sleep. Science is fake and it's cancelled. All Google knows is that if we don't sleep all of our organs start to malfunction and we get all ratty and mean and our eyes go pink and then eventually we die. This isn't super helpful or inspiring, Google, but thanks for trying.

But whatever it is that we need sleep for, it's important. So here are some tips to help you sleep better, and to make sleep a restorative and significant part of the day, rather than just that thing that you do in the night-time. And these are all just suggestions. Like everything else in the book, if you think it sounds dumb and unhelpful for you, forget it. I don't care. Do your own thing. But these are all things that I've tried and had some mild success with, so I'm not just throwing spaghetti at the fridge here.

♣ Do less work in bed. I'm writing this on my laptop in bed because I'm a fucking hypocrite and a liar and I simply cannot be trusted at all, not one single bit. But also there's stuff all over the sofa and the plug socket is over here and I can't be bothered. But I'm trying to cut down here, I *swear*. In my many years of Bed and Sleep Experience I've found that sitting at the table to do your school or uni assignments, or your taxes, or whatever dumb adult shit you need to do, can make a real difference to your sleep. When you keep work out of your bed (and bedroom altogether, if you can), your brain starts to associate bed with relaxing, reading and maybe even the occasional sex-bonk, who knows. It stops being a place where you spread out your stressful papers in a stressful arc and feel STRESSED ABOUT ALL THE STUFF. It's a place that your brain starts to think of as safe from all that hoopla and nonsense. And YES, bed is very comfortable and very reassuring and when you're depressed even getting out of the thing to get a glass of water can be an epic battle against fatigue and misery. I get this. I'm not asking you to transcend your deepest, darkest depressions to work elsewhere. But whenever you can make it happen – make it happen, all right? All right.

♣ Download a mindfulness or meditation app. There are so many different ones out there you can take your sweet time deciding. If you can't be bothered to read reviews online, just hit me up on Twitter and we'll talk options. And then any night you struggle to sleep (possibly every night if you're like me), you can fire up that bad boy and let some lovely soothing lady talk you into a sleepy slumber. Or if you don't feel like you're ready for the commitment of a whole entire app download, just get on to YouTube and type in 'meditation for sleep' or 'sleep mindfulness' or 'sleepy time speak man snooze fest' or whatever combination of words you feel will lead you where you need to go. I've found some absolute gems on there that have distracted my stupid anxious busy brain for just long enough for sleep to sneak gently in and smuggle me away, which has saved me from some sleepless nights and horrific exhausted mornings.

♣ Consider changing when you take your medication. I started taking my current medication at night because there was less chance of me forgetting it completely, but then I found that despite feeling very tired I couldn't fall asleep until 2 or 3 a.m. I switched to taking it late morning (with the help of a reminder on my phone) and within a week my sleep had improved. So have a little tinker with your medication if you've found yourself having extra sleep troubles since you started taking it.

♣ Eating at different times in the evening, or seeing whether replacing certain snack foods with other more sleep-friendly snack foods can make a lot of difference for some people – but it can also be really disruptive and harmful for others. Food is delicious and great and useful in all situations, so don't feel like you're not trying hard enough if the thought of not eating past 7 p.m. is super unpleasant (also if your work or life schedule means you have to eat late at night – don't fret). But for anyone who thinks this might be something they could try, give it a whirl and see how you feel.

♣ Set your phone to switch off at a certain time of night. Try keeping it plugged in on the bedside table, rather than under your pillow. If you're like me and you've fallen asleep with your phone clutched in your hand like a priceless, haunted gemstone, then you probably need to find a way to work this advice into your routine. It won't be easy and it'll take a lot of trial and error, but your sleep health stands to benefit a lot.

♣ Weighted blankets are a godsend. If you're unfamiliar, let me explain. A weighted blanket is a kind of quilted duvet lined evenly with weights, and can help the user relax or sleep better by mimicking the feeling of being hugged or held. They can definitely be on the pricey side, though, so this might be something to save up for or to ask your family to help you buy. They can help offset feelings of panic or anxiety at night, and give you a sense of safety that you're currently missing. They can help by increasing your levels of serotonin and melatonin overnight while you're sleeping – improving your mood and your sleep health.

♣ Let me tell you about blue light. It's light that's blue, basically. That's the whole science. I don't think I need to learn a lot more about it. Your phone and your TV and your laptop screen make this so-called 'blue light', and it's not good for your sleep health. Since most people spend around twenty-six hours a day staring at their phone or laptop, you may need to do something to make sure that blue light doesn't ruin your sleep health forever. Like setting up your device to change that nasty blue light to some delicious yellow light.

♣ Spend a week getting into your optimal routine. Brush your teeth, turn the lights off and get into bed at the same time every night. Set your alarm for the same time in the morning and try to get up. By creating a consistent sleep pattern you're conditioning your body to get prepared for rest and relaxation without you having to prompt or beg or bargain with it.

♣ Try listening to a playlist or audiobook before you head to bed. A big problem that I have when I'm trying to fall asleep is Overthinking Every Single Thing That's Ever Happened Until I Want To Die. Distraction helps. When my head is filled with a reassuring voice or some relaxing music there's way less room for obsessing.

♣ Aromatherapy is cool. I'm serious. I heard some teens talking about it at the skate park. Find some oils online and give it a go. I have one of those little mist-making oil diffusers and it's brilliant. It was only about a tenner and it also functions as a mood lamp. Bloody brilliant.

♣ Before-bed yoga and stretching can help you wind down. There are heaps of ideas online from actual Yoga People, so see what Google has to offer. Also you can do it in ACTUAL bed which is a real bonus.

You are allowed

♣ To leave any situation that makes you feel uncomfortable or unsafe.

♣ To ask for help when you need it. This might mean texting a friend, writing a tweet asking your followers to send you cute pictures or links to resources or calling a helpline – all are absolutely okay, allowed and very much encouraged.

♣ To rest when you feel tired, or even when you aren't technically tired but do feel in need of a dark room, a lie down and a break from the world.

♣ To eat what you want to eat and to do so without having to 'earn it' through punishing or restricting yourself or justifying yourself to anybody on Earth. Unless what you're eating is the hot dog they're holding and they're a stranger just trying to have a fun day at the fair until you launched yourself out of a bush and took a bite. In my experience people get really touchy about that one.

♣ To be bad at something. You're allowed to be totally, utterly rubbish at performing a task or executing a skill that other people seem to manage with ease. You can absolutely suck and it's completely allowed and doesn't affect your overall worth. Go out into the world and be terrible.

♣ To say no to things because you're feeling under pressure, overworked, too tired or you just plain do not feel up to doing them. Or just because you don't want to.

♣ To have been wrong about something in the past. To have misunderstood the complexity of an issue and fallen on the bad side. You don't get a medal for getting it right, but you do get room to be a flawed person.

♣ To disagree with your doctor or anyone else with strong opinions or ideas about your treatment or recovery. You're the one who exists inside of your brain and you're the one who has the illness. Your opinion is important and it matters.

♣ To have contradictory symptoms or to not fully understand your illness or illnesses. Mental health is a strange, strange soup, so it's totally okay if things don't seem to align perfectly or fit a textbook diagnosis. It's normal. You're normal.

♣ To take it easy. Some days you'll be less able to push through inertia and exhaustion, and on those days it's okay to step back, to postpone plans, to put off a chore and just do nothing. Resting when your brain and body are begging for rest isn't a weakness: it's a skill to be honed. As you recover you'll learn better pathways, you'll be more aware of your body and its signals, and you'll catch and manage these feelings before they cause you to crash. Until then, give your body what it needs and try not to be a jerk about it.

♣ To cry. Crying isn't an outward sign of inward weakness – it's a normal and healthy physical response to distress or sadness or frustration. It can also be really cathartic and cleansing. Sometimes I put on a sad movie just so I can have a good cry. Crying can wear you out enough to take the edge off whatever terrible thing you're feeling, or it can give you time to process and accept the true weight of a feeling or a loss or a situation. It can do a lot of things besides making your face wet. Just remember to rehydrate after you're finished.

♣ To protest or disagree with any treatment that's cruel or neglectful, or that ignores boundaries that you've already established. This remains true whether the treatment comes from a stranger, your doctor or therapist, or a friend or loved one. Nobody has the right to treat you badly and carelessly.

♣ To make mistakes or fall short of your own or other people's expectations. This doesn't invalidate your values or your progress. This is all happening at your pace. Your pace is the only one that matters. As long as you're taking steps and trying, you're succeeding.

Learn from bad days if you can, but if not, just be glad they're over.

♣ To express pain, anguish or disappointment or anger at a person or situation that's unfair or unkind to you. There is no time where you should simply have to swallow the feeling and allow them to do this. Wrong remains wrong even when you're mentally ill or when your illness tells you that you deserve to be hurt.

♣ To change or ditch your therapist the minute you feel unsafe, poorly taken care of, or even just don't feel like it's a good match. You don't need to worry that it will hurt their feelings or make you look silly. This is your recovery, and it's a normal and expected part of their job. They have to be able to help you, and if you don't feel like they can: *au revoir*!

♣ To show symptoms. You don't have to be perfect and suppressed and on your best behaviour all of the time. This is nonsense talk and it's also totally unrealistic. You're a person with an illness and that illness will not always be perfectly managed. Having a bad day or feeling irritable or tearful or having a string of anxiety attacks doesn't make you bad at this. It doesn't make you unlovable or unmanageable or beyond help.

♣ To half-arse a job. You don't always have to go all the way with everything. You're allowed to give up when something's making you feel miserable. You can pick it up again later. Life is short and sometimes it's just not the time. Forgive yourself.

♣ To be assertive: to tell anyone at any time that you're not willing to do something or explain something or go somewhere that you don't want to. Even after a whole life spent being very non-assertive and letting other people call the shots, you're allowed to change your mind and put your foot down.

♣ To put a pause on an argument or conversation that you feel too overwhelmed to continue at the moment. If you're too panicked or scrambled to think straight, then you're allowed to stop and exist in silence for as long as you need to regroup.

Things I've stopped doing

♣ Weighing myself. I'm not a playful little seal in a sanctuary that's recovering from a bout of fish poisoning and needs to be closely monitored. I'm a person who has no legitimate personal reason to know what I weigh at all times. Plus it makes me miserable and it causes me to assign moral judgement to a totally unimportant number. So I threw out the scales and never looked back.

♣ Pretending that my antidepressants are antibiotics or vitamins or small pill-shaped sweets whenever anyone asks me about them. They're medication that I take for an illness. And it's an illness that I work hard to manage and that I'm not ashamed of (on most days, at least).

♣ Buying clothes that don't fit me properly as some kind of weird incentive to work harder to make my body look different or take a different shape. This is a strange waste of money and it also does not work one bit.

♣ Beating myself up for things that are just features of my personality or neurology. Like being very clumsy, or liking reality television, or having trouble sleeping, or being kind of awkward and shy with new people. It's a slow road to fully accepting all of these harmless quirks but I'm getting there.

♣ Incentivising weight-loss or damaging amounts of exercise. I want to be on the same team as my body. I want to work with it and I want to like it. Running until I hurt myself or I want to throw up isn't discipline or commitment. It's self-harm. It's sad. It doesn't make me stronger.

♣ Considering some of my interests less worthy just because they aren't academic. I've stopped hiding the things I love out of embarrassment. Learn to confidently tell anyone who asks that, yes, you do keep up with the Kardashians, and no, you are not ashamed of that. Life is short and joy is joy.

♣ Following anybody online who doesn't make me feel good about myself. And yes, this includes every tall, skinny, even, perfect-skinned model on Instagram. And this isn't to say that I don't really love and cherish my five-foot-four, acne-prone, slightly-uneven-boobs self. But still, an endless feed of supermodels doesn't make me feel good. I don't get mad, I don't send any hateful messages to said models, I don't find ways to disparage or put them down. I just hit unfollow. And in their place I find other people who do make me feel good, who challenge me to expand my own ideas of beauty and success, and I let that magic do its work.

♣ Sending messages when I'm at the peak of my distress. Those texts are never reflective of what I really want to say and who I really want to be. They're panic signals, and they rarely (if ever) help to improve my situation. Instead I write long drafts, or scribble in my journal, or tweet from a private account about how cross and frustrated I am. I use my coping and distress tolerance skills. I list reasons why future-me would be hurt if I lash out now, and I remind myself of the impermanence of this feeling.

Your three minds

This concept comes from Dr Marsha Linehan, the American psychologist and author who created DBT (dialectical behavioural therapy), which I mentioned briefly at the beginning of the book. If you've ever pursued help for your mental health, you're likely to have come across some DBT teachings or techniques. There are a lot of free workbooks or techniques online that can be modified or adjusted to fit into your recovery plan or schedule. This is just one of many, and it's something I've found increasingly helpful for understanding my emotions and my approaches to problems.

Emotion Mind

Emotion Mind is a state of being where your emotions are controlling your actions and responses. There's no room in the equation for facts, logic, reason or any other of those sensible little critters. You're acting entirely based on your ruling emotion and taking nothing else into consideration. When you find yourself stuck in Emotion Mind, you may find yourself making impulsive or harmful decisions. Your ability to think beyond the immediate might be compromised.

Rational Mind

Rational Mind is essentially the opposite of Emotion Mind. Rational Mind is controlled by – you guessed it – logic and reason. Facts are in charge over here. Emotions aren't invited to the party when Rational Mind takes over. It's a rigid and unbendable thing. It's ruled by what is true and logical, rather than what you might want or need emotionally. When we're stuck in Rational Mind we're likely to invalidate or ignore our emotions, which is unhelpful when we're thinking about our overall well-being.

Wise Mind

Wise Mind falls somewhere in between these two states and draws from both. Wise Mind is the ideal mind. It helps us make our most positive and long-lasting changes. We can't inhabit Wise Mind at all times, but we can make an effort to get there from our Emotion and Rational Minds using our mindfulness and DBT skills. Even the most mentally healthy and stable person doesn't live in this mind all of the time. Nobody does. But the aim is to access this mind as often as possible, and to be cognisant enough of your other minds that you can use Wise Mind to solve problems and shine light on difficult situations where possible.

Coping statements for obsessive thinking

Below are some thoughts that you can use to help counter or interrupt cyclic or obsessive thinking. They won't always shut it down completely, and may need one or two tries, but repeating them whenever a thought gets exhausting or too much to bear can help.

'This thought isn't necessary or helpful, so I'm going to put it aside for now.'

'I'm perceiving this situation to be stressful or urgent when in fact it isn't. This situation is chilling. It is relaxing. It's having a big ol' margarita on the beach. I can take my time here. I can gather myself and wait to respond. Nothing terrible will come from me waiting, and it will make me feel better about my eventual response to this situation.'

'I don't have to respond to this thought. I don't have to defend myself against it. I don't have to engage with it at all, in fact. It's feeding me false information that's giving me a sense of urgency and unease, but really it requires no immediate action.'

'I've made a mistake. I'm thinking about it as much as this because this is the way that my brain works sometimes. In reality, I'm just human, and mistakes are a part of life for every single person who is alive on this strange rock. The same goes for being wrong – everybody goes through it. This feeling will get easier, and in future I'll learn to deal with it better – and more comfortably – than this.'

'My thoughts are irrational at the moment and as a consequence I'm feeling irrational and wanting quite desperately to do irrational things. This sucks, sure, but the feeling and the urge will pass and I will feel rational and in control again very soon. In the meantime, I can practise the self-soothing, distraction and endurance skills that I've learned. What's more, every time I do this, I'm winning a small but important battle. This is all true even when it feels completely the opposite.'

'Contrary to whatever I may have been told by myself or others, I deserve to feel safe, comfortable and happy. This is true now and forever, whether I can quite accept it yet or not. On days when I'm sad or scared or isolated, I deserve this. On days where I can't get out of bed, I still deserve this. My deserving these things doesn't change, no matter my internal feelings. What changes is my attitude to myself, and the behaviours and skills that I practise.'

'Aiming for perfection is unrealistic. I'm good enough as I am now and I'm working on getting better at the things that are dysfunctional or that won't bring me joy long term. My work is not just about getting better at everything, it's also about accepting my limits and celebrating what's different about me.'

How to deal with rejection or fears of abandonment

In a situation where someone treats you in a way that triggers an overwhelming feeling of fear or rejection, your impulse may be to act on that feeling at once, to seek immediate validation and reassurance. This is a natural and understandable impulse, and it doesn't make you weak or crazy. But it's not a healthy or intelligent impulse, and acting on it won't work in your favour long term.

♣ Consider every single neutral reason why the person in question might have behaved this way. For example, if someone hasn't responded to a text that you sent them, the most neutral reasons would be: they're busy and haven't seen it, they're driving or watching a film, they're asleep or in a different room, their phone is on silent, or perhaps it's out of battery. Perhaps they're dealing with something unpleasant or time consuming themselves and need space to deal with it. Think of them all. List them in your head. Maybe twice if necessary. And then simply say: 'I can't predict the future, I don't know exactly what's happening, but I'm going to accept that these are as likely explanations as any for what happened.'

♣ Don't act immediately on feelings of abandonment or rejection. You'll be incredibly tempted to. You'll feel as though you can't breathe until you say something. You'll be longing to react to the situation, to lash out, to call and call and call until someone gives you an answer as to why they've done something or not done something, to confirm or deny, to comfort, to reassure, to fix what you perceive to be shattered. You might want to apologise for nothing, or demand an apology for something that you've perceived as a hurtful or intentional rejection, but may actually just be nothing. But don't act on your most heightened and terrified impulse here. Doing better in future requires that you resist acting now, and wait out the worst of the feeling until you're able to think more clearly, and then choosing a course that's informed by what we'd like our life to look like, and not what it necessarily looks like now. If you've been drinking, your ability to control the impulse to act may be even more diminished. It cuts the fuse shorter and it hands you the match. Practice and determination are how you defeat this impulse.

♣ Remember that your brain lies to you. We cover this elsewhere but it bears repeating (and then repeating again and again until eventually we start to believe it). Your brain can be convinced of things that are utterly untrue and based in sludgy ridiculous falsehood. Your brain can be very convincing when it gets a hold of something. It's like a puppy when it takes a liking to a certain chew toy – it's not giving that sucker up easily. And no, this doesn't mean you're crazy. It is categorically NOT CRAZY for you to feel totally convinced of something that isn't actually accurate – not at all. It just means that you need to set up a kind of internal auditing system for your thoughts, and take the time to step back from very distressing convictions and subject them to a little line of questioning.

How to practise distress tolerance

Distress tolerance means protecting yourself physically and mentally during an incredibly unpleasant or upsetting time. It means learning skills, exercises and activities to practise when you're feeling deeply distressed and unsettled that will hopefully tide you over and keep you safe until you feel better or the situation is resolved.

Distract yourself

There are lots of ways you can distract yourself when you're feeling emotionally terrible. But let's be real: none of them are going to give you the immediate relief that striking back at the person or people who've hurt you would give. It just doesn't work like that. You have to choose to try these methods rather than firing back or engaging in unproductive confrontation or self-destructive activities. And you'll do this because something in you wants to be better and feel better and get better.

So what are your options for distraction?

You can keep yourself busy with an activity. It can be a chore, like hoovering your room or tackling a pile of ironing. It can be dancing madly or going for a run or doing an exercise video on YouTube. It can be something that is intended to be fun, like a game or a puzzle or an online quiz. You can watch a lecture or some stand-up comedy online. Anything that partly shifts your focus away from the distressing event and onto something else is a winner. It works because it helps relieve the immediate pressure of your situation and keeps you from acting impulsively or saying something that you don't fully believe or support, something that will cause you further pain down the line. And no, it's not going to make a huge immediate difference, or turn your mood or your feeling about the person or the event around, but it might buy you some time and keep you from doing something that later hurts you further.

Soothe yourself

It's time to get sensory. Think of all of the indulgent things that women get up to in TV advertisements for chocolate bars. That's the shit you need to get into – no matter who you are or how you feel about chocolate. Engage your senses. Put on your comfiest and cleanest clothes. A pair of warm socks. A light flannel shirt and boxers. A big romper that makes you feel like an enormous baby. Engage your sense of smell with a candle or a room fragrance or a bag of salt and vinegar crisps. Spray your favourite scent on a cushion and scream-cry into it. If you can stand to eat, have something delicious. If you're too upset for food, try drinking a glass of cool water and brushing your teeth slowly and deliberately. A shower can do wonders, even if you just stand under the warm water. If you have the energy to wash your hair and give yourself a good scrub and then cover yourself in body butter like a marinating aubergine – do it. It will engage your senses, distract you, and it's an ENTIRELY positive act, so you don't need to feel an ounce of guilt. Same goes for a bath. If you can focus on filling the bath, getting it the right temperature, adding bubbles and maybe a few salts if you're trying to show off – go for it. Doing something indulgent for yourself, even if the distress is still present, is like a big middle finger to whatever it is that tells you you aren't deserving of good and nice things.

Change your environment

If it's the middle of the night or you don't feel like leaving the house is an option, try changing rooms. Go and have a lie-down on the cool bathroom floor, or have a sit on the sofa under a blanket with a big glass of water. During a very distressing event your bedroom will probably feel like the only safe place on Earth, but those same four walls are going to start bugging the hell out of you if you don't change your scenery for at least a little while. If you're able to go outside, muster up as much energy as possible, and give it a go. Maybe just for a sit in the garden with a drink, or a walk around the block to give you something else to focus on for a while. Being outside in the world can also help keep your mind busy enough that the distressing thought or situation gets a little lost in the noise and the sensations of whatever public space you go into. (Though this isn't always the case, so make sure you consider whether your mental state might be put in more danger if you overwhelm yourself by being around crowds or in loud public spaces.)

Disrupt the thoughts

Snap a rubber band on your wrist. Splash very cold water on your face. Put on some headphones and play loud music. Speak to yourself very firmly – either out loud or in your head: 'This is going to pass. You are not going to fall into this, you are not going to get trapped. You are going to feel calm very soon. I promise you.' Repeat as necessary. Repeat through tears. Repeat until you fall asleep.

How to set (and achieve) clear goals

Here's what you want:

To get a new job. To move house, or city, or country. To date without risking emotional immolation at the first hint of rejection. To laugh more. To go places on your own. To sleep through the night before a big day. To not burst into tears when you can't figure out how a door works. Is it push? Is it pull? WHY AREN'T THEY ALL BOTH?

Talking clearly to yourself about your goals can help. It can also feel like trying to text while wearing oven gloves: frustrating and ridiculous and honestly why the fuck are you even bothering? But you should bother, because having something to work towards makes living through the present's nonsense a lot more bearable. Knowing that there's some potential shining future might make you stop and think: 'This could be worth staying alive for. If there's even the slightest chance of things looking and feeling a little like that, then fuck it: I'll stick around. I'll give my all for that.'

1. Decide a baseline. My everyday baseline is really simple – it has to be. It has to be as realistic on my worst day as it is on my very best day. My baseline is this: get out of bed, try to take a shower, brush my teeth, make my bed, eat as nutritiously as I can, get as close to full hydration as possible, leave the house at least once, take my meds. That's literally it. With your own baseline you need to be realistic and you also need to be prepared to have to wrestle with it some days.

2. Break goals down into their most basic parts. For example, getting the job of your dreams almost never involves just turning up somewhere and asking for it. If you'd need a qualification,

write down every part of that particular process. Then think about what else you'll need to do. For example, you'll want to do your research. You'll want to find people already working in that field and reach out. You'd need to make sure your CV or résumé was strong and appropriately formatted. Whatever the goal is, look critically at it and ask what steps it involves, then work out an individual plan for each step.

3. Be prepared to be a bit overwhelmed at times, and know that this feeling doesn't indicate weakness. I get really freaked out by anything I've never done before, and it takes a few shockingly executed attempts and a lot of coaxing and reassuring before I can do it for real. And that's okay!

4. Give yourself more time. Rushing yourself will not end well. Seeing happiness and success as places that you're going to arrive at and then never leave rarely ends in anything but disappointment. Instead, remember that life will always be shifting. Things will go one way and then they will go the other way. Life doesn't care about your timelines. Far better to commit to working on something a little every day (or week) and putting no further pressure on it.

5. Ask for help. People rarely get anywhere good by forging ahead completely on their own. This is your life and there are no extra points for refusing to ask for help. Things just take longer, you feel more frustrated, and you're less likely to make it where you want to go. So ask your friends and your family for guidance and opinions and thoughts about your plans. Talk to teachers or colleagues about what you're aiming for, and see how they can help. Discuss your objectives with your doctor or therapist and ask them what they think.

How to practise the ABC Skill: part 1

Firstly: what is it? The ABC Skill is actually three skills. I've tricked you. I've trapped you. I've deceived everyone and I would do it again. The three skills are all in the pursuit of the same kind of thing, though, so I think you can let me off this time.

The whole point of all three of these skills (separately and together) is to help you to grow and nurture your emotional resilience so that you're less affected by triggering situations when they arise and more able to handle the inevitable low periods and fluctuations that can be part and parcel of many mental illnesses.

A stands for Accumulate positive experiences/emotions
B stands for Build mastery
C stands for Cope ahead

Let's start at the beginning. How do you accumulate positive experiences and emotions?

Simply by doing things that you enjoy doing and doing them in a mindful way. These things should be things that increase your quality of life, things that you can take genuine pleasure and joy in, and things that don't later come back to hurt you or cause you shame or displeasure. For example, taking an absolute boatload of drugs and committing crimes might make you feel great in the moment, but overall it's probably going to hinder you and your recovery. So pick something else. Here are some options: you can go for a long walk or a drive somewhere scenic and relaxing, you can eat something delicious, you can spend quality time with people that you love, or with pets, you can write in a journal, you can sketch or draw, you can write poetry or stories, you can watch a favourite film or TV show. There are plenty more things you can do, but I got tired of listing them. I wandered off to get an ice-cream sandwich. You get the gist, though.

And you may be at a place in your life and your recovery where positive or pleasant experiences are thin on the ground. You might have little to no interest in going out and doing the things that used to make you happy. So you have to do things that are in reach. You have to accumulate positive experiences that are small before you can accumulate positive experiences that are bigger. Do good and pleasant things that are possible now and at every possible point going forward.

Make a list of things that you find fun or pleasurable. They can be small and easy to accomplish: things like sketching or baking or playing a musical instrument. They can be long, hot baths. Carrot cake with extra icing. Playing five-a-side football. Painting your nails. Styling your hair. Singing loudly in a karaoke bar. Meeting new people. Sleeping in late. Waking up early and going for a swim in the freezing-cold ocean. Maybe you love nothing more than finishing an outrageously difficult cryptic crossword or a 9,000-piece jigsaw puzzle. Whatever it is, do it often and do it without shame.

How to practise the ABC Skill: part 2

A stands for Accumulate positive experiences/emotions
B stands for Build mastery
C stands for Cope ahead

Build mastery: this skill is here to remind us to keep working on getting better and stronger and more in tune with our talents. To put it in basic terms: achieving things makes us feel good. It makes us feel stronger and more powerful and more able to survive.

It demonstrates to us that we're capable of things beyond barely scraping by. It sets us apart from every past version of ourselves who wasn't able to do what we wanted to do when we wanted to do it. It lights a little spark and keeps it shining.

Building mastery is about making a commitment to a task and then seeing it through to the end. So set aside some time every day to work on something that you're good at or want to be better at. This can be as simple as downloading a language-learning app and using it on your commute home, or when you're on the toilet, or in the fifteen minutes before you go to bed.

Take time too to do the things that you're already good at, things that you know you can succeed at, things that will make you feel proud of yourself without much effort. So if you're a whizz at Sudoku or can do a Rubik's Cube in sixty-nine seconds, then indulge the part of your brain that lights up when it achieves something tricky. Don't neglect it in favour of doing things that you aren't very good at.

Always give yourself permission to take a step back and do the slightly easier thing. If you're feeling overwhelmed or out of your depth, then dial back the difficulty and work back up to where you started from. This is how we get better and how we eventually thrive.

How to practise the ABC Skill: part 3

A stands for Accumulate positive experiences/emotions
B stands for Build mastery
C stands for Cope ahead

The purpose of this coping ahead skill is to help us be cognisant of difficult or stressful situations before they happen, so we can prepare ourselves for if and when they do arrive.

These situations don't have to be worst-case scenarios. They can be traffic jams or big family parties or being in a busy public place. Knowing that you've thought ahead and planned for these commonly triggering moments can make a big difference to how you feel when you're thrown into them again.

So start by describing the situation that you're going to face. Be specific and factual and try to steer clear of looking at it through an emotional or anxious lens. Channel your logic mind. Consider and then work through all of the skills and the strategies you know that may help you to cope with the situation ahead of you. If you're able to write out the steps of these skills, then do so. And then try to visualise yourself using them. Research what you'll need to do and say and then imagine yourself doing and saying those things perfectly, and getting through the situation with ease and poise and courage.

Knowing what situations or factors trigger feelings of vulnerability and fear is the first step, so try to make a list of all the things that you know you don't cope well with at the moment, and whenever you have spare time, try to write a few action plans. Are there certain meditations that you can download onto your phone? Can you carry earplugs with you wherever you go, or something sprayed with your favourite scent? Can you reach out to certain friends or family members to let them know that you're worried about something, and ask them to have your back or cover for you if you need to dip out of an event for a little while?

Caring less can be a
life's work

Caring less what other people think requires a lot of work, especially after a lifetime of caring very, very much what other people think. It can feel like unlearning something vital and important, and your brain and heart may work very hard against you on this one.

Repeat after me: the people who don't like me don't have to like me. These people don't have to think I'm the most wonderful person on Earth. The lens through which these people see me may very well be inaccurate, and it may always be inaccurate. Mental illness confuses some people, and they don't know enough to look beyond it and separate the symptoms from the person. And that's actually okay. Because you know enough, and there are enough of us around who also know enough. And that's enough.

Your best is good enough

Instead of telling yourself or other people that you're bad at something, try saying that it's something that you need help with. Living with a mental illness or a learning difficulty or a disability makes things hard and they'll often make having help or learning new shortcuts a necessity.

Your best is good enough. Your best may not bring you up to the same pace or the same quality as other people around you, but that doesn't mean it's worthless and you should pop yourself into the nearest dustbin. It just means you'll need ways to bridge the gaps, to figure out ways to make your day-to-day life easier. This is something I need to do, and will need to do for the rest of my life. In the past I wasn't happy to admit this, but I can now that I know where to look for help and how to ask for it, I'm able to stand up and admit to the things that don't work quite the way I'd like them to. Talking helps. Finding a community of people who are similarly impaired or struggling also helps.

Because your deficits may absolutely be an enormous pain in the left tit, and they may make certain areas of your life really bloody difficult to navigate. But they're genuine problems, and the only way you'll make headway with them is by finding new and better solutions (and then practising really damn hard). There's no universal system; there's no one solution or answer. There's you, and there's what you're up against, and there's the things that you can try to make them less disruptive.

And forget that nonsense about loving and embracing all of your flaws. You don't have to love the things that impair and disrupt your life. You just have to see them as workable, and never just unique to you. Everybody's fucked and everybody has a brilliance in them.

Let yourself be good and honest and committed to life and know that this is all you can do. Know that it's enough.

PART THREE: *Sunrise*

You're probably already doing all right

You're not wrong for not exercising 'enough', for watching TV instead of reading Russian literature or doing yoga in the park while eating an organic avocado and listening to a podcast about the moon. THE MOON IS NOT EVEN REAL, PROBABLY. So let's just forget about it. Let's forget about the perfect life, too. Let us instead commit to making a real effort to accept reality, and to not be a jerk to ourselves about it. Because being a jerk to ourselves about stuff is a waste of precious daylight.

Recovery and getting better have to involve checking the way we talk to ourselves, the way we frame pleasure and how often we allow ourselves to do nice things without lashing out at ourselves afterwards. Having a good relationship with ourselves means learning to enjoy the things that we do for comfort and accepting the fact that we bloody deserve them. We were not built to suffer, despite what we've been telling ourselves all this time. I want you to know this about yourself: you were not built to abstain and restrict and seethe and hurt and refuse and suffer. You were built for loveliness and goodness. You deserve pleasure and grace and joy. But you also deserve the hard-won rewards of recovery, so make time for the hard things too. Set aside real hours every week in which to work on your wellness, your craft, your learning, your curiosity. All of it. Go to the doctor's. See if physical activity or pushing yourself to go outside every single day helps. Take your medicine on time. Try meditating. Write down every single thing that makes you anxious and then gradually expose yourself to them, little ones first and then bigger ones. Swap your coffee for green tea for a week and see if your anxiety chills out a bit. And when you're scared – pull back. Sink into safety. Text a friend who gets it. Tweet me! I'll revel in your accomplishments and send you the trophy emoji and tell you how proud I am of what you did, even if what you did was leave the house and walk to pick up your prescription. Reward little steps. But never never stop wanting to move forward.

On bad days, do your best with what you have. Push through as much of the fog as you're able to and grab at whatever progress or goodness you can. Then later, when you've reached your limit, you can sink into bed and watch a movie. Because you're allowed to do that too! You're allowed to decide to go back to sleep, to watch TV, to skip something that fills you with dread. And when Netflix asks 'are you still watching this?' you're allowed to say, 'HELL YES, I AM, YOU JUDGEMENTAL ROBOT BITCH. MIND YOUR BUSINESS *POR FAVOR*.' You're allowed to have a big long cry. You're allowed to mess up at work, or skip a family event, or flake on a friend when you're feeling utterly hopeless and rotten and too depressed to deal with people – just make sure you explain and make it up to them when you're feeling better. These are human things, and not a single one of us is capable of getting everything right all the time – especially not when we're depressed or anxious or mentally shaky in some other way. So repeat after me (aloud, or if you're on the bus you can do it in your head): 'I am a person who makes decisions for comfort. This is not a problem. My self-care will involve doing the boring necessary things that I need to do, it will involve making a real effort to do things that I know need doing, and it will involve facing up to times when I fail, and learning instead of punishing myself for it.'

Self-identification

We're all too quick to define ourselves by the things we don't like about ourselves. We're all like: 'Well, I fucked up that one time eighty-four years ago so I guess I'm a fuck-up FOREVER.' This kind of talk is nonsense and it needs to be flushed back to hell where it belongs. We have to unlearn this language and replace it with a sensible, considered language, one which is honest, but also optimistic – one that's rational, but also as hopeful as you can stand it to be.

You need to work out a way to define yourself as all of the positive things that you are. I am Good. I am Kind. I am Talented. I have depression. It makes a lot of stuff suck sometimes. It's something I will have to live with. I will live with it with as much grace as I am able. I am also a writer. A friend. A daughter. A person who likes pickles a lot and is deeply suspicious of postmen.

Now you try it. Maybe you're a person who believes in something. An activist. A poet. An inventor. A singer. Someone who makes miniature ceramic penises that you sell online. Whatever it is, say it loudly and say it firmly. Say it with as much conviction as you can muster. Say it even when the walls are tumbling and your heart is breaking open. Eventually you'll start to believe it.

But what else are you?

Well – you are a person, firstly and foremostly. You are not a lamp or a clock or a decorative pillow on a sofa, sitting, tipping over, being plumped and righted and leaned against night after night. You're a person with blood and a brain and a heart and a combination of experiences unique to you.

You're so many things. Perhaps you're a person who feels things incredibly strongly. Perhaps you're a person who cries, who makes mistakes, and then over-identifies with them for years. A person who does the wrong thing still, despite knowing better. A person who drinks too much. Who doesn't know how to scramble eggs, or what size bra to wear, or how to parallel park.

You are a person who has struggled and struggles still.

You're very tired.

You're very hopeful.

You're very scared somedays by the way your brain works.

You're tentatively, gently, fearfully exploring the idea of feeling better.

What else are you? The truth is nobody on Earth is capable of seeing themselves quite right. There's too much water under that bridge: too much history. But honestly, just the act of trying to know yourself is almost guaranteed to make you feel less and less yourself. A truly wild fucking ride, right?

So, listen.

If you go about self-defining as a worthless bag of bees then the world will collude in this fantasy and your misery will be real and you will struggle to get out of bed. It will be your go-to excuse for everything. It will be your Get out of Trying Free card. Do Not Pass Go; Do Not Collect Any Single Chance of Making This Weird Life At All Bearable or Interesting.

So stop it. Instead I want you to try to self-define as a question mark, a work-in-progress, a shape-shifter, a magical egg that cannot be defined. THESE THINGS HAVE POTENTIAL. They're not inherently good or inherently bad. They have wriggle room.

These things are allowed to make mistakes, they're allowed to learn, they're allowed to have friends and hobbies and potted plants that they feed with water and sunlight and talk to every single morning. They're allowed to have really bad days slap bang in the middle of recovery. They're allowed to be selfish, and make mistakes, and be human. Because they can recognise that they are a wonderful work in wonderful progress.

So please don't settle miserably into one definition. Be like water: slip between states. Ice cube in the morning, steam in the afternoon. Go to bed and wake up changed. Wake up and be bewildered and awed at the constant changing and improving of you. Delight in the mistakes and the learning and the long, arduous nonsense of it all. It will all of it be weird and new and terrifying – that's pretty much a guarantee. The universe requires life to be these things. And there will still be long stretches where it all goes to hell and you go back to unhealthy coping strategies and self-destruction and misery. You'll slip back into this un-living, uncertain, unbearable in-between and it will feel like it's going to go on forever and ever and it won't ever stop. It will stop. Go there and then come back again. Let it happen to you and then when it's done happening, take a deep breath and start the whole process over again. Figure out what trips you up and then make knee pads. Metaphorical knee pads.

These knee pads might be realising that you get more depressed after getting drunk, or finding out your medication interacts with alcohol, then deciding you won't get drunk so much any more.

These knee pads might be finding that you're oversharing with strangers and partners because you're lacking an outlet for your feelings, and then reaching out to a counsellor or therapist or your friends and family. The padding is small but deliberate everyday actions. So pad yourself up. Be the pad you want to see in the world. You're a pad bitch, baby, you were born this way. That's a Lady Gaga reference in case you're one of my grandmas who is reading this. Hi Nan. Love you. Sorry for doing so many swears in the book.

So here's the real truth of it: having an unfixed sense of identity will trip you up time and time again in your recovery. Low self-concept (not being able to firmly identify who you are, what you like, what you believe in, what makes you truly happy) is a monster that I'm still wrestling with. But what I do know is this: if I do more of the things that I know to be good and brave and in pursuit of happiness for myself and others, I'll figure myself out quicker than if I don't.

That's all I have to be and that's all I have to do. I just have to try, and I have to be kind and good as often as possible. That's all. That's everything.

Failing better

Recovering from any mental illness involves getting a lot of stuff wrong. I've personally got it so phenomenally wrong so many times that it's a wonder that the Queen of England herself hasn't tried to chop my head off with a royal spork.

But it's like that man said in that thing that one time: 'Fail, then fail better. Then fail worse. Then cry. Then eat a plate of toast and try again.' It's one of the most beautiful quotations of all time and I'm actually crying just writing this. You're crying too.

Well, anyway, it's just like that. You have to fuck up. Not like, 'Well, alrighty then – HEY HO – failure and mistake-making are inevitable so better get used to it.' No, it's more like it is absolutely imperative that you make mistakes, fuck up, get it terribly, horribly wrong, because that's how you learn. You don't learn by reading about it in some dumb book. Hell no. Reading is for NERDS and WIENERS. Writing is even worse and you must never do it.

Anyway. Mistakes are where the lessons are. To live a better life you've really just have to get stuck into the failure and the mess and the confusion and the hell of what's happening right now. You have to get more than familiar with failure. You have to take failure to a show. You have to buy it a steak and kiss it on the mouth. That's how you heal. That's how you make better decisions in future.

So you have to apply for a boatload of jobs and you have to get turned down for a boatload of jobs. You have to relapse in your recovery and you have to fall all the way back down again. We all do it and we all suffer and hate ourselves and declare ourselves fuck-ups and losers and space-wasters and nonsense-cobblers and mistake-squids, and we lie down on the floor and give up for a while. And then sometime later, when the shame and the sadness have worn off a bit and we start to feel a bit peckish, we get up, dust off and we go get forty chicken nuggets and start the process all over again. And this time we know more. We know where the traps are and we know more of what we're up against and we're tougher this time around.

Rejection and failure never stop happening. What can change, though, is how we process them, how we automatically react, and how we talk to ourselves about what's happened. We can explore (non-judgementally) what we feel and what we'd like to do differently going forward. And this is something we can get very good at. But the simple act of not getting it right? Yeah, that happens forever and ever. Even while writing this chapter one of my editors emailed to politely tell me that an article I'd written that I thought was solid gold was actually no good at all and needed almost totally rewriting. Earlier this week I approached a dog and it turned its back on me. I was devastated. Life can be really painful, my friends, and we must learn to bear it together. The only alternative is to just flee civilisation and live a solitary life in a cave, surviving on moss and rainwater. And even then you're not totally safe. What if a judgemental wildebeest trots along and insults your cave decor? What if a rhino tells you to fuck off? It's honestly too much to bear. So you might as well stick with us here, where there's running water and microwaves and all the refrigerated yoghurt tubes we could possibly want.

Because life is not only painful and terrible. It's also having wonderful days with wonderful people. It's unexpected kindness from strangers. It's falling in love with someone who treats you like a precious thing. It's achieving something that you never believed possible. It's recovering from addiction or trauma and making your brain a space that you can exist and thrive in. It's seeing the world. It's realising you're really good at something – lots of things, actually. It's cycling along a canal and whistling a little show tune. It's eating a delicious crouton in the sun. It's giving your tiny nana a hug. It's waking up in a good mood, and celebrating the little chemical upswing, and not worrying or wondering when or if it'll swing the other way. It's all of these things and it's even more.

So let's toughen up right where we are. Here, among all the other nut-bars and failures and screw-ups. Not so tough that we become horrible armadillo-faced people – but just enough so that we can bear to live in this strange and ridiculous world without being devastated and distraught every time something doesn't work out exactly right. And that's really hard, *obviously*. A lot of the stuff I'm asking you to try is really, really hard, and if you haven't already chucked this book into the nearest swamp then I salute you. There's still time. But not just yet, because I'm about to drop some hot soupy knowledge into your lap.

You have to meet yourself where you are now. You've got to have goals, but if you treat them as places where you can arrive, rest, and never move from again, you're going to fall flat and you're going to fall hard. Instead you've got to let your goals be soft and pliable, rubbery and willing to go where you go, to shape-shift, to shrink and grow, depending on how the universe is behaving that day. You've got to let them burn bright, and you have to let them fall away. Let your goals tell you No. Be ready to accept this answer and adapt, but also be ready to stand your ground, and tell them Yes, Actually. Be ready to ask for help. Be ready for things to take longer than you wanted them to. Be ready to let joy in long before success.

Be ready to fail – a lot. All the damn time, in fact. Depressed brains love failure. They always want more of that delicious failure. They want us to internalise that failure as something that we deserved, something we did. In rejecting that idea outright you take a lot of power back from your depressed brain.

You will fail. You will have bad ideas that will crash and burn and you will have good ideas that will do the same. And your creativity and your drive and your ability to function will have seasons. You have to just survive your winters as best you can.

Therapy

Disclaimer: Therapy isn't accessible to everyone. It's an expensive aspect of treatment, and unless you're wealthy enough to see someone right away or there are other resources that you can gain access to through subsidies and waiting lists, then you may not get the therapy that you need. This is just how things currently are in mental health treatment. This doesn't mean I want you to feel guilty if you *can* get therapy. I'm glad for anybody who can reliably access any treatment, but we can't ignore that it's not for everyone. Also let's remember that therapists aren't a magical group of people. They aren't automatically good. Therapists can be shitty. They can be judgemental and bigoted and classist and rude. And I hope that there's a day not far from now where someone reads this and thinks, 'Wow, things used to be really shitty for people with mental illness. I'm glad it's a lot better now.' I have faith in that future – but we're not there yet.

How you expect therapy to go

You turn up at your therapist's office. There are bookcases on every wall and everything is draped in thick green velvet. Your therapist appears. They're wearing those teeny little glasses that look like they were made for dolls. They sit in a leather wingback chair while you recline on a couch. You talk, they listen. They ask you: 'How do you feel?' and you tell them. They nod. Do they have a goatee? Perhaps. Perhaps they have two. They make notes on a pad while you talk, and as you talk you feel less burdened. Any minute they'll speak, and you'll be cured.

How therapy will probably go

It will probably be really fucking awkward, and involve a lot of discomfort as you slowly get to know your therapist. There will be no green velvet and the room might smell vaguely of luncheon meat. You'll spend a few sessions talking through the basics, and establishing some sort of rapport with one another. Your sessions may go by very quickly, and feel very far apart. You might dread going, or daydream about better things you could have spent the money on. A new lava lamp. Ten enormous gummy bears. A mustard-coloured beret.

This is normal. Stick with it and try your best to trust the process.

How to get the most out of therapy

♣ Tell your therapist how best to communicate with you. Be as assertive and straightforward as you can. Identify what makes you shut down and feel uncomfortable and what kind of questioning you find it easier to be responsive to. Tell them what nicknames or pronouns you prefer. Are there any words or phrases that elicit a particularly negative response with you? Let them know. Make it as easy as possible for them to know and understand you from the start.

♣ Set goals for yourself and your therapy. Even before you have your first session, try to write out a list of things that you'd like to work on with your therapist, goals that you'd like to work towards, and topics that you'd like to broach.

♣ Be as honest as you can. It's tempting to lie, especially when you've had a bad week or done something that runs contrary to what you've been trying to achieve in therapy. But lying isn't helpful. It's also freeing to have a space in your life where you don't need to be polite and think about what you say. This isn't work. It isn't a catch-up with the girls. It's a safe space where you're allowed to tell the truth, even when that truth is embarrassing and a bit ugly.

♣ Be prepared for it to be exhausting. A friend of mine used to cry for a full hour after therapy and then fall into a deep sleep. That was her process. Another went on her lunch break and carried on her day as normal afterwards. Therapy can be incredibly cathartic, and it can also bring up a lot of very difficult and very unpleasant emotions. So give yourself permission to relax and restore yourself afterwards. Practise self-care and plan for a little dip in mood after certain sessions. This is okay. This is very normal.

♣ Prepare for your sessions. Take notes in the days leading up to therapy. Think about what issues are most pressing and obstructive to your immediate life and then tell your therapist that that's where you'd like to focus if possible.

♣ Try not to frame your therapist as someone whose approval needs to be earned. They aren't a cool older kid at school who you're desperate to impress and please. They're a professional whose job it is to guide and assist you with bettering your mental health. When you mess up, you don't need to worry that you're failing them or letting them down. Try to stop worrying whether your therapist thinks that you're weird or uncool, and keep your head in the game.

A therapist should never

- Open up unnecessarily to you about their own personal problems, especially if those problems or stories are of a sexual or intimate nature. A lot of therapists will tell you about themselves and their experiences and this is normal and okay, but there are clear lines that shouldn't be crossed.
- Belittle or embarrass you for any reason.
- Share details with you about their other patients.
- Refuse to explain certain elements of your treatment – such as the medication they're recommending or the kinds of questions that they're asking you.
- Attempt to see you in a social setting outside of your sessions. This can include one-on-one time unrelated to your treatment or inviting or accepting invitations to spend time with you in a larger group.
- Tell you that you're their favourite patient and that they feel strongly and particularly towards you.
- Insult or mock you for any aspect of your life, personality, interests or history.
- Suggest that you engage in behaviour that you know to be harmful, dangerous, triggering or contrary to your recovery in any way.
- Threaten to reveal things that you've told them to others, or use this information as leverage against you in any way.
- Position themselves as your ultimate protector or guardian, and vow to keep you safe or be the only person you need.
- Ask for an inappropriate favour – like to borrow money or stay with you or have you pick them up from a bar or a party.

- Pursue any kind of relationship with you outside of your sessions. They're a professional and it's imperative for your recovery that they maintain a proper and professional distance at all times.
- Ignore or blame you when you express discomfort about the things that they've done or said, or ask for clarification about something that you're finding troubling about your sessions.
- Show up unannounced at your house, work, school or any other place where you aren't meant to be meeting.
- Ignore your boundaries regarding touching or mentions of highly triggering topics.
- Forbid you from researching your own illness or talking to other people besides them about your treatment or diagnosis.
- Tell you that you're a lost cause and cannot be treated.
- Tell you that you clearly don't want help or to get better, and suggest that suicide may be a reasonable option for you.
- Offer you special discounts or free sessions because of a special liking towards you.
- Exchange therapy sessions for favours or other services from you.
- Ignore you during your sessions to text or take frequent phone calls, or do anything that detracts from the purpose of your visit or wastes your time and money.
- Encourage you to break ties with non-abusive people in your life with the intention of fostering a more dependent relationship with them.
- Suggest you make changes to your physical appearance to please them – such as getting a haircut, changing your way of dressing or losing or gaining weight.

- Demand or require you to hold the same beliefs as them for your treatment to continue, or tell you that their belief and practice will hold the key to your recovery.
- Use hypnosis or similar techniques without your express permission and before explaining what to expect and what will happen.

For more information about this you can find patient abuse checklists online, or by visiting www.survivingtherapistabuse.com. Hopefully you'll never experience any of this, and this list will just be a handy guide to keep you vigilant of what should and shouldn't happen in a therapy session. But if any of the things on the list do happen, or have happened, to you, please know that you are not to blame and you were not at fault. This was not something that you deserved or encouraged or should have known how to stop.

Things that might help lift your mood (but also might not)

♣ Exercise. I didn't think this would work for me at first. Mostly because of my own twisted, toxic history with eating, working out and body image in general. My only experiences with exercise growing up were being forced to do it at school, or forcing myself to do it to lose weight and become 'worthy' (i.e. the most bullshit reason to ever do exercise). It had always been a competition between me and me, and neither of us ever seemed to come out winning. So for a long time exercise was out. Total non-option. I wasn't good at it, for one. I didn't enjoy getting all sweaty and out of breath and whatnot. No thank you very much at ALL. Also, the idea of going to a gym where other people were made me dizzy with anxiety. Same with running outside. I just didn't want any part of the whole horrible nonsense. But then I started running. I did it out of sheer frustration at first. I'd tried everything else. And it ended up helping a lot. I do still need to be mindful and make sure I'm not pushing myself too far or getting competitive with it, but it's a great mood booster and sleep aid when I'm able to do it.

♣ Taking up a creative hobby. This can be anything from writing poetry to sketching to handcrafting ceramic egg cups on your days off work. I say this as someone who is really bad at most creative endeavours. Once I made a blue Play-Doh dog and someone asked if it was a dinosaur. I was twenty-three years old. The indignity. But if you have even the slightest inclination – then give it a go. Engage the part of your brain that isn't busy running the logical day-to-day nonsense operations. Give it some clay to play with. Put a paintbrush in its hand. See what happens.

♣ Meditation and mindfulness. Anybody with a brain that's always working is usually pretty sceptical about these two. The idea of sitting still and doing nothing might fill you with dread and apprehension, which is the opposite of what we're trying to do here. But try to suspend your disbelief long enough to try. They're not just for naturally Zen or easy-going people. They're for the neurotic, mile-a-minute thinkers as well. Maybe even more so.

♣ Journaling. You can do a daily dated journal if you're the kind of person who can commit to keeping up to date. Or, if you're like me, you can use an undated and relaxed journaling system. I'm not going to harp on about it because Google exists and also my microwave potato is almost done, but if you're at all interested, do some research. There's so much out there. Journaling can be a great way to keep up to date with the basics of your recovery – your medication, your doctor's appointments, your CBT or DBT exercises. It can also be a place to put your hopes and your ambitions for wellness and life. Or you can write an erotic novella.

Questions to ask after you've made a mistake

♣ How many other people in the history of the world have made this same kind of mistake and got through it? How many millions upon millions of people have made a far worse mistake and survived?

♣ Do you know even one single more thing about yourself or the world than you knew before you made the mistake?

♣ Imagine that the person you love most in the world was the one who made this mistake – what would you tell them right now? However reassuring and encouraging you would be towards them, try to direct that energy and support towards yourself.

♣ Does fixing this mistake require any more than a little time, energy, money or an apology to fix? If not, great. You can access those things without much difficulty. Put it in perspective. If it does, that's okay as well. You have it in you. Grab some of that tasty perspective again. Consider how many other people have done the same thing, and how many different ways they've found through it.

♣ If you take the mistake out of its current context and remove all fear of other people's judgement or disapproval, does it really seem so much of a big deal? Is it just a series of normal human behaviours that didn't quite end how you hoped? I thought so. Let go.

♣ Did the mistake happen because you were trying to cause harm, get one over on someone else, or do something shady – or was it simply a product of being an imperfect human on Earth? If the former, then own it. Accept that in that moment you weren't being your best self, and that you suffered because of it. Take the lesson as graciously as possible and when the universe serves up a similar opportunity to act slyly, you can reject it and redeem yourself to yourself.

Things you can unlearn

- Caring quite so much about what other people think of you.
- Negative and hateful self-talk.
- Needing to please everybody else, regardless of whether or not they deserve it.
- Taking drastic measures to keep your mental health problems hidden, even in contexts where you're not at risk of being judged or punished for it.

Mantras

Words to repeat to yourself when you're feeling low

'This will absolutely pass. There is absolutely no feeling in the world that is final or permanent, and that includes this one. As enormous and terrible as this is, it has an end, and I'm probably far closer to the end than I am to the beginning.'

'Moods are evidence of nothing. The most special, worthwhile, brilliant people suffer from depression or episodes of low mood exactly like this. I am worthy of life, I am worthy of happiness, and sticking around through these times is total and absolute proof that I am stronger than this.'

'I'm learning through all of this. Even when it feels like it's just bottomless, soulless, endless darkness, my resilience and endurance are teaching me something. There will be a point where I can fight back. Maybe now is not that time. Maybe next time won't be. But the time is coming. I am learning what I need to learn to eventually come through this and feel good.'

Words to repeat to yourself when you're feeling awkward

'My worth doesn't depend on my ability to entertain or amuse other people. If I'm having a bad or foggy day and my words aren't coming out right, I have my own permission to not be my best self. I'm allowed to tell people that I'm not feeling so good and I'm allowed to bail and go home.'

'Everyone notices their own mistakes most acutely. I'm feeling awkward and hyper-aware and I'm spiralling a little. Chances are that enough of my real personality is coming through that the people I'm with are totally unaware that I'm feeling like this. I need to be more forgiving of myself and allow myself room and time to warm up to a new social situation. So many other people feel exactly the same way and understand this feeling. I'm not an oddity or an abnormality. I'm just figuring it all out.'

Words to repeat to yourself when you make a mistake

'I learn very little when I don't fuck up. Fucking up and making mistakes can be terribly painful and distressing, but they teach me lessons for the future, lessons that will undoubtedly save me from pain further down the line. I feel confident in my ability to live through this, learn from my mistakes and, most importantly, forgive myself for making them.'

'Brains don't always tell the truth, and right now my brain is exaggerating in a way that turns a small and understandable mistake into a huge mess. This isn't because I am broken, it's just faulty logic that I've picked up along the way and will have to learn to correct. My brain might be telling me I'm a failure when really I've just been human. This might not help me feel better right away – my impulse to feel deep shame and embarrassment is still very present – but it's not going to be like this forever. I'm fine, I'm safe, and I'm just human.'

'Every single person I admire or think of as better or more capable than me has made WAY worse mistakes than the one I just made. They've totally messed up, failed, made errors, and they've probably felt very similar to how I feel now. And just like them, I will endure this, learn from it, and become better for having been through it. I may not be able to totally let myself off the hook right away, but I'm going to do my best to treat myself with the same patience and loving kindness that I would anyone else in this situation.'

Words to repeat to yourself when you feel lost

'What's happening in my life now is confusing. I'm figuring out how to go forward; I'm figuring out what does and doesn't work for me; I'm figuring out what's wrong with me. I'm being tested from every angle, and that's extremely frightening. But whether or not I can see a clear path right now, it doesn't matter. Because the only thing I need to do is keep putting one foot in front of the other.'

'Not having a clear goal or a clear destination in mind is what's making me feel like this. My recovery has to be open and free to take me at the most productive and healthy pace, and while I understand this, it doesn't stop me feeling frustrated and lost at times. But that's okay. Because having a wobble and needing reassuring and setting right doesn't mean my recovery is doomed or even in danger.'

Words to repeat to yourself when you feel betrayed or hurt

'Whatever happens, I deserve kindness, respect, communication and basic decency. My mental illness does not negate this or make me any less deserving of fair treatment. When someone behaves poorly towards me it really sucks – but it's their decision and it has nothing to do with me or my worth. When I treat people with patience and dignity I deserve that in return. That is non-negotiable and I am right to be upset when someone disrespects me or treats me carelessly.'

'However distressed or upset I feel right now, it will pass. Someone else's decision to betray or treat me unkindly does not mean I have to self-destruct or hurt myself in response. I'm entitled to my emotions and I will respect myself by letting myself feel them, but

I will not allow them to overtake my recovery or my wellness or put my safety or peace of mind in jeopardy.'

'I'm allowed to feel hurt and betrayed while also wanting an explanation for what happened from the person I feel has betrayed me. I need to honour and work through my own feelings about this, but I can also be open to the fact that there may be miscommunication or misunderstanding on both sides.'

Words to repeat to yourself when you're feeling anxious

'I've been this anxious before and I've lived through it. This will pass just the same as that did. If I need to take some time to breathe and gather myself, then that's totally fine, and the people around me will understand that.'

'Anxiety is an overwhelming feeling and even thinking about facing things today is courageous. Pushing myself to do things in spite of anxiety is brave, but I need to remember that it's also brave to know my limits and to recognise that I might not be ready to do something just yet.'

'I am here. I am present. I am safe. My feelings of intense anxiety are always, always temporary.'

Words to repeat to yourself when you're feeling self-destructive

'Feeling as though I want to self-harm or engage in toxic and self-destructive behaviours is a very normal part of recovery. I am learning new ways to cope and react, but in the meantime it's understandable that my brain still takes me here. I will do my best to resist the urge to do this, because I know it is a very important part of my recovery to transition from harmful coping strategies to productive ones, but I will also do my best not to shame or judge myself for my urges or my decisions at this point. I am learning and I am doing my best.'

'Before I hurt myself or engage in other self-destructive or self-harming behaviours, I promise that first I'll try to reduce or manage my distress or other overwhelming emotion through constructive methods, such as distraction, self-soothing, changing my environment, or seeking help from someone close to me. I know these aren't as immediately effective or satisfying and aren't what my brain is urging me to do, but I'm going to try them anyway. Because I know now that they can work, and a part of my commitment to myself is working on and reinforcing healthier behaviours.'

'If I do self-harm or engage in self-destructive behaviours, I will be brave enough to accept that it happened and that it does not make me any less worthy or suited to wellness. I am not lost to happiness or recovery and, even though this feels like a huge setback, I was doing what I felt I needed to do in that moment to get by, and I won't attack myself for it. I am one of so many people fighting an illness, and having a relapse or a low moment does not make me any less deserving or likely to get better.'

Words to repeat to yourself when you're feeling rejected

'Not everyone thinks about things in the way that I do, and that's okay. But it does mean that what I perceive to be a sign of dislike or rejection may in fact be something harmless and completely unintentional. An important part of my recovery will be learning to be open to more than one possibility and more than one explanation for the situations that make me uncomfortable.'

'The way that other people treat me is entirely their decision. It's about them, and as terrible as it may feel to be treated like crap, it is not reflective of my worth or the way I deserve to be treated. Even on days where I don't feel worthwhile, I know in a deeper place that I am.'

Words to repeat to yourself when you feel unsure about the future

'Life will get better. I will get better. The reason that it doesn't currently feel like this is true is because I've been unwell for a long time. This feeling of hopelessness comes from my illness, not from reality.'

'Whatever situation I'm in now, it isn't forever. Small changes happen every day, and whether or not I'm ready to make the big changes necessary to move past the unpleasantness of right now, eventually I will be. There's nothing that I can't look at, address, ask for help with, and gradually overcome. Not a single thing. With a mixture of learning, brave and decisive action and patience, things will change. They will improve. They may look nothing like how I once expected them to, sure, but they will still be great.'

'This isn't a problem that's just specific to me. This happens to so many other people – it happens to so many great people, in fact. Everyone I admire has felt the way that I'm feeling now. Lost, confused, a bit hopeless, as though the future is dark and unwelcoming. And so many great people have survived this period of confusion and pain and they have gone on to be happy and functional. This will be true for me, too. I just have to survive and gradually try to work on what scares me and figure out what might make me happy.'

Words to repeat to yourself when you don't want to go on

'This feeling won't last, and on the other side of it there's hope and recovery and learning and peace. When this feeling is over I'll feel less destructive and miserable and I'll be able to cope with what's happening to me. This is temporary. This is a temporary situation and a temporary feeling. I will just have to do things differently when I'm able to.'

'I've survived every single difficult situation I've been in so far. This is incredibly hard and I'm not going to pretend it's not happening to me, but I will try as hard as I can to just accept that it's going to pass – because it will.'

'So many other people have felt like this before and I'll never be alone in this suffering. What I will do is give myself a day or so to recover, to put space between myself and this feeling, to try to reach out to the people who love me. I will recover gradually, and with self-acceptance and patience. I will feel a bit better soon, and then even more so. Eventually I will feel okay and able to continue.'

Words to repeat to yourself when you feel silly or embarrassed

'Every single person on Earth feels like this at some point or another. Everyone makes mistakes, everyone gets flustered and embarrassed and feels like they're the most ridiculous and awkward human to ever blunder across the face of the Earth. But they aren't, and neither am I. I'm a normal human being who has a history of being too harsh on myself for normal human mistakes. This is what I need to work on, rather than trying to make sure I never do another "embarrassing" thing.'

'The only way to avoid doing silly or embarrassing things is to stay inside all day – to do nothing and know nobody and keep quiet. In short: to waste my life. If I want a full and colourful and wonderful life, then I have to take the embarrassments. The trade is worth it. I know this. It might not make me feel any better just yet, but it will. I just have to be patient, dust myself off and try to laugh if I can – or if not, then just try to put it behind me and move forward. Being out in the world, even when I do something silly, is always far better than shutting out the world.'

Words to repeat to yourself when you feel like you're letting someone down

'Sometimes my illness will mean I'm unable to do things. Sometimes I will just need to rest. When this happens my impulse will be to beat myself up, or to try to push through it. But I have to honour where I am in recovery, and be very honest with myself and my loved ones about what I am and aren't ready to do yet.'

'If I explain what's happening and I commit to making it up to them another time, I've done all I can do. And yes, they're allowed to be annoyed and upset and disappointed. But I have to honour my limits, and that might sometimes mean resting and rescheduling.'

Some good things: part 1

♣ Taking a warm bath. A bath that is just the right temperature, in a bathtub that is clean and deep and full of something hot, bubbly and comforting. Maybe there are some candles flickering. Maybe Billy Joel is playing softly from a stereo. Maybe you have a box of chocolate-covered raisins to snack on at your leisure. The options for comfort are endless with a bath.

♣ That period after being really unwell when you finally start to feel better. Even when you're still a little bit of a disgusting snotty sweat monster, some part of you is content and happy in the knowledge that you do not feel as bad as you did earlier. You are healing. Your pain is dulling. Your skin is cooling down.

♣ Figuring out what food you really, really want to eat and then getting to eat that exact food. Not that food's cousin. Not its mate. Nope – that exact food. And nobody else is even trying to get in on the action, either. No way, pal. Because this is your food.

♣ Having a good chat with someone where nothing feels forced and nothing feels exhausting or insincere and you guys are just chattering away like a couple of old parrot pals on a tree branch without a single care in the world.

♣ Showering at the end of a hot, sweaty day and putting on clean, dry clothes and then sitting outside in the late-afternoon sunshine and feeling like the sun is holding you in its hands like a hot lovely doughnut hole. You are the doughnut hole. You are the lovely doughnut hole.

♣ Reading a great book in a great jumper with some great socks on while it's raining outside. And the rain is ALSO great because it's just living its best life making all the plants grow and giving us water for drinking and washing our feet in. And those plants and those drinks and those feet are all extremely great too. Everything is SO flipping great.

♣ The smell of baking bread. It doesn't even have to be an exciting, horny-sounding Italian type of bread. It can just be a regular brown loaf with one lone seed in it. The point is it smells fantastic when it's being baked and this will always be true forever and ever. Even when the dolphins (a far superior race to us) have finally taken over this godforsaken planet and wiped out the human race, they will continue to bake our humble human loaves. That's how good the smell of baking bread is.

♣ When a cat or a dog or a large lizard shows a special liking towards you, almost as though it has chosen you out of all of the other weird-looking, two-legged flesh people and has decided that it will be your friend now. It's beautiful and magical and a moment to be cherished.

♣ Saying something funny and making everyone around you laugh. And maybe the funny thing didn't even take you a second to come up with. It was just there. It was just waiting in your brain ready to be said.

♣ Having someone compliment your work when you know they really, really got it. When you know that they aren't trying to ask for a favour or hit on you or compliment you because they think it'll help them down the line. You know that it's because they really dug what you made and they just wanted you to know that.

♣ Going to sleep when you're exhausted. It's a bonus when you know that you don't have to be up super early the next day. It's getting into bed and finding that elusive comfy spot among your pillows and feeling cradled and supported and ready to snooze. And then before you know it, you're just drifting off, peaceful in the knowledge that you are the marshmallow that you were always destined to be.

♣ When a kid thinks you're cool and you didn't even have to try hard or bribe them to make them think that. You literally just had to show up and talk to them like they were a person and make them laugh a little and ask them questions that weren't completely stupid and patronising. And sometimes the kid is wearing their shirt inside out and back to front and it's like, Wow, you are the future, my dude. My small innovative buddy. Thank you for validating me.

♣ Having a succession of good days – days where you manage to do things without getting too overwhelmed or disheartened or scrambled by it all. Days where you feel in control of yourself, days where your hands feel like your hands and not strange arm hams. Days where you know that that is what you're aiming for, this is the future that you're working so hard to get to, and that even if you stumble and have to leave this feeling for a while, you will be back. You will return here more and more as you recover and it will feel just as good each time.

♣ Realising that something that used to scare the shit out of you just isn't that big a deal any more. Like catching a train or speaking aloud in front of more than one person or ordering in a restaurant or going on a first date. It's just a thing that you can do now. It's just a battle that you have quietly and courageously won for yourself.

♣ Going to see a movie on your own, or for a walk, and realising how comfortable you feel in your own company, more comfortable than you've ever felt before. And how nice it is to be by yourself and to know that you're enough, and that your company is enough, and that you can do this.

♣ Knowing the answer to a question in a quiz that nobody else knew. This is an especially good thing when you didn't have to dig or scramble or second-guess yourself for it – you just knew. You just had that little quiz-winning bit of trivia squirrelled away in your little nut box already. You bloody champion. You hero. You god among mortals.

You can't control

- Whether or not someone loves you.
- Whether or not someone wants to be with you.
- If it pours with rain on the day of your birthday barbecue.
- If you break a nail eating a corn on the cob.

You can control

- Whether you have soup for lunch or an entire pineapple.
- What colour socks you put on in the morning.
- How many doughnuts you buy, and whether those doughnuts contain jam or chocolate sauce or custard or other, smaller doughnuts. Doughnuts inside doughnuts. A Russian doll-type baked goods situation.

- Whether or not you say fuck it to the rain and have that damn birthday barbecue anyway.
- How you use your good days.
- How you use your bad days.

How to use radical acceptance

Radical acceptance is the practice of accepting the reality of what is, without trying to resist or deny the parts of it that we don't like or don't want to believe are happening. It's not about dwelling or self-pity or focusing on the negative: it's just accepting that what's happening right now is happening, and we don't need to hide from it.

The opposite of radical acceptance is total refusal to face what's happening in your life and in your recovery at this exact moment and in this broad general time in your life. It's reacting angrily to what you see in front of you, which is just another way of denying it (pretty tempting when your entire life feels like a dumpster fire and you want answers, but ultimately it's not going to help you make progress).

Radical acceptance used to annoy the absolute tits off me, if I'm being totally honest. I struggled to get my brain around any of it. It seemed to me that radical acceptance was asking me to be passive in the face of tremendous difficulty and suffering. To just let it happen to me. To stop fighting and lie down. It seemed like inaction, which in turn seemed like giving up. In reality, radical acceptance is nothing of the sort. It's a loosening of your grip on control and allowing the present moment to exist exactly as it is, without any fabrication, wishful thinking or sense of rightness or wrongness on your part. It's saying, 'This is what's happening right now,' and accepting it without piles and piles of judgement and shame and longing for an entirely different reality. Because reality doesn't change with longing. It changes with gradual and deliberate action.

Resisting reality can't make you happy long term. It's like planting half-chewed sticks of gum in your back garden and expecting sunflowers to grow. It's just not realistic. Radical acceptance means taking an honest look at whatever situation you're currently in. You are here. Here is where you are. This is what's happening at this moment in time. If you're having a bad time, it means accepting that.

Accepting doesn't mean shrugging your shoulders and not trying any more. Accepting is not approving, and it's important we get that in nice and early. ACCEPTING DOES NOT MEAN APPROVING. You can yell it if it'll help. You can yell it in Spanish or Ukrainian or Urdu. It doesn't mean that you have to like any of what you're accepting. You aren't becoming the present's bitch. It's not your boss now; it can't make you bring it a little cup of steamed milk and call you Tiny Michael.

No, you're just going to decide to stop pouring anger and denial and pain into it. You're working to cut off its supply of power and take some control back. You're saying: 'THIS IS WHAT IS HAPPENING RIGHT NOW AND I AM ACCEPTING THAT WITHOUT FIGHT. MY FIGHT AND MY POWER AND MY ENERGY WILL NOW GO INTO MINDFULLY AND DELIBERATELY CHANGING THE THINGS ABOUT THE PRESENT THAT I DO NOT WANT TO BRING WITH ME INTO THE FUTURE. BITCH.'

The bitch is, as always, optional.

You can practise radical acceptance by using coping statements, like the ones listed below:

'This is the situation I'm in right now. I can accept that reality while still working hard to create a future where I'm happy and in control.'

'There will never be anything I can do to change the past, and even just attempting to accept this might help me to feel better in the present moment.'

'I can control the present, and I can choose to sit with it and be patient. Even when I feel as though there's nothing to be done, there's always something to be done. Even if that just means working on my own current mood.'

How to distract yourself

♣ Get a blank sheet of paper or a fresh notebook page and go quote-hunting online. Write down any quotes that make you feel something that isn't depressed or anxious – hopeful, less alone, understood. They can be short quotes or they can be whole copies of whole articles that you've loved, or tweet threads that you've retweeted a dozen times because you liked them just that much. They can be literally anything – any words that make a little bridge across the void and help you feel like a person again. You can jot them down in biro or paint them in beautiful watercolour.

♣ Go on YouTube or Spotify or your iTunes library and make yourself some playlists for different occasions. You could make one for sleeping, one for waking up, one for exercise, one of your all-time favourite songs, one for getting yourself out of a bad funk, one of all the songs that you've always meant to listen to but your short attention span means that you've never found the time. Spend an hour or so doing it. Remind yourself of old favourites and discover new songs to love.

♣ Bake or cook something. You don't have to go all out, not unless you want to. Maybe you're the kind of person who finds attempting the perfect soufflé a relaxing experience. But if not, then some Rice Krispies squares will do just fine. Maybe a batch of cornflake cakes, or a sheet of puff pastry covered in whatever delicious random junk you've got in the fridge. An old favourite meal can be wonderfully comforting, something that's second nature, where you don't need to double-check any of the ingredients or the instructions. Or you could try something brand new, something with a whole bunch of ingredients. Something that requires all of your attention to get right.

♣ Try to learn a new skill. This could be something that requires you to use your hands, like knitting or cross-stitching or playing an instrument. It could be learning some basic conversational phrases in another language – ideally in the language of a city or country that you know you'd like to visit some day. It could be learning how to properly blend your eyeshadow, or it could be a forty-five-minute tutorial on how to properly shampoo a Shetland pony. (You know, just in case.)

How to make a self-care plan

♣ Make it flexible. Because when you're totally, ridiculously depressed out of your swampy, ridiculous mind, it'll need some pretty serious adjustments. It's not going to be yoga in the mornings and a probiotic on those days, NO, SIR, IT IS NOT. On bottom-of-the-barrel days it's going to be forcing yourself to stand up, stagger to the bathroom and drink water straight out of the tap before going back to bed for another twelve-hour sleep. It's going to be sobbing as you feebly brush your teeth for the first time in days. It's literally staying alive while wave after wave of terrible terror washes over you. So your self-care plan needs to allow for fluctuation; you have to have a back-up for when you're feeling your worst, or when you're otherwise unable to stick to your usual routine.

♣ Focus on the basics at first. This means covering the barest minimum of things that you'll try to do for yourself every day of your recovery, however good or bad you're feeling. For me this includes taking my medication, eating something, drinking water and trying my best to leave the house at least once. That's it. And that probably doesn't seem like a lot to a well person. It also doesn't seem to fit the typical magazine model of what we've come to expect from 'self-care'. I didn't even mention taking a bubble bath or eating an entire treacle tart? What gives?

♣ Make sure you balance the tough and boring life-maintenance stuff with the indulgent, fun, pleasure-focused stuff. Make sure everything is represented. The plan needs to help you take care of yourself in all ways, not just the warm, toasty, immediately enjoyable ways. On a typical day try to do an equal amount of both. On a difficult day, balance it more in favour of the sensory stuff, with a set amount of life maintenance thrown in for good measure. But on any day, make sure you remember that self-care is about an overall managing of all the things. That's a clumsy way of putting it but I think you know what I mean. It's taking the necessary action to make life better, easier and safer to navigate for you – a person who has a mental illness.

♣ Remember that there's nothing shameful or embarrassing about asking for help. This probably won't stop you feeling embarrassed or ashamed about it, but still it's worth remembering. A collaborative self-care plan can be the mother-effing motherload. If you think a box of notes from your friends and loved ones might help you, then ask them for help. It's a small act from them that might help pick you up on a bad day somewhere down the line.

Survival tips for university

♣ Find out early what mental health resources your university has for its students. Get on whatever waiting lists you need for counselling, DBT sessions, group meetings. If there's any kind of support network between students, then get involved – it can be incredibly lonely and isolating not feeling like you can be open with any of your flatmates or course friends, especially in the early stages when you're not really sure of who everybody is and whether or not they're a potential ally.

♣ Lean on your family if you can. It's not a step back to need a daily call with your mum or your siblings or to head home for the few days when you don't have lectures (or anything else compulsory). There's a lot of new stuff to learn and to take in and to adapt to. When you're feeling like a tiny fish in a big bowl of Jägerbombs, it's okay to step back.

♣ Find a doctor that you can actually trust and talk to. Often this will mean seeing a few GPs and enduring some frustrating ignorance from people who should know better. This is okay. It's irritating and disheartening, sure, but it's also normal and doesn't mean there aren't decent doctors out there.

♣ Tell your closest friends what you're going through. Because at some point you're going to need some kind of help and support with the whole mental illness thing. Maybe you'll need to ask someone to walk with you to a lecture or go to the library with you when you're feeling anxious, or bring you some food when you've been too depressed to get out of bed.

♣ Try to find an ally within your course – someone who's sympathetic and understanding and who can send you copies of notes and reading that you've missed, or even make recordings of lectures that you're not able to get to.

♣ Contact your department directly. Take them medical proof (e.g. a doctor's note) when you've got it, and explain to them exactly what your illness might mean for attendance, deadlines and your ability to always perform at your best. If you have a personal tutor or supervisor then email them directly as well. You're entitled to support and you're not being a handful or a nuisance by asking for it. Ask them what assistance they can give you, who to contact about missed deadlines, how often they'll need medical proof, etc.

♣ Be prepared to miss out on some things. There may be days when you're not well enough to get up and go to the lecture or seminar that you've been looking forward to. You may need to flake on nights out when you're not stable enough to endure being in a big crowd with lots of noise and alcohol and flashing lights. This is okay. Nobody worth knowing will think anything of it, and your well-being may depend on taking these nights off.

♣ Be smart about drinking and drug use. I'm not making any assumptions or judgements about your lifestyle or the way that you have fun, but if you're binge drinking or abusing drugs in a way that's interfering substantially with your daily life and making you more depressed – that's a problem. Try to err on the side of caution and moderation. That doesn't mean you can't have fun or do things your way.

♣ Don't worry if you're not having the time of your life. It's a myth that you arrive at university and then spend three or four years having the most incredible experiences, meeting people that you'll know forever, dancing on tables all night and then somehow attending every lecture and getting perfect scores in all of your exams. It's fucking unrealistic. Some of the most wonderfully put together, successful and happy people had a terrible time at university. I personally had a terrible time at university and look at me now. A sexy billionaire. A genius.

♣ Learn and practise some basic life-maintenance skills. If you're confident in your ability to do laundry, do a full food shop, cook some nutritious and enjoyable meals and keep your room fairly clean and tidy, then it makes it easier to feel like you have a handle on the whole living-away-from-home thing.

♣ Find some neutral or 'safe' spots on campus or in the town or city where you can go and just exist when you're tempted to self-isolate. Perhaps a coffee shop that has plugs and a good wifi connection, or a little study spot in the library that isn't too noisy, where you can comfortably read or work. Spending days and days alone may be what your brain is begging you for, but at a certain point it can become damaging. These places can act as brilliant compromises. Anywhere that isn't holed up in your bedroom is a win.

Sucking the poison out

Getting to a place where things are easy and comfortable takes hard work. It involves a lot of sucking the poison directly out of the places it hurts. And these poisons are old poisons. They're poisons that have got warm and comfortable living where they are.

To get these poisons out we first have to know their names and how they got in in the first place. And then we have to work very hard and very deliberately on making our lives an unsuitable environment for them to continue to exist.

The poisons are all the things we do and think and say that legitimise our misery and put us in situations that are unsafe and endanger our recovery. The sucking part of the metaphor is just the deliberate and repetitive actions we take to avoid the triggering people and situations that do all this damage.

So suck away, mate, suck away.

Highly sensitive person

I am a highly sensitive person. I have a thin skin. Emotionally, I bruise easily. Like a peach who cries when criticised. This has been my deal for as long as I can remember, and it may be my deal (in some ways) forever. But that doesn't mean I'm not tough in my own way, it doesn't mean I give up and curl in on myself like a beetle whenever things get rough.

Build your own armour out of everything you ever learned and every strong thing you ever did. Some people are born with skin that is the right thickness to feel everything almost entirely the right amount. That's cool for them. Very groovy and cool. Good job, Other People Who Are Not Like Me. But some people (lots and lots of people, in fact) are born with an emotional skin that BURNS when it should just prickle, and bruises black at the lightest touch, and just feels the absolute hell out of everything in general. These people are The Big Feelers. Technically that's not the real name for them, because medical doctors and scientists are idiots who refuse to return my calls. But whatever. It's what I'm calling it. Being a person who feels everything acutely and devastatingly strongly is, to put it mildly, INCREDIBLY TERRIBLE AND THE WORST.

But there is always a light. There is always something else we can try.

Survival requires compromise

Survival requires compromise. It requires us to put a lot of stuff on hold while we deal with the very real and immediate terror of our serious mental illness.

And then later when we're doing a little better we take a peek at the stuff that we've neglected and it's SO BIG AND LOUD AND SCREAMING.

And then we start screaming.

And everyone is screaming.

And the cycle starts again. So why try at all? Why start to stack the cards if the cards are only going to come tumbling down some time in the near future?

Because life gets good. It gets really, really brilliant. When we're prepared for it and when we're confident in our survival skills, life can be so open to us.

This is how it goes

This is how it goes. This is how it goes for me, for you, for anyone with a big juicy dose of depression. You'll feel better and you'll feel worse. Some days you'll try everything and do everything right and you'll still feel like crap. Some days you'll feel like a monkey in roller skates going the wrong way down the motorway. Some days you'll feel numb. Some days you'll feel too fast and too much and everyone you speak to will seem very far away. Some days will just go wrong from start to finish and no amount of mindfulness will seem to make a dent.

But some days you'll feel peaceful. And the progress you've made will shine clear and beautiful like a freshly glazed doughnut. You'll feel strong. You'll wake up, eat breakfast, look at the sky and feel all right with it. You'll work on your projects, call a friend, take the bins out. You'll go to work and feel inspired. You'll smile at a lovely chubby baby.

In this way, you will live a human life. In this way, everything will be okay.

Because absolutely nothing has been called. Nothing has been decided. You need to catch yourself every time you start projecting weeks, months, years ahead into your life. Your life is decided by your actions now. It's new actions every day. It's new days every day. The sun comes up, it's like, 'Hello, I am here, I am the sun.' It sits in the sky making us warm and melting our ice creams and feeding our plants. Later on it says, 'I am going now, the sun is going. Goodbye,' and it sets. The time in between is yours. Worry only about the day you are existing in. There is nothing else, and acting as if there is is just another form of avoidance, and it's another distraction that you don't need. Sometimes it's just daydreaming, imagining a life as perfect as the lives of those models on Instagram that you won't stop looking at (side note: please remember that nobody on Earth is living that life); sometimes it's gut-wrenching fear like, 'Oh GOD, my life won't turn out anything like I want, OH GOD OH GOD, what if the future is just more of this? Oh SHIT, OH SHIT.' That's the kind of panic that we can really do without. Because it's nonsense gibberish and it will cause you to not get shit done. And as we already know, getting shit done is really the only way to climb out of this hole. And what a hole it is. A hole of every bad decision, every self-destructive act, every toxic self-defeating behaviour we learned. It's a big scary hole and we do not like it and we did not invite it to be here but it is here.

But guess what:

YOU DIDN'T PUT YOURSELF IN THE HOLE. And even if you did, who cares? What are you? The hole police? The sheriff of holes? Look – the hole is there. It exists. And so long as we're just like, 'Wow, what a large hole,' nothing at all gets done about it.

You're in a hole. You've been sad. You've been really, massively depressed. Like millions of people today, you've been suffering. And it fucking sucks. You can say that. It doesn't make you pessimistic or negative or doomed. Say it. Say, 'FUCK! THIS SUCKS AND HAS SUCKED AND I FUCKING HATE IT AND WISH IT HAD NEVER HAPPENED TO ME.' It has sucked and does continue to. But this is the way it goes. You're depressed. You behave in all kinds of fucked-up ways because of your depression. You watch your potential bleed out behind you.

But then you realise you can't live like that any more. You know this for a long time and do nothing, but then you start to make changes. You learn. You do this every day. It's mostly boring but sometimes it feels like you own the entire sky, stars and comets and aliens and all. Your life starts to resemble something worthwhile. You don't feel as scared any more. You feel different. You still have your bad days, but they don't suck all of the air out of the world the way they used to. You can see beyond them, into the good place. Into the light.

Wellness is relative

Wellness is relative. Anything that isn't rock bottom can feel very much like wellness to some people, even if it's only rock bottom plus a few extra feet in a general upwards direction. To other people, not actively self-destructing and needing round-the-clock monitoring is very much wellness.

This sucker is absolutely relative.

And it means a lot of different things to a lot of different people. Some people won't consider themselves truly well again until they're back to being high-functioning, happy all the time, never ever depressed, never struggling with intrusive or unpleasant thoughts or urges. But that's not always realistic – or even healthy. Wellness needs to be subjective. It needs to be open. It needs to allow for bad days and relapses and those particularly deep emotional wounds.

Your wellness is valid, wherever it lands. And it's changeable, too.

Practise your gratitude, not your guilt

Instead of saying, 'I'm sorry for going on and on about myself,' say, 'Thank you for letting me talk to you about this, it's been really, really helpful.'

Instead of saying, 'I'm sorry that I'm so useless. I can't do anything right,' try saying, 'I really do appreciate your help with this. Thank you for being so patient with me while I'm learning.'

Instead of saying, 'I'm unlovable. Why are you even with me?' say, 'Thank you for loving me. Thank you for being there for me. Let's work on ways that we can be there for each other. However bad I feel, I never want you to take on more than you can deal with.'

PART FOUR: *Eclipse*

Bad self-care

There's good self-care and there's bad self-care. Or, more accurately, there's avoidance and toxic behaviours that we've conveniently dressed up as self-care. So here's a true thing that I absolutely did not want to accept for a very long time: loving yourself and taking care of yourself has to include real attempts to make life better, smoother and more secure. And making these attempts will often feel really stressful and bad and not at all loving and caring.

It's not self-care to sit and watch TV for twenty-seven hours straight while your life melts into goo around you, and your responsibilities go unresponded to. That's called depression. I may have mentioned it a time or two. And doing that when you're depressed is fairly normal. But calling it self-care is not the groove at ALL, so don't start that shit with me.

Doing your life in a mindful and deliberate way is self-care. Cutting out stress-triggers and verifiably harmful people is self-care. Rewarding yourself for trying (even if you crash and burn) is self-care. Drinking half a litre of water and showering and brushing old tomato sauce out of your hair is self-care. Dragging your depressed ass outside and walking it around the park for an hour after being inside for days is self-care. Taking care of yourself is self-care.

So take care of yourself as much as you're able to. Push your tired body out into the sunshine. Force your hands into the fridge. Get food. Get water. Get your meds. Put them in your mouth-hole. Drink. Swallow. Care for yourself as deliberately as you can.

Because looking after yourself and getting on your own team doesn't just mean eating delicious sweets in the bath (although I think you should do this too). It's also going to mean making some really difficult decisions to do the hard and uncomfortable work that will eventually make your life better. And you're going to have to cut toxic people out and you're going to have to endure the mess they make as they go. You'll have to have potentially upsetting conversations with people you love. You'll have to ask for more, and if more isn't an option, you're going to have to think long and hard about whether that person can stay in your life, and in what capacity. It's all a whole mess of stuff.

Because depression isn't a cold. It's not a broken arm. It can be helpful to compare it to a passing physical illness when you're explaining it to someone who has no real context, but we can be real here and say that it's not really anything like those things. It's days of feeling better, of doing better, of behaving better. And then it's days of feeling terrible and doing really badly. It's both. With the right work it's an upward curve, and it's more and more and more good things. But it's some days of real struggle and I'm not going to dress that up in a little hat and Crocs and call it Lil Marco. That would be revolting and I won't hear another word about it. Good day, Lil Marco. I said good day. It's a chronic, serious, unpleasant illness. Classic brain lols, you know?

Our self-care needs to take all of this into account. Our self-care needs to care for us in the current moment and in the moments that are going to come afterwards. It needs to be forward facing as much as it needs to keep us safe in whatever immediate situation is threatening our sense of peace and ability to keep going

Replacing negative thoughts

Your life isn't a trap: your brain is the trap. Which is actually way scarier, and I'm deeply sorry for saying it. But as the old saying goes, you have to know your enemy to squash your enemy into goo. And your enemy is the bad brain habits, trauma, and chemical nonsenses all trapped in your brain egg.

Work out what can be solved and what can't.

Throw as much peace and acceptance at the latter as you're able to.

Some problems require our focused attention (or that of a trained professional). Other things are baseless and impossible anxieties that will only ever make us suffer the more we look at them and pick at them and try to work them out. Some things you just have to trust will vanish as you become happier and more functional.

The big things, the big feelings of worthlessness or insanity or total wrongness, can't be solved by thinking your way out of them. You can think all day about them and all that will happen is you'll obsess and make it worse and dig deeper into yourself and your self-hatred. Put that over there and focus on what you can do. Because some things aren't meant to be solved. They're scams. The more you look directly at them the worse they make you feel. Like the sun. So let it be. Don't stare at it. Put on the sunglasses of Trying Your Goddamn Best and get on with doing something that isn't picking away at the fabric of your life until it's in ruins. The more you agonise about why you're wrong, the more wrong you feel. Like I said before, it's a whole scam. So cut that shit out by doing more and keeping your head and your heart too busy to ache. Or let it ache alongside the doing. Just do. Do, do, do, and eventually you will feel better. That's a real-life guarantee (when done alongside the other things mentioned in this book, of course).

I know what it feels like to try to get better. Nothing ever happens as quickly as you'd like. You're not fixed yet, you're not whole and normal and well. You're not Instagramming your perfect-looking life. You look around you and it feels like everyone you know is out there having a golden, pure, exciting time of it – enjoying a life of doing, and living, and not struggling like you're struggling.

Thing is, though – this is nonsense. Yes, some people are more functional than you. Some people are out there doing things that you would like to be doing. But do you know why that is? It's because they're not up against what you're up against right now. If they were, they'd be where you are, or somewhere nearby. What you're up against is big and it's giving a good fucking fight. And before you fight back and smash your way through it and defeat it, you have to learn how to do that. And then you have to do it slowly and deliberately. It won't be like in your Mario and Luigi computer games. It won't be one big punch and the bad guy's dead and you're the winner and oh wow now you have a crown on. Nope. No such luck. It's day after day after day of doing as much of the right thing as you can, making good choices whenever you're able to and talking to yourself with unflinching respect and support. It's still making mistakes! Loads of them! But it's about not letting them derail you. It's living a human life, better and better and better each day until it's mostly good and mostly whole. It's doing a bit more right every day and a bit less wrong, and feeling things getting better. It's going through the steps of your treatment with as much patience, willingness and acceptance as possible.

This is what's ahead. I promise you. Through the swampy, heavy, awful present, you eventually emerge somewhere that makes sense.

It's going to turn out. Please stop looking to the future for answers. There are none there. Look at your own hands, your own heart, your own will to survive. That's where the answers are. The answers are in the work. The work you're just figuring out how to do.

Self-harm

Trigger warning: mentions of self-harm and drug abuse.

For me, self-harming happened mostly between the ages of twenty and twenty-three. My actions were self-destructive, rooted in my desire to shake myself awake, or to matter, or even just to feel something. I drank too much. I hurt myself physically, or didn't eat for days. For months I would sleep from 9 a.m. to 6 p.m., then wake up, eat whatever I had to hand, whatever was easiest (usually cereal but occasionally dehydrated noodles if I was feeling adventurous). Then I'd go back to bed and open a bottle of wine. I went weeks without seeing sunlight. I watched a lot of *Grey's Anatomy*, then a lot of *Gilmore Girls*. I watched the headlights rush across my ceiling and wondered if this was how I'd always feel.

Waking up was painful. Walking to the corner shop (approximately forty-eight seconds from my front door) often required more than an hour of building up to. I had to know exactly what was about to happen. Which aisles I'd need to go down, exactly how much it would cost, how long I could spend outside before I shattered into sharp, jagged, terrible pieces.

I stopped going to university for months at a time. I passed exams by staying up studying for twenty-four straight hours before each one. I didn't make a single deadline for two years. I lied to everyone I loved. Even now, years later, just thinking about it brings me out in a cold sweat. My heart beats faster. Shame crawls its way down my spine and then up again. It still feels like I wasted the time, even though I know now that I was seriously and chronically ill and didn't have any of the tools I needed to pull myself together and access the help and support that could have made a difference. I was two essays away from getting the first-class degree that I was always predicted to get. I just had to hand them in. I just had to pass. I didn't write them. I got blackout drunk for a weekend, took a handful of Xanax and slept for a day and a half in a kind stranger's spare room. My mum reported me missing to the police. It was my rock bottom, and the work to drag myself up out of it almost killed me. But I did it. Here I am, doing life. Hello.

People self-harm for different reasons, and in different ways. Some people abuse drugs or alcohol, or engage in reckless behaviours that have nothing to do with fun and everything to do with hurting or devaluing themselves. Sometimes we do it to stop the other pain, the worse pain, the inside ache of anxiety and depression. We self-harm because it's almost blissful to feel something that isn't that.

Sometimes it's as punishment, because that's really what we think that we deserve. A way to outwardly show what's been bleeding out inside for as long as we can remember.

Sometimes we do it simply to stop the clock. To slow down time enough so we can catch our breath, gather ourselves. In this way, it's cathartic. It makes the invisible physical. It also helps bring us out of whatever desperate, angry, fugue state we were in when we did it. And yes, it's also more shameful than anything we've ever done before, but the shame of it exists elsewhere, in a different dimension, so far off the map that we don't even feel it. We do it, it's done, and the immediate pain of it pulls focus from the hell you're going through inwardly. It puts you to task. The patching up, the cleaning, the bandaging, it all gives you something to do.

And it's not for attention, either – or at least not in the way that people think. It's both totally in our control and out of it at the same time. We do it because that's what we need to do in that moment to get by. To be a person on Earth. To be awake. Sometimes, pretending to be fine in every other space requires you to be totally un-fine in this private space. And I don't say 'need' lightly. It's really truly that. It's compulsive and addictive. We do it because we're trying to survive, and then sometimes we do it because we can't stop. It's the pound of flesh that balances the scales. And some people will recoil from the very idea of it. This will be their limit and they will be unable to comprehend it or accept it.

In the past this has devastated me, but now I'm beyond wanting everyone to understand. If you think the scars make us broken or empty or ruined, then think that. Eat that particular poison and stay ignorant forever. I can't hurt about other people's ignorance any more. I just won't do it. I can't beg for your empathy. I don't have the time. None of us do, actually. I self-harmed and I'm neither proud nor ashamed of that fact. It was a way to survive, and I did survive. I don't do it any more but if I ever do again, I will forgive myself and I will work twice as hard to stay well.

Self-harm is not

Trigger warning: mentions of self-harm.

- Attention-seeking behaviour.
- Necessarily a sign that a person is feeling self-destructive.
- Limited to just cutting yourself. It can involve heavy drinking, engaging in potentially harmful sexual behaviours, starving or refusing yourself food or pleasure or company, or putting yourself in potentially harmful or dangerous situations.
- Inherently shameful.
- Just a cry for help. It can be a way of privately maintaining mental stability.
- Always easy to understand. It can be an incredibly complex thing.

Staying safe with self-harm

Trigger warning: in-detail descriptions of self-harm wounds.

People who self-harm often do so to manage their mental health, not to exacerbate their pain or punish themselves. Self-harm and suicide attempts are often worlds apart: both are intended to stop the pain, but self-harm is also very often an attempt to stay alive. But it has its obvious inherent dangers and although I can't necessarily talk you out of doing it today, or convince you to go cold turkey right now and never self-harm again, what I can do is help give you some tips to stay as safe as possible when you do feel the need to engage in it.

Basic precautions

If you're cutting yourself then please make sure what you're using to cut yourself with is sterile. Your intention may be to just alleviate some of the mental pressure and then go about your day, but when you're dealing with an open wound there are more things that you need to be wary of. An infection, unlike the cutting itself, is not in your control. It can get very bad, very fast and can put you in a lot of danger. It can force you to expose your illness to people that you don't feel ready to expose it to yet. So please take care to keep anything you use sterile and then properly clean yourself up afterwards. It's easy to access information online about how to keep different kinds of wounds safe, and it's important to at least have a basic understanding of what's required to minimise the chance of infection. It's also not that difficult – it just requires a few easily procurable items and a few minutes of your time. Keeping the wound clean with water is important, and applying some kind of bandage or covering is essential to the healing of many injuries.

How to treat a cut

- To stop the bleeding, hold a clean cloth to the wound and apply pressure. Be careful not to take the cloth away until the bleeding has stopped, as you can disrupt the clotting. If you don't have any clean fabric to hand, sanitary pads are a great alternative.
- Raise the injured area above your head to slow bleeding.
- When the bleeding has stopped, gently remove the cloth and wash the area – saline solution is great if you've got it. Be gentle and don't scrub at the wound.
- When the bleeding stops or slows down significantly (usually after ten minutes or so) try to cover or bandage the area – but never wrap so tightly that it stops circulation to any extremities.
- Once the bleeding has stopped and the wound is clean and covered, get yourself something to eat. This is especially important if you've felt at all dizzy or light-headed during this process.

What to do if you think you've cut too deep

If you're bleeding heavily and for a sustained period of time, you'll need to seek some urgent help. If blood is spurting, is a very dark red or has been flowing for more than twenty minutes, you need to either call an ambulance or get to A&E as soon as possible, and keep firm pressure on the wound during this time. This will be an incredibly difficult thing to do, I know, but you need to do it. Listen to me: you need to do this, and you can do this. Everything will be absolutely fine once you do. They'll get you patched up and straightened out, and they won't be seeing anything that they've not seen a hundred times before. If you can call a friend or a family member to take you there or to be with you, then do it. This is not a time to be alone if you can help it.

If you're not bleeding heavily or for a sustained amount of time but you can see fatty tissue in the cut, then you should ideally get some stitches, though you're not necessarily in danger if you don't.

Additional things to be wary of are cuts near joints or tendons, or cuts that may have damaged your nerves. Get to a doctor so you can be sure that there's no lasting damage. Always err on the side of caution.

How to care for second-degree burns

The first step is to rinse the burn with cool water (though not freezing or icy) until the pain stops. This might take anywhere from fifteen minutes to half an hour. You can also effectively rinse an area by placing the burned area into a basin or tub of cool water. Alternatively, you can use cool compresses if that's more convenient.

Always wash your hands before you clean or touch a burn, and try to keep any dirt or unclean objects away from your burn because they're easily infected. Let your burn heal by not interfering with it by touching or pressing it or by trying to pop, slice or drain the blisters. Use clean, cool water to gently wash the burn as it heals and then pat the area dry with a clean, smooth cloth. Don't scrub at the burn or use an abrasive material. Also, don't use any sprays or butters on fresh burns as this can just trap the heat inside the burn and interfere with the healing process.

If you're wearing any jewellery in that area, gently try to take it off as soon as possible, as your skin might start to swell or feel 'sticky'. If this has already happened, try to leave any jewellery or item of clothing that can't easily be pulled away. Seek medical help in this case.

For chemical burns you'll need to rinse the wound under cool, slow-running water for at least twenty minutes, before ideally seeking medical help as soon as possible – no matter the severity. See somebody.

Signs that you're in shock

With significant blood loss or any severe injury, you have to be cautious of going into shock – which just means that your blood flow in your body is significantly reduced. Signs of shock are rapid and shallow breathing (feeling breathless) or feeling nauseated or dizzy. Shock can be fatal, and it's important to know the signs.

If you think you've overdosed

Call an ambulance, or a friend, or get yourself to A&E. If you're worried about loss of consciousness or confusion later on, write down anything that you've ingested, so that your friend or the medical professional knows what's happened and what they're dealing with.

Common signs of infection

- Increased or unusual discharge coming from the wound.
- Swelling that continues after five to seven days post-injury. It may also feel hot and painful to the touch.
- A wound that looks as though it's healing but is still unusually painful or sore.
- A wound that doesn't seem to be responding to any of the recommended treatments or creams that you're using.
- An unusually high or low body temperature or a faster heart rate than usual.
- An older wound that's still prone to bleeding.

If you experience any of the above, see a doctor. You might need antibiotics or a different topical treatment. Be as pragmatic as possible: they're doctors and they've seen it all before. Take a big breath, walk into the surgery or the hospital and be brave. Show them the wound, tell them how it happened, and let them help you.

How to treat scars

If you have scars and you're interested in fading them, this advice is for you. But before I get into it, I just want to say this: you're under absolutely no obligation to hide or fade your scars. Other people may find them uncomfortable or confusing – we all know that happens. But it's your body and other people's comfort isn't an important or relevant factor here. If you're proud of your body for healing and don't have a problem with the appearance of your scars, then don't for a second think you're obligated to change a damn thing. All right, sermon over.

Bio-oil, vitamin E and cocoa butter can all be relatively inexpensive treatments for fading old scars. Applying them daily after your shower or bath or before you go to bed is an easy way to incorporate them into your routine. But you can also use special types of acids or oils as topical treatments. If you can afford to see a dermatologist, they'll be able to help with more specialised treatments.

Alternatives to self-harm

Trigger warning: mentions of self-harm.

Self-harm can be a very effective method of managing depression and anxiety. That's the truth of it. It's quick and sharp and to the point. It does the job. But it's also something we can't continue to do long term into our recovery. Because while YES it might make us feel better in the moment, it's still a violent and destructive act in the long term. No shame, no pity: that's just how it is. So we need to gradually replace it with other methods that can help us wean ourselves away and eventually stop completely.

Disclaimer: I know that when the urge to hurt yourself is looming really large, most of the things I list below won't be viable options. But I'm listing them anyway because they might help, they might take the edge off enough that the damage needed won't be quite as severe. So here they are. Just in case.

- Hold or squeeze an ice cube.
- Snap a rubber band against your wrist or arm.
- Splash or submerge your face in icy cold water.
- Eat or chew on something sour, like a chunk of lemon or a bag of sour sweets.
- Rub or massage your usual self-harm site (if it's free of current injuries).
- Make a physical list of why you're trying to stop self-harming, the benefits of being clean of cuts, and how you can reward yourself for your new milestones.
- Try getting your heart rate up with a quick sprint or burst of movement.
- Scream or yell into a pillow.
- Write a cathartic letter or email – something that you'll never send but that you'll imagine you will. Swear and be pissed off and write as furiously as you want to. Then delete it. Or burn it. Or eat it. Or feed it to a goat. Or throw it into the ocean. Whatever feels best.
- Spend time with an animal.

How to help friends and family struggling with self-harm

Trigger warning: mentions of self-harm.

An important thing to remember whenever trying to help anyone with issues relating to self-harm: leave shame and disapproval and disappointment at the door. It has no place here. So leave it behind. You don't need it. It is not welcome. Flush it down the toilet. Throw it into the swamp. If you're using shame to try to help your loved one stop hurting themselves, then you're doing it all wrong. It's not even just unhelpful – it's risky and damaging and completely messed up. I'm mostly finished yelling about this now but please don't cross me on this again or I may fight you.

♣ Don't try and emotionally coerce someone into not self-harming. Don't bargain with them, or bribe them, or tell them that you'll be disappointed and upset if they do it again. Don't threaten to hurt yourself if they hurt themselves. Don't threaten to take away privileges or possessions if they can't get it under control right away. Not only will this not work, but it's also incredibly alienating, hurtful and plain out of line.

♣ Do ask them if they feel like a distraction might help, or if they feel in any immediate danger. Do ask if there's anything specifically that you can do to help. Do encourage them to be as safe as possible. Do remind them of the importance of cleaning and covering their cuts. Kindly and gently nag them about this.

♣ Remember that self-harm and self-neglect isn't just limited to cutting or burning. It can involve people depriving themselves of sleep or food or other basic necessities. It can be binge-eating or exercising until they're sick and exhausted. It can be intentionally putting themselves in stressful or triggering situations, or getting back in touch with people who were abusive or unkind to them in the past, or depriving themselves of positive human contact or pleasurable experiences. So when you're trying to be vigilant about self-harm in your loved one, try to think more broadly.

♣ Remember that they're still a whole person – a person with a whole personality, hopes, dreams, interests, skills. They're a hell of a lot more than the sum of their symptoms, and they definitely aren't a cause or a charity case for you to work on and fix.

♣ Don't make decisions for them. If they're open to suggestions, tell them what you think (especially if you've been in their position before). But don't insist or nag or tell them that they're wrong for not following your advice.

♣ Try to understand that this isn't something they're doing to spite you or upset you. It has nothing to do with you, in fact. You don't need to totally understand why it helps or like it one bit, but you should try to accept that, for now at least, it is an effective skill for minimising their pain and helping them cope. This doesn't mean you have to think of it as a healthy long-term coping strategy. It's not! They know it, you know it. But right now it's doing the work, and until they can learn to replace it with something else, you may need to get used to the idea that this is something that they do sometimes.

♣ Be their cheerleader. You may not be able to help them stop self-harming. That will probably take a lot of time and a lot of treatment with a trained professional. But what you can do is remind them of how great you think they are. You can plan fun things for the two of you to enjoy – things that you know that they're good at and won't make them spiral.

Suicide and suicidal ideation

Trigger warning: mentions of suicide.

In this next section I'm going to talk about suicide. It was pretty difficult and upsetting to write, so be prepared for it to be upsetting to read. If any part of you feels that you're not ready to read it, or that you might be triggered: skip it.

Nobody knows how to talk about suicide. Wanting to die is the big no-no topic for small talk. You can't just bring it up at dinner parties and expect not to ruin the tiramisu. It's not realistic.

For a start, finding the language to use is nearly impossible. And even if you know exactly what you want to say, you don't want to worry your friends and family, or risk them trying to make you go to the hospital or push you further than you're ready. You also don't want to risk the potential shame, the possibility that you'll open up to the people you love more than anyone else and get nothing but rejection in return. You worry that they'll give you The Look – you know the one I mean. The look that says, 'This isn't normal. You're not normal. The way I think about you is irrevocably changed – all because you opened your mouth.' The look that makes you think maybe you SHOULD just do the thing and end it all and never bother the rational, normal, non-suicidal sector of society again. You're probably even reluctant to talk about it with your doctor. What if they react the same? What if they try to get you sent away? What if they say they can't help you and then that's it – there's no more hope?

Feeling suicidal is a generally indefinable thing. People ask you to show them where it hurts, but where it hurts is nameless. It hurts somewhere off the map. It hurts within the hurt and it has done for a long, long time.

The panic and the shame of feeling like this is overwhelming, and long before you find any peace and understanding with it, you'll feel utterly and completely alone.

But you're not alone. That's what I'm here on Earth to tell you. I'm here to say that despite the very convincing feeling that you ARE alone – YOU ARE NOT ALONE. And sure, it feels like you're in an endless awful infinite darkness and you are there entirely and completely by yourself in this odd and empty place. The land is barren. The horizon is empty. You're there by yourself and nobody knows what it's like but you. I'm here to tell you that's bullshit.

You think I'm full of it. You think anyone who tells you they understand what you're going through is similarly full of it. You wish we'd leave you alone in the dark, strange land that is yours and yours alone.

But I won't leave you alone. You are wrong. The dark, strange place that you're in has had a million previous occupants before you got here. It is dark and strange and familiar to a truly astonishing number of people. That's the big ridiculous secret here.

I've been where you are. I've spent months there at a time, actually. I've got a motherfucking timeshare in the dark, strange land of suicidal ideation. There's a whole-ass community of people who know exactly how this feels.

Feeling suicidal when you're depressed is not unusual. Suicidal thoughts, fantasies or images can spring up from a bad day, a change in your personal life, or even premenstrual distress. And it's scary how not scary it is sometimes. It's unnerving that it can be comforting to think about dying, about stopping existing, about nothingness forever and ever and ever. That can't be normal? That's totally fucked, right?

Well, sure. But also, no, in fact, it's not. When you're in a huge amount of pain, it's understandable to be desperately casting your mind around for a way to end that pain. It's not a huge leap. You're not broken. You're reacting naturally to a really terrible thing and your reaction does not make you frightening or broken.

So why do people end their own lives?

People end their own lives because they're very unwell. They do it because they're receiving the wrong treatment, or because they're receiving no treatment at all. They do it because they're triggered by something and they make a decision in a moment and then that decision sticks. I could go on, but naming reasons why people do it is as exhausting as naming reasons why people die of any illness. They died of the illness because they had the illness and it killed them.

When a suicide happens a lot of people reach straight for blame. They want someone to be angry at, someone to point the finger at. Sometimes they blame themselves, either for doing or for not doing something. But very often they blame the person who's gone, the person who died, the person who took their own life and isn't here to give any answers. They blame them for not trying hard enough to survive, for being selfish, for causing so much pain, for leaving so many unanswered questions. For wasting the great, wonderful, brilliant gift of life. Because sure, life can be the most wonderful and brilliant gift, it can be joyful – but in very depressed and mentally ill people, this is very often not the case.

As sufferers, we're here fighting. We're learning better and better ways to cope, but very often there's no light falling where we are.

As a society we treat the mentally ill and the suicidal with frightened disdain. We don't want them to come any closer. We don't want to catch what they've got. We don't want to lose the people we love to something that we can't see or understand. We don't want to comprehend the kind of pain it takes to lead someone right up to the edge and then over it. It's easier to look the other way. But it's the reality for millions of people. It's not a dark underbelly. It's everywhere. All over the place, people are feeling like this. Even people who are outwardly successful, financially stable and apparently have everything they need to have a happy, brilliant life can feel suicidal. They can finish work every Friday and spend their train journey home figuring out how not to be alive by Monday.

So we need to collectively do better by each other. We need to let go of the idea that a suicide happens because of weakness. Let that idea go and let it stay gone. This isn't what happens at the edge. You aren't there because you were given a choice and you chose wrong. You're there because you're sick and your options feel limited.

We also have to stop moralising suicide the way we do. It is a death from a serious illness. It's not selfish or short-sighted or weak. It's no more selfish a death than that of someone who had an aneurysm, or diabetes. The treatment available for mental illness simply isn't good enough, and so people fall through the cracks. It happens. They get sick and they have no access to treatment. They're routinely shamed and judged and ignored. And then they get so sick that they die. They're in so much pain that they die. And if that isn't something worth talking loudly and non-judgementally about, then I don't know what is.

Life can be very hard and ugly, and responding to the darkness by feeling bad is not a mistake, or a blip, or something to be ashamed of. It makes all the sense in the world in that moment. We honour the people who've died by refusing to feel shame on their behalf. We shed the stigma and we reach out to one another.

There is light ahead. It's coming.

Misconceptions about suicide

Trigger warning: mentions of self-harm.

♣ 'Suicide is a selfish thing to do.' Suicidal feelings are a serious symptom of a serious illness. A death from suicide is no more selfish than a death from any other illness. It opens up so many questions, so much pain and regret and wondering whether there was more that could have been done. Culturally, we still don't know where we stand on suicide. It's either romanticised or vilified. But it's not selfish, and that's all we need to work hard to remember.

♣ 'Only really messed-up people think about taking their own lives.' We're not all on separate teams here. Suicidal ideation can happen to anyone. It's not a sign of deep wrongness and it doesn't separate us into an abnormal category.

♣ 'Suicide is choosing the easy way out.' There's nothing easy about any of this. When a suicide happens it's just very, very sad. There's no sense or justice in moralising it or making assumptions about what the person was up against or what they should have done differently.

♣ 'Suicide is too serious and awful to ever be spoken about openly.' It's not! I mean, let the depressed person lead the exchange, and try to read the room if you're planning to crack any jokes. But when they bring it up, don't be surprised or scandalised. Listen to them, ask questions. It's a symptom of depression, and talking about it helps a lot. Because it's the kind of thing that goes without being talked about for years and years – not even alluded to. Years and years of shame and denial about it takes its toll – and talking about it at last can be a release and a relief.

♣ 'People who attempt suicide but don't succeed are attention-seeking.' The term 'attention-seeking' is kind of a cop-out in itself. It means very little when applied to mental illness. It's rooted in the bizarre idea that attention is an unhealthy thing to seek when you're in pain. When you're suffering and you need help, attention is necessary. Attention helps other people see that there's a problem, and this is how we access care.

♣ 'Suicidal people are weak people.' I believe with my whole heart and soul that the opposite is true. Continuing to exist when your whole self is hurting and you're desperate to give up – that's strength in its purest form.

Suicidal ideation is not

- Selfish.
- Proof that you're too ill to ever get better.
- A deep and terrible character flaw.
- Something you need to feel ashamed of or to keep to yourself.
- Necessarily a sign of intent or that you're in any immediate danger.
- Something only you are going through.
- A rare or unusual symptom in people who have suffered from depression at some point in their lives.

Relapse

Relapses happen. They've happened to me plenty of times, and every time I think: 'Well, this is it, isn't it. This is the end of everything. I've really definitely absolutely fucked it all up this time. It's hopeless.' And every single time that turns out to be untrue. It's a relapse, and a relapse is a slip. It's falling back a few paces, but it's not the erasure of everything you've accomplished in your life and your recovery. Those good days – the days where you made the right choices and leaned into wellness and happiness – those days are banked. You lived them and nobody can take them away from you. When you slip up and self-harm, or fall back into depressed patterns for a week or two (or even longer) – it's not the end of your recovery. It's not the end of the world (though it definitely feels like it is while it's happening). It's not game over. Nobody yanks you up and forces you back to the start to begin the whole process all over again.

You just have to put yourself back together right where you are. You've done it before and you can do it again. You can and you will. You will because you have to. That's our collective burden and our collective talent: reassembly after the storm, an innate ability to return to wellness from a place so bad that even a brief glimpse would terrify the uninitiated. And yes, okay, sure: I wish we had a collective talent for snowboarding or making erotic origami instead, but there you go. It is what it is. We know which way is up as far as recovery goes, even on the days where we're burning with shame and a desire to vanish completely forever. There is some innate sunflower urge that knows where the light is, knows how to start undoing the damage and swimming back to shore.

Reality vs perception

Your brain lies. Your perception of things differs because of what you've been through, and the things that your brain invites you to believe, even when they're really convincing, can be absolute bullshit.

Your brain will make a very compelling case:

You're not loved by the people you love.
Your friend cancelled because she doesn't care about you.
Your partner isn't texting back because they've found someone else.
You're too sick to get better.
You'd be better off giving up.
You'd be better off dead.

So you have to learn to talk back, to consider this voice as an unwelcome, but ultimately irrelevant, visitor to your brain. You have to learn to say, 'Uh huh, sure thing, thanks,' and roll your eyes at it and carry on with the boring functional tasks of existing and getting better.

You'll need to say, 'I feel this way, but this feeling is not proof of anything. My brain needs correcting sometimes. This is me correcting myself.' Then you correct yourself. And then you fight crime. AND THEN you get a smoothie. Also you get me one. And it isn't particularly glamorous, and it gets repetitive having to deal with the same brain-nonsense week in, week out, but it's necessary, and it helps to get us where we want to be in recovery. Because you're fighting back, and in fighting back you're saying, 'No. I'm not broken, I'm not ruined, I'm not doomed. I'm good. I'm worth this. I'm worth the time it takes to get better.'

Rejecting your own thoughts is a difficult thing to do. It can feel like rejecting a part of your literal, actual self. But you have to learn to reject them anyway, because in rejecting them you can learn to filter negativity out a lot more easily in future. And also: because I said so.

Thoughts influence feelings. Feelings influence actions. Actions can either help or hinder our progress and our recovery. Accepting that the root – the thought – can be based totally outside of reality is a game-changer. What it suddenly means is this: we aren't obligated to listen to the thought or do what it says. We don't have to act on it, in other words. Instead, we can pause. We can give ourselves time to understand and identify the thought for what it is, and then we can choose the best actions to take going forward. We can identify an unhelpful or toxic thought and then firmly refuse to do what it suggests, on account of us now knowing that it doesn't have our best interests at heart. This rogue thought stops having as much power as it did. It gets demoted from big boss to little boss, then to no boss at all. Before you know it it's packing up its desk and clearing the hell out.

So interrogate the thought. Ask it where it came from. Ask it where did it go? Ask it did it come from Cotton-Eye Joe? Ask your thoughts for proof. Be firm and calm but don't let yourself get away with the same nonsense any more. You're probably full of at least a certain amount of shit. And that, my friend, is fine.

On some days

On some days you're going to feel worse than you can ever remember having felt in your entire stupid stinking life. Everything you encounter will feel stupid and pointless and ridiculous and you'll even hate the very idea of things that you know you love. Babies laughing? Trash. Tiny dogs wearing costumes? No thanks. Free ice cream? You can fuck right off with that.

Getting out of bed will be laughably difficult. You won't be laughing, though, on account of how your entire head is full of lead and lava and flesh-eating bees. Objectively, though, ha ha. Out of bed is not happening. Get real, universe. You slag. You horrible, rude, high-expectations-having slag.

Clenching your fists and crying will be the only exercise you're able to do. If there's water in reach, you might take a sip. If not then you'll lie thirsty and hateful in bed for hours like an angry little desert crab.

On some days you won't be able to see beyond this feeling. The wire-wool-brained misery of it will consume everything in its path and leave no room for empathy or joy or patience.

These days can come out of nowhere. They stomp their feet and demand to be noticed.

There's not much else you can do on days like these but endure them as best you can, knowing that you are never alone in the feeling and that it will absolutely pass.

Reasons why you might be feeling terrible

♣ Are you dehydrated? If you haven't had a glass of water or a drink within the past hour – go and get one now. Heck, go and get two. Treat yourself. If you'd prefer juice or squash or tea – that's cool. I'm not your beverage boss.

♣ Are you hungry? If you've not eaten at your usual times today (or not at all), go and grab a snack right now. Eat something and then wait a while and see how you feel.

♣ Have you changed your medications recently? Your body needs time to adjust to a new medication, and it's likely in the early days that there'll be all kinds of side effects.

♣ Have you been taking your medications on time lately? Even a difference of an hour or two can mean a spiral for some people. Try setting an alarm on your phone to remind you to take it every day.

♣ Are you avoiding doing something because of anxiety or worry? Go and do the thing. Look right at the thing and ask it what it needs from you. Then do everything that you can to take the sting and the panic out of it.

♣ When was the last time you expressed how you felt emotionally, whether in a conversation or a letter or a diary entry? Putting your current emotional position into words can help keep you focused on where you are now and where you want to be. It can stop you from amplifying and exaggerating. Have a cry if you can. Let this out.

♣ Is there something that's really stressing you out lately? Something that you've put to the back of your mind but is still giving you little jolts of panic? Sometimes we bury these fears and try very, very hard not to think about them instead of just facing them and getting them sorted and out of the way. Left unattended they grow into terrible, twisted, miserable plants. Ask a friend for help.

Productive things you can do without leaving your bedroom

♣ Plug in all of your devices to charge. This includes phone, laptop, iPod, camera, portable chargers – everything. Anything that you can cram with delicious electricity, do it.

♣ Put away all the clean clothes that are scattered around your room. Then put all the dirty clothes in one place too. I know they're there. Don't you try to lie to me about this. I don't care if you just make two piles on a chair or by the door. But get them off the gosh-darn floor right now now or else I will stuff you into a toilet. Don't you think that I won't.

♣ Open the blinds or the curtains, then open a window if you can. Whatever you're doing and whatever your energy level, fresh air will help make a room less stale and energise you a little. If you can stick your head out of the window and get a couple of big chomps of fresh air then that's a bonus. Go straight to the source. Take a big hit of that ol' air flow.

♣ Moisturise your whole body. Take your time doing it. Use a different moisturiser for your face than your body, like a famous celebrity might do. Even a jumbo tub of E45 that's been sitting under the sink for as long as you can remember will do the job.

♣ Try some basic meditations. For this one you can just fire up the old YouTube Video Machine and you're hot to trot. You don't have to expect any groundbreaking results: just recognise that this is a thing that helps a lot of people (many of who may be wired very much like you) and that you lose nothing by trying. Scientifically speaking, doing some controlled breathing and learning to filter your thoughts is a REALLY GOOD AND HEALTHY THING FOR YOUR BODY AND YOUR BRAIN. Plus you can do it while you're lying in bed in your underwear and it passes the time slightly more interestingly than just staring at the ceiling and waiting for the world to end.

♣ Dust something. This can be a single shelf or a side table or the top of a picture frame. Maybe spray a cloth with some cleaning type stuff and then run wildly around the room, swiping indiscriminately at every flat surface you see until things seem a little shinier. Dusting is a fairly low-stakes cleaning activity. You just lift up an object, wipe then put the object down again. It's great.

Templates for better days

If you wake up early

Try jumping straight out of bed. Trick yourself into thinking you're the kind of person that jumps out of bed. Have a cup of something hydrating. Water or a healthy juice or a hot herbal tea. Then have something to eat. Your body functions best when it is hydrated and fuelled.

Turn off your phone (or place it far away on a high shelf) while you eat your breakfast and drink your hydrating drink. Focus on the tastes and sensations.

Go for a walk. It's a good way to start the day, and getting your heart pumping will release endorphins. Endorphins are very tiny blood horses that gallop around your human body and make you feel all nice. Or something. Fuck it. Who knows.

If you wake up very late

Take a moment to breathe, and to repeat to yourself that no day is wasted and done until the very final minute. You have plenty of time to make today good. Your body wanted sleep, and so it took it. There's nothing to panic about now.

If you feel groggy and fuzzy, then jump in the shower and be thorough about getting everything cleaned. Take deep breaths and let the steam and the water wake you up. Unless you're meant to be officiating at a wedding or piloting a spaceship, then you're good to take a few extra seconds in there.

Don't rush to catch up. If you're able to, slow down and mindfully do the things that you intended to do early in the day. Have something small to eat, and a cup of tea or coffee, and think about your plan for the day. What can you do with the time left? What steps can you take to improve your mood and feel more in control of the day?

If you wake up in a good mood

Practise gratitude for this feeling. You're a good person who deserves these good feelings and there are so many more good feelings ahead for you in life. With this in mind, get some breakfast and a cup of something warm and energising. The idea here is to keep the good feeling around for as long as possible, and so you need to nurture it with something tasty and full of vitamins (a very tiny and helpful kind of ghost found in certain foods and plants).

If you wake up in a bad mood

Practise patience and wilful endurance. You're in a bad mood right now, you're feeling bad, and badness is mostly all of what you can feel right now. In the face of that, you're allowed to curl up and hide. You're allowed to honour the shitty, terrible, miserable feeling in your heart. You don't fail when you honour your emotions. So admit that feeling to yourself. You feel bad. But also admit that you're still able to do things on bad days. Bad days are difficult, but they aren't impossible. They just require more patience and a bit more grit and determination.

If you can leave the house

Try to do something useful for future-you, like get a food shop in, or run a couple of errands – return parcels, take money to the bank, buy cards and stamps for upcoming birthdays.

Or just take a walk. It doesn't need to be a walk to anywhere in particular or for any particular purpose. Just try to enjoy the air and the sky and the feeling of the ground under your feet and the deliberate forward motion. Choose a new route, or an old favourite route, and just go. Walking for walking's sake is always worthwhile.

If you can't leave the house

Commit now to at least trying to do some very basic things today. These things might include brushing your hair, cleaning your teeth, making your bed, opening a window, catching up on a little bit of work or replying to at least four emails or text messages. No saving the world or leaping through burning hoops today. No sir. Those things can wait. What today is asking of you is that you try and that you do one or two things to exist above the gulf of deep, endless misery. Today is asking for no more than that.

Try to be somewhere outside of your bed and your bedroom – even just for an hour or two. Set up shop in the kitchen or the living room. Staying in one room is likely to make you feel even worse than you're already feeling.

Things that feel shameful but are actually just symptoms of your illness

♣ Not having the energy (or the inclination) to shower or wash or brush your teeth or your hair or moisturise or shave or put jeans on. This might go on for a day or two days or it might go on for weeks at a time. And it will feel gross and shameful and otherising, but it's a symptom. It's a part of the worst of this, and you're never alone in it.

♣ Feeling nothing but indifference when someone gives you good news, or at other times when you know that you're supposed to be happy. Depression apathy is a very real thing. It doesn't mean you don't love your friends or your family and don't feel happy for them when something good happens. It's just a symptom of depression and exhaustion. The colour will come back.

♣ Sleeping for most of the day. Depression and anxiety use up a hell of a lot of energy. Also, being awake when you're feeling that shitty isn't the world's most appealing option. Look, when people are incredibly depressed, they sleep. You are a people. You are feeling depressed. So if you can't stand being awake right now – go to sleep. Or, if you're on the bus or operating heavy machinery, wait until you're home and then go to sleep. And when you wake up you might feel a little better, and then you can work on doing better. Because when you're flat-out exhausted and utterly miserable, you're in no position to do much good for anybody. Rest.

♣ Thoughts of self-harm or suicide. Ill and depressed people often want to vanish. Ill and depressed people often believe they're deserving of their suffering, and that inflicting the same suffering on themselves is totally normal. Ill and depressed people are under a huge amount of pressure, and imagining a future where that pressure doesn't exist isn't an unbelievable or shameful thing.

♣ Not being able to tidy or clean up around you. At the height of a bad spell you might find yourself living in a fairly horrific mess. Lots of dirty bowls and cups and old food packaging. Lots of dirty clothes and underwear. Some stuff will have been spilled along the way and you will not have cleaned it up.

Things to consider not doing any more

Trigger warning: mentions of suicide.

♣ Checking in on your exes' social media. It's tempting on some bizarre self-harming level, but there's absolutely zero need for you to do it. Whether it causes you pain or just informs you of things that are of no use to you, it's pointless. Let it go. Cut yourself off from the supply and don't do it any more. Be really firm with yourself about this. Instead, try following a couple of extra-cute animal accounts. Check to see what your favourite tiny monkey did. Maybe that adorable hippo did something really funny today. Only one way to find out!

♣ Weighing yourself. Unless you're a baby koala at the zoo that is under observation because of a stomach infection there are very few reasons why anyone needs to know their exact weight. Numbers don't mean anything and I am actively working to have them all destroyed and replaced with little dog drawings. Poodle doodles, if you will. But until that day you're going to have to try your best to join me in throwing away the scales and caring less about it.

♣ Using the term 'committing suicide' in any of your speech or writing. There's no crime when a person dies from suicide. It is not an abhorrent or criminal decision. It's death from suicide. It's death from an illness. A person had an illness and the illness killed them – this is what suicide is.

Some signs that you might need to ask for help

- Your medication doesn't feel like it's working any more, or the effects of it are different – and more unpleasant – than they used to be.
- You're sleeping a lot more than usual.
- You find yourself self-medicating with drugs or alcohol.
- You can't seem to find the energy or desire to do life-maintenance things like going to school, university or work, tidying up, cooking, cleaning, showering or even fun things like seeing friends or doing an activity that you know you enjoy.
- You've noticed an increase in thoughts of self-harm or suicide.
- Close friends or family have expressed concern about you.

When it goes wrong

Even when you know better, even when you have all of the skills and the methods on hand to deal with a blip or a hard moment – they don't always do what they're meant to do.

1. Name the thing that you've struggled to correct or work against – is it self-harm, is it restrictive or self-punishing behaviour, is it negative self-talk, is it engaging in toxic and risk-taking behaviour when under the influence of drugs or alcohol? Figure out where your recovery is snagging.

2. Take a closer look at what happened. Were there any contributing factors to this behaviour? Were you under any additional stresses? This could be immediately before you acted, or it could be in the weeks or days before.
3. In an ideal world, how would this situation have been handled?
4. What happened after the problem behaviour? What were the negative or neutral consequences of behaving in this way? Did it have any ill effects on relationships, on your career, on your physical or mental health? Were you able to practise self-compassion and self-care or did it cause you to double down and treat yourself even more poorly?
5. Make a plan for the next time this happens. What will you try to do differently? What will be your priority?

How to practise self-care when you can hardly get out of bed

There are so many cheerful and encouraging resources for people who aren't feeling great but are still functional enough to leave the house or run a bath or head to the corner shop for some snacks and face masks. There are fewer resources for when you're all but immobilised by illness and can barely face moving enough to pick up the glass of old water on your bedside table and taking a sip. Which makes sense, I guess. It's harder to make that shit sound cute. There's no adorable panda sheet mask you can throw over that bad boy. So here are some alternative suggestions.

♣ Plug in your phone to charge. If you can face it, plug everything else in as well.

♣ Get some water (or other non-alcoholic fluid).

♣ Drink that water (or other non-alcoholic fluid).

♣ Address your most immediate physical pains: headache, stomach pangs, any physical wounds that need cleaning and covering.

♣ Catch up on some basic social maintenance stuff – text your partner or best friend, or a family member that you can trust with this stuff, and give them an update. Let your boss know that you're ill and might not be in this week. Text a co-worker and ask if they can cover a future shift. Email your tutor or professor to explain that you're too ill to make it in today, but you'd appreciate any help catching up. Contact someone in your class and ask if they can let you know what you've missed and email you any homework.

♣ If you can't face getting up to brush your teeth, then grab some chewing gum or have a quick swill of mouthwash (both of which you should start keeping by your bed). It'll make you feel slightly more human almost immediately.

♣ Push back your duvet and swipe all of the crumbs and other bits of depression debris out of your bed and onto the floor. You can deal with them later when you're feeling better, but in the meantime it's important that you're not feeling any more physical discomfort than you have to. One time I found four coat hangers, a battery, three chocolate-bar wrappers and a stack of books in my bed. That's way too much stuff, man. It will make you feel cleaner and more like a person to have your bed free of all this junk, and it may help you sleep better.

♣ Make an effort to change out of any dirty clothes and into something clean. Even changing your underwear is a win. If you can't manage this, then spray what you're wearing with something that smells good. If you're not feeling up to getting fully dressed, even just changing out of one set of pyjamas and into another is a step in the right direction. Or find some middle ground with a comfy pair of trackies and a jumper rather than the same set of pyjamas you've been wearing for four days.

♣ Grab a handful of baby wipes and give yourself a quick clean with them. Because we all know that there will probably be days and days when you can't face showering. We've all been there, it's nothing to be ashamed of, but it's definitely not heaps of fun. It's one of those very real aspects of depression that can't be ignored. Like how we can all communicate with animals and sense when someone's about to sneeze.

♣ If there's someone you can text to ask to bring you food, text them now. If not, try to order something in. On days when you can't cook, you still need to eat. On days where you think you're too depressed and useless to deserve to eat, YOU STILL NEED TO EAT. Your body has to have food. It is its fuel and its joy and what it needs to keep moving. So give it food. There is no 'deserving' about it. There is no 'earning it'. There is just need and want and providing for yourself if and when you're able to. Honouring your need for food even on the most miserable and lethargic days is how you look after yourself here.

And next time you can get to the shops, you'll stock up on some energy bars or little snack packs. But for right now: do what you can to get food in your body. If it's simple and easy, so be it.

Rejoice at living in a world where you don't have to chase after your food with a spear.

♣ Do some light stretching, either in bed or standing or sitting on the floor of your bedroom. Start with your feet and your toes, then work upwards until you're gently rolling your shoulders and moving your head from side to side. This will help loosen up any stiffness caused by lying down for a long time, and might help you feel a bit more human.

♣ Watch a few YouTube videos – these can be related to mental health, but they don't have to be. You can watch compilations of cats doing hilarious things, or some stand-up, or inspiring speeches. You can watch a porpoise happily play in the ocean, or a video of a baby eating marmalade. I like watching make-up tutorials, personally, despite knowing nothing about make-up. They're all so beautiful and shiny and they use big soft brushes and sparkles and it's just so soothing to me.

♣ Let some light or fresh air in. Get out of bed and open the window or the blinds. Then you can go back and lie down. The light and the air won't totally mend your mood, but they can help with the groggy, brain-foggy feeling that comes with debilitating bouts of depression.

♣ Try to connect with somebody – either on the phone or by text or email. Text your best friend, or your mum, or someone who you know can relate. Or if you don't feel like talking about what you're going through, text a friend just to catch up. Ask them what they're doing. This can work as a great distraction, but it's also very low stakes. You can do it from your bed, and you can put a pause on it at very short notice. Just tell them you're going back to bed and will talk to them soon.

How to check that you've taken care of the basics

- Have you eaten in the last few hours or at all today?
- Did you shower today or yesterday?
- Did you brush your teeth today?
- When was the last time you drank any water? Have you had a glass of water in the last hour?
- Is your laundry done or do you have at least enough clean clothes and underwear to last you the next few days?
- Are your pets fed, walked, cleaned out and generally taken care of?
- Have you washed your face, brushed your hair or used deodorant today?
- Have you done at least one of your daily chores? Is the bed made, for example, or does the dishwasher need loading or unloading?
- Have you taken your medication today or at all for the last few days?
- Have you been to see if there's any post for you?
- Are there any bills or payments due today or this week that need taking care of?
- Have you been out of the house, even for five minutes, in the last twenty-four hours?
- Have you called or texted a member of your family or friendship group in the last few days, either to let them know that you're all right or to ask them for help?
- Have you stretched your arms or your legs or been for a walk longer than a few minutes in the last day?
- Have you missed an appointment or meeting lately that you need to reschedule?

- Have you done something that you enjoy or that brings you pleasure in the last few days?
- Do you need to speak to a doctor or a professional about any developments or changes in your mental or physical health?
- Have you tried meditating or using any mindfulness or DBT skills in the last day or so?
- How much time have you taken away from your phone or laptop today? Are you feeling any strain or discomfort in your eyes or head that might be related to how much time you've spent looking at a screen?
- What's your current environment like? Are you sitting among dirty dishes or clothes or in a stuffy and stale room? Can you let in any fresh air or light a candle or incense? Can you make the bed and move all rubbish into a bag outside of the room or out of sight?

How to reduce and replace negative thoughts

Reducing and replacing negative thoughts takes a lot of deliberate effort. It involves naming and recognising cognitive distortions and then doing a lot of work to get around them in future.

You need a better way of talking to yourself, first of all. Those negative beliefs about yourself sit brutal and deadly like icebergs in a dark, dark sea. Unchecked, those motherfuckers are prone to sinking massive ships and KILLING beloved actor and environmental activist Leonardo DiCaprisun. We just can't let that happen any more, you guys. We need to either chop those fuckers down and make them into tiny slushy cones, or we need a better plan for navigating around them without tearing a massive great hole in the middle of our progress. You get me? Me neither. It's fine, though. Let's sail on anyway.

1. Write down the negative belief that you have about yourself.

2. Examine the belief closer. Ask what evidence you have for the belief. Be critical and scientific when you do this exercise, and reject common vaguenesses such as 'because I am' or 'because I know it.' This is science camp and you're being foolish. Facts and rationality are what you need to be working with here.

3. Look at the language that you're using. Is the language critical, cruel or negative? Does it lean towards giving yourself the benefit of the doubt or does it automatically assume that you're bad and awful? Would you ever use this language about a friend or loved one?

Look: we all believe some wildly inaccurate things about ourselves. Even those of us who outwardly seem to have no problems with self-love can be quietly and secretly seething inside. We believe that we're broken or rotten or bad or unworthy or unlovable or too stupid to do anything worthwhile ever. And our evidence for believing these things is extremely sketchy, and wouldn't stand up in any court of law. But we go on believing them anyway. They're comfortable discomforts. Old friends that don't treat us well or support the things we do, but that we've got used to and wouldn't know how to begin to be without. But now is the time to boot them out. To show them the door. To murder them in their beds. Too dark? I thought that as I was writing it. I'm sorry. But it is time to give them the old heave-ho. We want to go forward, and we want to tolerate (and then like) ourselves as much as possible, and to do that we can't keep entertaining the same old broken and faulty trains of thought. We need to get off those trains and call a motherfucking self-love taxi.

How to manage unpleasant or intrusive thoughts

♣ Don't suppress them. Suppressing a thought is as effective as trying to sew a wet paper bag shut while wearing oven gloves. Is it sexy? Absolutely. Is it a good use of your time? No. Instead, try to engage with it in a new way. Perhaps with a little comedy, or with a strong but stern, 'That's not at all what I believe and it isn't what I think.'

♣ Try treating the intrusive thought like an annoying (but ultimately harmless) ghost or spirit. Because that's all it really is. Imagine that it's all whispery and formless and its only power is to haunt the Earth and try to send perfectly pleasant people entirely insane. It's a candy-floss demon. When it pipes up with some unpleasant thought or comment, mentally roll your eyes at it. 'Okay babes, cool. Are you finished? I'm trying to watch TV here.' Then you have to deliberately shift your attention back to what you were doing and do your best to refocus on the matter at hand. As mentioned before, simply pushing down these thoughts will do little to keep them away for good, so looking right at them and saying, 'All right, thanks, moving on. . .' is a new form of attack that might work better.

♣ Talk back. Feel free to engage with your intrusive thought. It's an intruder, yes, but it's not armed. It doesn't have any more power than a beetle with a tiny revolver telling you to fill his tiny bag with money and nobody gets hurt. It's alarming, sure. For a start, how did the beetle get the licence for that gun? And how did it acquire human language? How did it learn to talk at a volume that the human ear could pick up on? So many questions. But ultimately – you're in no danger. So put on your cheeriest, most curious voice and ask the thought, 'Why, though?'

The exchange might go something like this:

'You should give up.'

'Why, though?'

'Um, because you're worthless?'

'Why, though?'

'Because you are.'

'Why, though?'

'BECAUSE SHUT UP, THAT'S WHY.'

Be like a toddler infuriating an older sibling with accidentally existential questions. If your brain wants to talk shit, then talk shit right back.

♣ Work out if there are any major contributing factors. For example, I find myself most troubled by intrusive and unpleasant thoughts when I'm low on sleep. Mornings can be a dangerous time, and a bad one will set the mood for the rest of the day. Realising this made me take my sleep more seriously and lets me plan ahead for potential danger in the mornings. Now I make sure to organise as much as possible the night before and play loud cheery music as I get ready for the day. A small thing, maybe, but it makes a lot of difference. Other contributing factors can be hunger, stress or a recent triggering event. Once you've pinpointed the thing (or things) that usher the terrible thoughts in, you can get to work figuring out how to push back against them.

♣ Understand that intrusive and unpleasant thoughts happen to us all. They happen in differing degrees, sure, but you'd be hard pressed to find someone who'd never experienced them at all (whether they'd be willing to admit it or not is another matter). And what's more: they're not evidence of anything. They're not evidence of an internal sickness or wrongness or brokenness. They're just an unpleasant symptom of an unpleasant illness or just having a human brain. Understanding and working to accept this fact has done me as much good as anything else on this list. It lets me treat myself non-judgementally and be pragmatic in the way I carry on with my day afterwards. Instead of feeling derailed and anxious (and in turn letting even more intrusive thoughts flood into my frantic, unguarded brain) I respond mindfully. I take it for what it is, and remind myself it's a human thing. I repair the damage by thinking good thoughts, kind thoughts, even if I really don't feel like it.

♣ Find a distraction. Sometimes engaging or trying to disprove or shut the thought down won't work in the slightest. It'll be a hopeless exercise and will just sap your energy and leave you tearful and ready for bed. Instead, try doing something that involves keeping your mind on task, but won't matter if you can't fully concentrate on it. I suggest a puzzle or a relaxing video game. Exercise can also help, if it's something you enjoy or can do without getting yourself further into a negative, self-defeating headspace. Or even just calling a chatty friend and have them update you about their life while you listen. Pop on a movie or a TV show, or take a walk somewhere while you listen to a podcast or an audiobook. Draw or make something. Bake an entire banana loaf. Find a simple origami tutorial online and learn how to fold paper antelopes. Get creative.

♣ Understand that you can have intrusive thoughts that go totally against your morals and your beliefs. You can have intrusive thoughts that you know you don't agree with, that repulse and horrify you, that make you feel unsafe or afraid. This can all exist in a mind that isn't evil or twisted. Know that your distress or horror about these thoughts is proof that they don't represent who you are, what you want or anything you would ever act on.

Some good things: part 2

♣ When there's a new episode of your favourite guilty pleasure TV show out and you have nothing to do except sit somewhere comfortable and enjoy it. Maybe with a bag of gummy eels and a big delicious cup of tea. Maybe under some kind of lovely IKEA blanket that the label says is called a SNURGENTRONK and it is VERY SOFT and EXTREMELY SNURGENTRONK and you deserve every single second of it.

♣ An act of kindness from a stranger. Like someone paying for your cup of coffee at the shop, or smiling at you on the bus, or complimenting your shoes as you pass one another in a bar. A small kindness for its own sake and for no other reason than that.

♣ The first real day of spring after winter when the weather stops being like 'NOOOOO' and starts being like 'ahhhhh okay all right yes maybe?' And also the trees are all flirty and the sky is all blue and the air is not yet hot but it's also no longer cold. It's just right. The perfect spring day.

♣ When a cat sits down like a human. Just totally slobbing out like a school teacher after a hard day at work. Totally maxing and relaxing. Sitting on the sofa with their big lovely tummies out watching TV or having a tiny, wee nap. I live for that sight. Ten out of ten personal favourite sight. And even though they have their entire feline crotch all displayed and out there for the world to see, it doesn't matter. It's just joyous. A real treat.

♣ Finding a fiver or a couple of quid in an old jacket pocket. It's like getting a little gift from your past self. A little nod across time that you can use to buy an ice cream or a very small pie or a new lip gloss. Whatever you like. That's magic time-travelling money, and it's yours.

♣ Making a new meal from scratch and having it turn out really good. Maybe you tentatively tried a little vegan curry that even your most meat-loving friend had to admit was delicious. Or maybe you baked up a batch of dairy-free cookies, and instead of being awful cardboard nonsenses, they were amazing.

♣ Putting on a jumper right out of the tumble dryer and feeling like the sun itself is giving you a toasty little hug.

♣ Falling asleep outside on a warm day. Maybe you're in some kind of sunlounger, perfectly designed for this kind of eventuality.

♣ Curling your toes into a really soft rug, or into some warm sand. Two similar but also subtly different sensations. Both pretty lovely, though. Toes don't often get a lot of pampering. We throw them in some shoes, we stub them willy-nilly, we don't really ask how their days went. But this is something just for them.

♣ Standing in front of a fire on a cold wintry day and feeling your butt get all warm and toasty. A warm, toasty butt is truly the peak of comfort and luxury and I'll hear nothing to the contrary.

♣ A huge bowl or mug of your favourite soup on a cold, foggy, miserable day. Soup, despite being a drink that insists on masquerading as a meal, is nonetheless very delicious and perfect on miserable days.

♣ Watching a cat lick its paw and then groom its face. The other parts of the grooming process, the whole crotch-licking thing, are less cute. But this is an adorable and life-affirming thing to see. They're so clever and innovative, those cats.

♣ Wrapping yourself up in a warm towel after a swim or a bath, like a lovely human spring roll.

♣ When you do something you've been scared to do and it turns out that it was actually no big deal. Or it was, and it sucked, but then it's finally finished, so who cares! Bye!

♣ Finding a brilliant bargain in a charity shop or on ebay. Maybe you find an old pair of designer clogs, or a denim jacket with a huge sparkly aubergine decal, and it's just the most beautiful thing you've ever seen and then you get to own it and wear it whenever you like.

♣ Doing something that really makes someone else's day. It's a bonus when the thing didn't even cost you a lot of money.

♣ Getting an unexpected day off – or even just a morning or an afternoon. Capitalism is such a scam and it also takes up a lot of time, so getting some of that time back to sleep or eat crumpets can feel like a real treat.

How to practise distress tolerance using the ACCEPTS skill

ACCEPTS

A – Activities

Getting yourself stuck into an activity when you're feeling bad is a brilliant distraction tactic. Having something to focus your mind on when you're in a bad place is a way to avoid sinking deeper into the bad place. Things you can try: going for a walk or a run or doing a quick workout, tidying or organising a section of your house or your room, playing an engrossing game on your phone or a console.

C – Contribute

Do something that sends a little positivity out into the universe. Not only is this distracting, it also breaks you out of whatever self-destructive, seething, furious brain space that you're in. Things you can try: write a letter or a card to someone who you love. Maybe an old friend or a grandma or your best pal who lives two streets away. Similarly you can make or bake something to share with the people you love. If you're not up to anything high energy, you could try just paying for someone else's coffee or donating to a charity.

C – Compare

Try comparing your current situation with you a few years ago, or at a time when you knew less and were worse off. You can also compare yourself to other people who have been where you are now – what did they do, what did they try, how did they break through that time and into a better present moment?

E – opposite Emotion

Identify the negative emotion that you're feeling and then practise the opposite emotion. You can find more information about this in the following section.

P – Pushing away

When you start to feel lost and overwhelmed by a situation or feeling, visualise the problem as a tangible and literal thing. Then visualise yourself pushing the problem away, crushing the problem down to size, putting the problem as far away from you as it needs to be. This isn't an avoidance tactic so much as it is healthy and necessary distress tolerance. Things you can try: verbally telling the bad feeling or problem to go away, to get lost, to give you a call on 0121-flipping-do-one.

T – Thoughts

Do something that gets your mental cogs turning in a positive way. Writing or journaling can be a great option here. Do a puzzle or a crossword or some other kind of word game. Nothing so difficult that it makes you want to smash a window, though.

S – Sensations

Disrupt the feelings of distress by engaging your other senses. Things you can try: splashing your face with very cold water, snapping a rubber band against your wrist, sprinting up and down the stairs or the garden to increase your heart rate. Or you can try to engage very pleasurable sensations, such as taking a long hot bath.

How to work out if your emotion fits the facts and then use opposite action to regulate mood

What is opposite action?

To put it as simply as possible, opposite action is the practice of identifying the negative emotion that you're currently experiencing, and then choosing to react in a way that is totally unlike that emotion. For example, if you're feeling angry and your anger *doesn't* fit the facts (e.g. if you can be certain that there is no reasonable or logical cause for it), then an opposite action would be removing yourself from the situation or doing something deliberately gentle or meditative to calm down. Or if you're feeling fearful or withdrawn, then the opposite action in that situation would be to face what's scaring you and go out into the world, maybe surround yourself with people, meet a friend, or just give yourself an errand to do.

Opposite action is a difficult skill to master properly, and at times it can feel like a pointless exercise, but the eventual benefit will be an increase in emotional control, and a reduction in the harm that we put ourselves in when confronted with an overwhelming feeling. Opposite action requires us to be open to trying, and willing to explore other options, even if early on we only find ourselves able to identify what the opposite action would be, rather than being able to actually practise it. It involves looking ahead, past the current bad feeling, and focusing on doing what needs to be done to pass through it as quickly and harmlessly as possible.

How can I practise opposite action?

First you need to identify what the unpleasant emotion that you're experiencing is. Whether you're angry or upset or jealous, to tackle that feeling you first need to name it, look it in the eye and accept that it's happening.

Then you need to ask yourself: does this emotion fit the facts? For example, you may have identified the unpleasant emotion as fear – asking if the emotion of fear fits the facts means asking if the situation is actually immediately threatening to your safety or the safety of those around you. If the answer is no, then opposite action can work.

When Anger doesn't fit the facts, take immediate space from the person or situation that's making you angry. Try doing something deliberately kind or gentle if you can, but even doing something neutral or distracting is a win.

When Jealousy doesn't fit the facts, practise being as magnanimous and trusting as possible. Give the person who's the focus of your jealousy plenty of space. Refuse to lash out and vocalise your non-fact-fitting jealous feelings. Instead, vocalise rational and fair feelings about them and about yourself.

When Fear doesn't fit the facts, take a deep breath. Nope, deeper than that. There we go, that's more like it. Then figure out how big a move you can make to counter the feeling. Do something brave. If what you're scared of is outside, get outside (even just into the back garden). If what you're scared of is making a phone call, write down a transcript and practise dialling the number, and then push yourself to try to make the call.

When Sadness doesn't fit the facts, do something intentionally joyful. Take a walk, smile at a dog, buy yourself a small pastry and eat it in the park. Spread the happiness beyond yourself if possible – send a card or a letter, leave a few dozen compliments on your friends' Instagram posts. Sit in front of the mirror and smile at your own reflection. Creepy? Yes. Embarrassing? Yes. Helpful for some bizarre reason? Somehow also yes.

When Resentment doesn't fit the facts, practise deep kindness. Force yourself to say something generous and kind about the person or situation at the centre of your resentful feelings.

When Suspicion doesn't fit the facts, resist all impulses to sleuth. Don't ask leading or accusatory questions. Be kind to the person who's at the centre of this feeling, and let go of your impulse to control and limit and hold on very tight to them so they can never leave you. Tell yourself that you're choosing trust in this situation, despite your desire to do otherwise. Tell yourself that you don't have anywhere near enough evidence to genuinely need to worry, and that your suspicion is born of some toxic impulse that you're now in control of. Being in control here means very firmly resisting and choosing non-action.

When Guilt doesn't fit the facts, remind yourself that you're innocent and good. Smile, breathe deeply, and commit to making a mental list of reasons why you've done nothing wrong here. Remind yourself, too, that no person on Earth is perfect, and that dredging up old mistakes is just a way for you to put yourself down. It's unhelpful and you are going to calmly reject it. Your guilt here is just a reaction to all the things that are going down in your brainbox. Guilt is not rational in this situation and you are allowed to reject it.

If it hurts you, it hurts you

Whether it's for rational or irrational reasons, if something is distressing, then you're entitled to be distressed. That's the bottom line here. Now, that doesn't mean you're allowed to react violently or aggressively to the hurt or distress. It doesn't mean that anyone else is obligated to drop what they're doing immediately to address it. It doesn't mean it's necessarily based in fact or reality. But if it hurts, it hurts – and you do need to address it. You're not crazy. You're not imagining things. Learn to feel your feelings and your pain and gradually do the work to heal them. There is no sense in denying yourself the reality of your pain. You'll hurt worse and nobody will win and everything will be a weird grey kind of misery. So cut it out. If it hurts you then it needs some light on it, simple as that.

I can't do this

Just because you can doesn't mean you *can*. Let me explain, because you look confused. That's okay. Not everyone can be as IMPOSSIBLY brilliant as I am. Okay, so, here's the thing. You might have the *ability* to get up out of bed and go to work today. Your legs might be *capable* of holding you up. Your arms might just *work enough* so that you can choose a shirt and put it on and button it up. You might be able to get on the bus and boop your travel card and then get to your office and type some words on a computer. But this doesn't mean that mentally you can face it. You might be right on the edge, and running on fumes, and pushing yourself to do things you don't feel okay about might just topple you over. You toppling over is a worse consequence than having to take the day off work and risk disappointing your boss.

Your limits are valid.

They're valid even when other people are sceptical. Certain people will always have their own weird and rigid ideas of how productive and normal other people should be. That's their business and their problem. Sure, I wish they'd keep it to themselves more, but this is the soup we find ourselves in. Listen to your body and do let it rest when it asks you for that.

You're already trying hard enough

There's no 'trying harder' when the reason that you're struggling isn't lack of effort, it's just a part of your neurology. So fuck the idea that you aren't trying hard enough, that you aren't putting in enough effort to be well, that you're somehow choosing this reality over a better and easier one. And don't forget, too, that sometimes trying harder will just burn you out, push you over edge and then fry you like a sad and exhausted little onion.

Trying harder isn't always the answer. The answer is often trying different things, switching it up, asking for help, giving yourself a break. Accepting and learning is the secret, not digging deeper and somehow accessing a magical source of new energy that simply doesn't exist.

In the night

Depressed-brain gets hungry late at night. Kept quiet most of the day, it stretches and yawns and scratches its belly. It feeds bad dreams and lets them loose. Negative thoughts jump over one another like sheep to be counted.

At night everything seems a lot worse than it does in the daytime, and so it's important to not make any long-term decisions at night. Put your phone on charge. Get a glass of water. Play a soothing mix of songs, or listen to a podcast to distract yourself. Save all judgements and decisions for the morning – because in the morning you'll exist in an entirely different skin. You'll be far more able to deal with whatever it is that's making the inside of your head all itchy and you'll be less likely to do something unthinking or harmful. Rest, now.

PART FIVE: *Illumination*

Dating when you're mentally ill: part 1

Dating when you have a mental illness can be a real pain in the tit. Mental illness can rob us of the ability to be ourselves for days and days on end, which naturally takes its toll on us and the people around us – even the people who already know and love us, people who understand that we're ill and are on board with us needing support. Bringing a brand new person into that equation is terrifying. There are no guarantees that they won't turn around and flee at the very mention of mental illness, or that they won't use our illness to exploit or abuse us like other people might have done in the past. We can't be sure that they won't scoff and laugh and pass our very real and very serious illness off as 'attention-seeking' or 'weakness'. It's really bloody scary.

When I date, I need to be with a person who will be able to see me clearly enough for both of us on the days when things are very bad. This is the deal we'll strike. I'll do the heavy lifting. I'll do the worst of it, the quiet hauling, the invisible work of recovery. In the middle of the night I'll grit my teeth and try to sleep. In the mornings when the room draws back, and the world's at its strangest, I'll do what I need to do to get up and dressed and go to work. That's my work, now and forever. And my partner's work will be to support me in that. To give me room to suffer and to let me take a break from acting strong. To give me simple and direct reassurances. To uphold their own boundaries and ask what they need of me without bringing judgement or unkindness into the equation.

They'll cheer from the sidelines, and I'll do the same for them, if and when they need it. This is the give and take of love for anyone, mentally healthy or not. Because I'm not a sinking ship – I'm a person with an illness. I don't want anything impossible, I just want a love that's good and honest. If you love me, then love me. Stay beside me when I'm crying, when something in recovery isn't coming together, or when I'm doubting if I'll ever feel well enough. When I can't move for fear, try your best to stay calm, to hold me and remind me to keep breathing. And if I frustrate you, then take some space – don't lash out at me. But also don't forget that your emotional well-being should never take second place, and it's not your job to exhaust yourself to make me better. This is a long road, and there may not be as many eureka moments as we'd both like. So don't give up your sense of peace for me, not ever.

I know what I want from love, and I know what it looks like when someone is unkind. I'm confident in my ability to date without risking my emotional well-being. But there are still so many associated fears. It's scary out here. Dating is terrifying. But it's so brave, too. It's brave to fall in love, to spend your time growing and cultivating that feeling with one person or consensually with several people. It's especially brave to fall in love after heartbreak, or abuse, or when you've lost someone that you loved. It's an act of courage unlike any other. It's also something that the body does almost without thinking. It's breathing, or falling asleep, or singing along to 'Africa' by Toto. It's an automatic human reaction. The world is big and odd and full of terrors. Good love, when you can get it, is a sustaining and illuminating thing like nothing else.

So nurture all of your loves. Nurture your love of other people, or your love of a book or a song or a work of art. Find what you love and go to it as often as possible. And when you're too ill to practise or really feel that love, just trust that it is there, as patient as ever, waiting for you to come back to it.

Here's what I know. Romantic love can't and won't save you from any of this. At best it can distract you, give you something besides yourself and your recovery to live for and pour your time and energy into.

But it will not climb into your brain and untangle the tangles that have been tangled for as long as you can remember. It will not wake you up and get you out of bed and do the work of getting better.

At best, it will be a warm and reassuring other place. A supportive, kind, mutually assuring thing.

At worst, it will siphon your energy into an already dead thing and keep your recovery from even getting started.

When a relationship is your lifeline, you panic. You hold on tightly. Too tightly. Something breaks, and then you break. Not into two pieces, or three, or even four. An uncountable, incomprehensible number of pieces. Like glitter, except no fun at all. Like sand, but you can't sit and build it into castle shapes. Like shattered glass, but every creative writing teacher I've ever had would slap me across the face if I described it like that. So I'll leave it nameless. You break. You break up. You cast the wrong person in the role as your saviour, and when they leave you you cast yourself as un-saveable.

I know this because I did this.

My way of loving was desperate and angry and rooted in a desire to be well and worthy and normal. A break-up wasn't just a break-up, it was an end to wellness. It was total relapse. It was proof that I was too sick to be loved, too crazy to be with anyone, too broken to be alive.

In reality none of these things were true: I'd just chosen people who weren't a good match for me and the break-ups (and the pain) were always inevitable. That's all it ever was. I'd used up too much of my energy on making myself lovable and not enough on getting a foot in the door of recovery. I was way too depressed to be a good partner to anybody, least of all the well-meaning but emotionally careless wallies that I had tricked myself into believing would be good partners for me.

And it hurt terribly. I felt completely abandoned and rejected and I internalised those feelings for a very long time. Rejection when you're mentally ill feels extra shitty. It feels like confirmation of your lack of worth. It opens you up and lets all your colour drain out and then you have to walk around everywhere in black and white until gradually you fill back up and then the whole cycle starts again. It's terrifying and I want to hoof it up into space.

Dating when you're mentally ill: part 2

So here are some tips to doing better in future. Here's the work. The hard, terrifying, gruesome work – the work to separate love from wellness, and to put yourself back at the centre of recovery. Here's everything that I (a simple but experienced egg roll) know about this.

♣ Don't base your ways of loving on anything you see in a Nicholas Sparks movie. Or a tampon advert. Or a magazine spread. These are just scams designed to trick people into settling for bad relationships and buying luxury socks. Forget movie love, book love, TV-show love. Love where you have to sacrifice your well-being to keep the other person safe is not the kind of love that any of us need or deserve. Base your ways of loving on kindness, on happy, long-lasting relationships that you've seen first-hand.

♣ There will be days where you feel utterly unlovable, utterly empty and utterly terrified. On these days it will be very tempting to seek out the people we love and ask them to re-declare their love and acceptance of us. It will feel like a necessary restoring of the balance, the harmless scratching of an itch. But we have to do our best to learn not to do this, at least not daily, at least not so often that it puts undue pressure on the people you love and who love you. We have to learn what's fair and what's not, what's rational and what's our own brain pulling tricks. We have to learn to stop testing people's commitment to us. We have to learn, through practice and patience and all the other things, how to do this work for ourselves.

♣ Communicate freely and patiently with your partner. If you're not able to face an argument or a long conversation, decide a time together when you will sit and talk things through. Try to be as present and open with one another as possible when that time comes.

♣ Stop showcasing the most ragged parts of your insides and asking other people to confirm that you're still worthy. OF COURSE YOU'RE STILL WORTHY, YOU EGG NUT. Learn to confirm that yourself. Your voice is the one that matters. I know it doesn't feel like that because of the years of cruel, terrible self-talk and people treating you like shit – but it's true. It is an objective and literal truth. And from the other side of things, it's exhausting to be tested. It's hard to be asked for validation when validation has been given already. When your partner is good and does their best to love you, it's hard for them to hear that it hasn't felt like enough for you. Go easy on your loved ones. Accept that your perception of things can be crooked and that they're doing their best. Practise putting down your phone, saying, 'I'm not feeling great, I'm going to shut my eyes for a while,' or, 'I'm going for a walk, want to come with me and tell me about your day?' or just the very honest and straight to the point: 'I am going to cry. The crying will begin now and end sometime in the future. Please brace yourself and remember that it isn't about you. It's just a natural response to what's happening right now.'

♣ Let bad days happen. Make sure your partner or partners know that it's not about them. It's not. It's you. You want more than any person on Earth can give you right now. You're bottomless today. You're a cup with a hole in. You won't get filled up. You'll both just get frustrated beyond belief and want to run in separate directions into the ocean. So switch off when you feel like this. Leave it alone and work crazy hard on soothing yourself. Self-soothing is an annoying way to put it because that's the term for when we leave babies alone when they're crying so they can learn to relax. Personally, I don't know many babies so I don't know if this works or is the world's dumbest idea. I am an adult, though, and I know that learning to bring yourself down from the edge when you're feeling terrible and terrified is the most incredibly difficult and valuable skill you'll learn. The support system is valuable, and there will be times when you need someone else to bring you back, but I promise that you can take care of yourself way more often than you think you can.

♣ Some people are not your people and they never will be. Learning to recognise these people and giving yourself full permission not to fuck with them any more is life-changing. But it can be hard to get to a place where you see these people for what they are. This is what I know: your people won't squint sideways at you when you say something silly. They'll laugh. They'll say something silly too. They won't shame you for the lovely, harmless parts of yourself. Not ever. They'll also never shame you for your mental illness. When you've been shamed and misunderstood for this in the past, it's a hard thing to believe. But I promise it's out there. It's a real thing. Your people are out there and knowing them will feel like coming home.

♣ Ask your partner clearly what they want and what you can do to be a better partner. You don't have to always be able to predict the way their mood is going to swing, or know without asking what they need to feel better. And when they tell you something that triggers or upsets them, remember it (or make a note somewhere) and do your best not to do it again.

♣ Safe words are not just for doing sex. Decide on some words and phrases that you can use when you're out and about that let you indicate you're not doing very well without actually having to explain the whole thing.

♣ Research one another's illnesses. Like I've said before, mental illness is a different wig depending on who's wearing it. Or maybe I've never said that, because it's very strange. But it's happened now, so let's just move on. You need to show an interest in what your partner's going through and how their illness manifests. Even with a very well managed and treated condition, it may still show up from time to time, and preparing for it will save both of you some anguish

♣ Fairly and calmly call out one another's mistakes. Being mentally ill doesn't let you off the hook for being shitty. It might explain an instance of frustration or flakiness, but it doesn't give you licence to hurt anybody. If your partner makes a mistake or says something that makes you feel invalidated or triggered, talk to them about it. And be willing to be called out, too, and be receptive and open to hearing what you might be getting wrong.

♣ Vow to be non-judgemental of other people's illnesses. The world asks us to be embarrassed more often than it asks us to be proud and unashamed. Within your relationships you should be able to expect a break from this, to have someone tell you 'well done' for getting through the day, rather than shaming you for needing that reassurance and support. When they're unable to do much, or when they can't find the energy to get up, and when they need help going to the shops or remembering their medication – help as much as you can without expressing exasperation or shaming them for not being able to do better.

Totally reasonable things to ask for from your partner

♣ For your needs to be met a reasonable amount of the time. They can't be met absolutely all of the time, of course not, but there needs to be a fairly clear split. And of course these needs do have to be reasonable and realistic. If you're worried that you're asking for things that aren't possible, then talk it over with a trusted friend or your therapist. But when one person's needs are met at the cost of the other person's, there is a problem. There is no situation where none or very few of your needs being met is a good relationship. That is not how this thing works.

♣ For your partner to work on the things that they do that trigger or upset you. It might be a total accident on their part the first time this happens, and that's something that can often be easily resolved and talked through. But repeatedly ignoring their role in exposing you to upsetting emotions is a red flag.

♣ For time alone when you're feeling overwhelmed. You can love a person with all of your heart and still need time by yourself. This is normal, and any partner who tries to make you feel guilty or tries to keep you from taking that time is not holding up their end of the deal.

♣ For them not to berate or humiliate you for your mental illness. Or anything, really. Not even once. The rest of the world will do its best to make us feel shitty for our mental illness, but our people are meant to do the opposite.

♣ For an apology and an explanation after unacceptable behaviour has occurred, and for your wishes during that time to be respected.

♣ That they never, ever, ever mock or put you down for the basic fact of your illness. It doesn't matter if they're tired or if they've had a bad day. There's no excuse for framing you or your illness as wrong or unacceptable. They're allowed to call you out on wrong or unacceptable things that you do, sure. But these don't include low mood, anxiety attacks, hallucinations or flashbacks. Frustration or eye-rolling when you're not well is crushing from anyone, but from the person that you love and trust it's world-crumbling.

Enduring what you can't change

Depression is a soup and sometimes you're just a crouton. This isn't a nice or pleasant fact. It's actually very bloody awful, if we're being honest. But it does happen. Sometimes you just have to buckle up and be that crouton. Sometimes you just have to float and sink and suffer. And then after the worst is over, when you're less crouton and more human – then you can pull yourself more effectively up out of the soup that you're swimming in and you can be a person again. You can stand up and wash it off and then you can carry on going. In the meantime, though, you're allowed to just be really, really depressed. Because you have depression. Your brain is a sticky, confused, sad place sometimes and in your scrambling to stay alive, or get away from the inexorable dark badness of it, you've somehow managed to make it worse. You've reached for the aerosol that says HAPPINESS and you've accidentally grabbed the one that says MORE MISERY. It's okay. It happens. It's very dark in there and the shelves are crowded and mistakes happen when you're *that* desperate to feel better.

You're not okay. And that's okay. I don't mean it's okay like it's good and it's fine and we should just let it happen because it's OKAY. No. It's bad and should stop as soon as possible.

But it's not evidence of anything, is what I'm saying. Listen – SO many of us go through this. Smart people, happy people, people with good jobs, parents, people who iron their socks and seem to have their shit together. Writers, chefs, snake charmers. People we love. People we hate. All your depression is is evidence that you're human. Also partly crouton. But mostly human!

And when you're depressed you may be a human in a way that feels so terribly, achingly UN-human. You won't wash. You'll eat without tasting, or you won't eat at all. You'll drink and then throw up and then drink more. You won't wash up. You won't do the laundry for six months. If a shirt has fewer than three stains on it you'll consider it a win. You'll pee in a jug, or a sink, or something else that was absolutely not designed for this purpose. You'll forget that the curtains can even open at all – that there's a whole world on the other side of them. You'll see a baby laughing in the sunshine and you'll feel absolutely nothing.

Here's the truth that all of us know: sometimes, you're just going to suffer. Sometimes you're just going to have a bad day, or a bad week, and you're going to fall all the way to the bottom of yourself and feel totally, utterly, ridiculously terrible. I'm writing this while having one of those weeks. I'm in it. I'm in the middle of the fog and I'm woozy and exhausted and numb with it. The peak of my functionality at the moment is rolling over in bed, scrolling through social media, and occasionally getting up to pace around and sigh very, very deeply. Thankfully I still get tiny and infrequent bursts of energy that allow me to get a glass of water or do a quick tidy-up or maybe even post a tweet, but nothing significant. It's a resistant type of depression, a steely, unyielding low mood. It stands like a bouncer at the edge of my life and refuses to let any help or joy through the doors. But it will pass, is the thing. I know from experience that it always passes. I also know that from inside it there are things I can do to help, to ease the worst of it and take the edge off.

And no, pervasive feelings of emptiness on days like this can't be solved with some of the softer self-care tips, like throwing on a face mask and watching a cheesy movie. These probably won't even touch the surface of what you're going through on those most terribly terrible of days. And not being able to connect with this kind of advice can also make you feel even more rotten and faulty. It's a really fun and sexy cycle all round, I would say.

So here are my tips for the worst of the worst days.

♣ Don't make big decisions today. Today is not the day for that. Don't decide you'll quit your job and buy a one-way ticket somewhere brand new and very far away. Don't get a Kermit the Frog tattoo on your neck. Don't end your relationship. Don't make any huge purchases or get a new credit card. You'll be tempted by a lot of these things, tempted by the possibility that doing something big might just jolt you out of the current agonising place that you're in. This almost definitely won't happen. Chances are you'll just make a big old mess for yourself to clean up later. So don't act. Let the desperation come. It's okay to feel desperate. It will pass. Acting on your most desperate impulses is not a panacea. On the worst days just try to survive. You just have to get from one end of the day to the other.

♣ Go back to basics. I'm talking bottom of Maslow's hierarchy type shit. Get food. Put food in face. Make it as nutritious as you can get, but don't worry if it's fast, easy and basic. Also hydrate. Get a large glass of water. Drink the large glass of water. Then fill the glass of water up again and drink more. Make a tea (or a hot chocolate if tea isn't your cup of tea). Whatever it takes to get fluids into your body. Food and water and physical safety – those are your basics today. Take care of them as best as you can and don't ask any more of yourself. The rest you can take care of when you're doing better. Which you will be soon. I promise.

Being your own ally

In the lowest moments of my depression, I used to imagine that I'd meet someone who'd take the worst of it away. They'd understand what I was going through and they'd know exactly what I needed without me having to say it.

Because when you're that low, all you want is for someone else to do the work, to swoop in like a heroic pigeon and fix you. Even now I still sometimes want that. It's a very human and understandable desire. But it's not *realistic*, is the thing. The heroic pigeon does not exist.

So you have to be the pigeon. You have to learn to be the first responder to your own anxiety. You have to learn to tell yourself that you're fine. To say that yes, you're experiencing something incredibly unpleasant right now, but that it will pass soon and you will feel like a person who's in control again. You'll have to learn these things because staying alive through mental illness means gritting your teeth and bearing the very worst of days and communicating kindly and reassuringly with yourself throughout the whole horrid process.

It's being very honest with yourself that, absolutely, the symptoms of your illness are real, scary and desperately unpleasant, but no, they aren't the only thing you'll ever feel or act on.

It's having two voices – one that is all suffering and fear and panic, and another that is calm, reassuring and firm. One that says,

'No, I can't and I never could,' and the other that says, 'You can, you have, and you will again.'

Cultivating this second voice is difficult – and most of the time it will seem pointless and idiotic. Like holding up a cocktail umbrella against a tidal wave. But you have to keep going with it. When you're panicking, tell yourself aloud that you're okay, that this will pass, and that you will be absolutely fine. Say it even though it sounds silly and doesn't feel like it's going to help at all. Say it again and again until the bad patch is over and then say to yourself, 'I'm proud of you. You got through that. You survived.'

Redefining recovery

What you think it should look like

In the early stages of feeling better you'll imagine recovery as a fairly straightforward process. You know that it'll have challenges and wobbles, sure, but you visualise a fairly consistent upward curve. It gets better and better and better until it's done and you are well forever. You'll think of each obstacle like something that can be conquered and buried and never spoken of again.

But it's not like this. This is not how it happens. Let's just rip this particular plaster off and get over it. This is not how it happens at all.

What it's far more likely to look like

Speaking in purely scientific terms, recovery can be described as both 'squiggly' and 'wiggly'. You will not get a sensible upward curve out of it. You will not begin at the beginning and then proceed rationally in a forward motion until you reach the end. This will not be what recovery looks like. Recovery does not care for your interpretations and assumptions. It is like a disobedient iguana. It will do whatever the goddamn hell it likes.

There will be massive successes, and stretches of time where you feel utterly invincible.

But there may also be years of your life that you spend barely making it through. There will be periods when the only way that you are able to survive is by doing some very dysfunctional shit. Unlearning these survival tactics will be the most excruciating exercise of your whole life, and it may be very messy and very ugly. This messy, ugly struggle to do better is the heart of recovery. It's the real fight of it.

Recovery is something that you live within. The minute you rush to get it over with, to overcome it and leave it behind you, that's when you've missed the whole ridiculous purpose of it all. Recovery is the tiny step. Recovery is the milestone. Recovery is the lesson that tears you open. It's the tangible successes, the deleted numbers, the forgotten terrors. It's today and it's forever. You will pick it up and you will put it back down. You will hate it and mistrust it long before you learn to walk alongside it. When you first start out, when you first go forward with the purpose and idea of living a better and more stable life, the whole thing will feel tentative and delicate, like a bicycle made of candy floss. But not forever.

Everything I know about recovery

♣ It needs to be taken slowly. Not to pour a big bucket of cold sewage over the whole thing. It's still all possible and it can and will happen for you – but it's also a journey. Odysseus didn't just jump on a speedboat and get back to his wife in forty-five minutes. Woody and Buzz didn't just find Andy right away. Dorothy didn't just realise her shoes were magical and go on her merry way home.

No. The journey was the whole point of that movie. And also to teach us that monkeys cannot be trusted and wizards are short, rude, and not our friends. BUT MOSTLY THE JOURNEY THING. She had to learn the lesson before she could live better. And so that's something that we have to do as well. We are, to coin a brand new term that has no second meaning, 'friends of Dorothy'.

A big part of recovery for me was admitting to the things that I just couldn't do yet. And admitting them without allowing guilt to enter into it. I was like a bouncer at the club and guilt was the group of drunk underage lads trying to get in. It took a lot of standing toughly and menacingly to send it on its way. And I won't lie to you – it was really difficult. It still is. Because I want to feel as though I'm doing things right, and living up to my potential, and achieving my dreams, and making my family proud, and on the days where I'm too depressed to get up out of bed, I struggle to remember that this is how it happens.

So let me remind us all: THIS IS HOW RECOVERY HAPPENS.

♣ Bad days are going to be a part of it. Some days are just bad. Some days you will wake up already knowing it's a bad day. You'll feel it in your bones. Your bones will be like, 'Um, yeah, so this day FUCKING SUCKS.' Your bones will be very convincing. And the bad day will feel infinite and unending like the universe or Cher's life force. You will flat-out refuse to believe that it's just a bad day. You'll dig your heels in deep and insist that ACTUALLY it's evidence of your inner wrongness and total and complete insanity and worthlessness. You'll be convinced that this bad day represents a return to depression forever and ever and ever, amen.

And you will, of course, be wrong. A bad day is a bad day. A flare-up of symptoms after weeks, months or even years of working very hard at recovery is NORMAL. You will go through it. You will still have bad days, no matter how far into the process you are. And when they come, you will probably want to retreat into your shell like a nervous snail. You will wilfully ignore any progress you have ever made. You will look upon the day as though it's spilled soup and you will say LOOK AT THIS DESTRUCTION. LOOK AT THE ENORMOUS MESS THAT I HAVE MADE THAT WILL NEVER EVER GET CLEAN AGAIN.

In reality that's nonsense. It will get clean. And you will feel better. Because this is just a bad day. As much as it sucks and as much as you wish these didn't happen any more – it's still just a bad day. Your personal world isn't ending. A bad day is as inconsequential in the grand scheme of life as spilled soup. And, sure, having depression may mean the only tools available to clean up said soup are a postage-stamp-sized napkin and MORE SOUP. But let's not redefine soup as something it's not just because for the moment we aren't able to tackle it. The soup will just be soup tomorrow and when you feel better you will be able to clean it up as easily as ANYONE can. Confused? So am I. I took the metaphor too far. Let's switch it up.

Your bad day is a monster to be fought. You either win the day or you don't. That's not the most important thing, though. The trying is the most important thing. Because you have to try. You have to push back against the bad, bad terrible feeling, and exist in the world. You have to put your shoes on and button your shirt and walk out of your front door and right into the storm. This is the boring and frustrating truth of getting better.

♣ Relapses aren't the end of the world. Relapses are actually pretty necessary milestones in most people's recovery. Learning how to put ourselves back together and get back on track after a relapse is as vital a lesson as any, and changing our way of framing relapses can help us be kinder and better and more resilient when the bad days come around. So remind yourself of this often: relapses are normal in recovery. Relapses happen to everyone. Relapses do not make us weak. Relapses do not undo the good days, or the work that we've done to make it this far.

♣ Recovery involves becoming something new far more often than it involves returning to a previous way of being. This can feel scary and unfamiliar, like visiting any new place for the first time. But the new place eventually becomes a place you know like the back of your favourite biscuit. The new place is wonderful. Who you become will be wonderful, too.

♣ Recovery will come in waves. There will be seasons to it. Just as often as you find yourself somewhere good and new and promising, you will find yourself back in bad and familiar swampland. Both states will be temporary and you will gradually learn to greet both with a mindful acceptance.

♣ Recovery may be a forever process. This doesn't mean that you won't ever be happy, or successful, or able to consider yourself doing well in life. It just means that you'll always have to do some wellness work. It means enduring a backslide now and then, and then doing the work to pull yourself back up again afterwards. It means having to tweak meds or try new ones from time to time. It means changing therapists when it's time to work through some things. It means rolling with it.

♣ Recovery is as much about the smaller battles as it is about the big ones. Finding small pockets of peace, building new friendships and learning to maintain them, discovering things that you'd quite like to make a career out of, conquering small anxiety triggers one by one. All of these cumulatively make up your recovery; it's never just one single solution that trips a switch in your brain and makes you normal. Soz.

♣ Your perception of life and recovery is wobbly and crooked from years of believing a bunch of untrue shit. The trick is to tell yourself very firmly that this is just how it goes sometimes, but that you will unlearn it. This is exactly the swamp you have to swim through. You are swimming through it just fine. Yes, you're getting mouthfuls of swamp water in your mouth but STILL YOU PERSIST. You keep swimming. In the swimming you will figure it out. You will reach for the land, and the land will reach back out to you. The land will say, 'Hello. I have been waiting for you. Here I am. There you are. Let's do this.'

The land is, of course, wellness and control and some semblance of happiness. Recovery will mean whole weeks spent on land, living a human life, going to the shops, eating an orange, making small talk with someone at the post office. Being okay in all the mundane and lovely normal ways. But it will also mean days where you go back into the water, back into the dark and the cold and the swampish terror. It will be days of crisis, or even just single hours where you feel as terrible and defeated as you felt when you were in the worst days of it, totally unrecovered, totally flailing.

♣ Recovery is great, but it comes with its own brand new set of problems. Your family and friends may start putting pressure on you not to relapse, and then acting disappointed and distraught when you do. You might start putting too much pressure on yourself as a consequence, and taking on too much to prove that you're just fine and that your recovery is working. When you're doing well in recovery, you'll also probably find that medication-doubters start to pipe up again, encouraging you to ditch the pills now that you're doing well.

So there's a rough blueprint for recovery. It will suck and it will be life-affirming. However lost and out of your depth you feel now, trust that you *will* find pathways through, pathways that right now seem impossible. You will do things in this process that right now seem out of the question completely.

It will not be linear. It will not begin at the beginning and end at the end. It may begin several times or several dozen times. It might involve a lot of false starts and setbacks and moments where you feel more unwell and more lost than ever. It may also feel as though it's ended, only for you to realise that, NOPE, still a whole heap more to learn.

I find it helpful to imagine it not as a line, or a journey, but as a daily commitment to action and honesty and – when possible – joy. On the days where I'm unable to do anything besides lie in bed, the thread doesn't break. I don't slide down the snake and go back to the beginning of the board. A bad day doesn't represent an interruption or a setback, it's simply a part of this process and a symptom of an illness that I may suffer with (on and off) for the rest of my life.

Treating yourself better

It might seem like no big deal in the grand scheme of things if you think good words to and about yourself, or if you scold yourself for being a fuck-up. Turns out, though, that it's actually a huge deal. The biggest, in fact. Because right at the heart of happiness and wellness and peace is your relationship with yourself and the effort you put into fostering something supportive and encouraging and kind. It's in the identifying all the terrible things we say to ourselves without even realising we're doing it.

Getting better involves understanding the value of a calm and peaceful and mindful existence, even when it's momentarily out of reach. That's what to reach for, to reach back to, to strive for. That's home, that's where you're safe and well protected.

BUT!! BUT! BUT YOU CAN'T JUST BE PEACEFUL AND RELAXED AND EXPECT ALL YOUR PROBLEMS TO GO AWAY!!!

No, you can't. Of course you can't. But if you work hard on practising genuine kindness towards yourself and verbally reminding yourself that your human problems are not terrible, awful impossibilities, you find that shit starts getting easier and easier to solve. And you get happier and less burdened and lighter and kinder and better all round. And you deal with your problems better, and you talk slower, and you consider what you're saying when you're saying it. It's an overall softening and strengthening of self by overhauling the way you talk to and treat yourself. And it's also a pretty difficult task that you'll probably need to work on almost daily for the rest of your life. But that's fine. Because you have that time. It all just opened up to you, like a flower or a Kinder Surprise. There is no rush to arrive, no matter how urgent it feels.

So here are some tips for being a bit bloody nicer to yourself:

♣ Watch the way you talk to yourself. Monitor your thoughts as passively and non-judgementally as you can. Note how often you insult and scold yourself. Note how often you make bold and definitive statements about how different and dysfunctional you are compared to everyone else. Note how often you verbally put yourself down, to yourself or others – whether out loud or via text or email or instant messenger or social media. Being aware of the language you use about yourself is an important first step. Often it's been going on long enough that we've learned to normalise it. It doesn't shock us any more. Bringing it out into the light and looking directly at it is how we start the process of undoing it.

♣ Write some mantras (or find some online or in this wonderful nutritious book) that feel like the type of thing you'd LIKE to believe about yourself. Start or end your day by saying these things to yourself. Say them with as much conviction as you can. Go to sleep saying them. Write them down in your journal. Spend time on circulating that intentionally positive and self-supportive language. Let it settle like snow on top of whatever landscape it finds. Let it sink into what's there.

♣ Take time to do the things that you like to do. On your day off, set aside real hours to do things that make you feel more excited to be a person on the planet. It's important to de-stress and sleep in and watch Netflix in your underwear, sure. But think of other things outside of this that actually make you feel powerful and inspired. Do those things for a bit as well.

♣ Pamper yourself in ways that make sense to you. This might be going to get your nails done every few weeks, or going to a fancy barber, or putting on a full and glittering face of make-up until you're shimmering like a beautiful exotic fish. Anything that makes you feel your best possible self is worth doing, and it's worth doing in some form forever. Doing your hair and putting on your most banging outfit can be a healthy thing to do. Forget what the nerds told you. They don't know you. They don't know what you need or what your heart reaches for.

♣ Stop talking shit about yourself. Nobody else wants to hear it, and you shouldn't want to hear it either. Enough.

Reasons to recover

- So you can enjoy the things that you used to enjoy again.
- So you can start enjoying brand new things, things that you've only ever been indifferent to, things that you had absolutely no idea you could enjoy.

- Trying new foods.
- Trying new drinks.
- Trying new bubblegum flavours.
- Travelling to new places and actually being able to have fun, and explore, and take photos, and eat delicious food, and buy ridiculous souvenirs for your tiny grandma.
- Conquering certain anxiety triggers and knowing what life looks and feels like beyond them. Like being able to travel to new places alone, make phone calls without freaking out quite so much, watch live music or films on your own, or stand up to people and not feel utterly dreadful and traumatised for a fortnight afterwards.
- Hearing new music that makes you stop and pause and tingle all the way out to your fingertips.
- Meeting adorable animals and having those adorable animals rush excitedly to lick your face.
- Falling in love – whether with one person or many people or this whole ridiculous world.
- Cold drinks on warm days. Warm drinks on cold days.
- Reading new books, new poems, new jokes on the back of ice-lolly sticks.
- New episodes of your favourite TV shows.
- New TV shows that don't even EXIST yet. But one day they will exist and they're going to be fantastic and all of us will be around to see them.
- Knowing more than you know now, and one day being able to use this knowledge to help someone.

Things you can change

In a day

- You can change your immediate physical situation by doing a quick tidy.
- You can change your bedsheets and put on a load of laundry.
- You can begin to rehydrate by drinking a few big glasses of water throughout the day.
- You can fill an entire bag with rubbish and throw that rubbish away.
- You can book an appointment with someone who might be able to help you access better treatment and advance your recovery.
- You can reach out to friends and family and ask them for the help and support that you need.

In a week

- You can focus on improving your sleep patterns, which will help your overall health and mental well-being.
- You can continue to drink enough water, and make sure you're taking your medicine every day, and eating things that give you enough energy to get through the day.
- You can start to pick up a good habit or practice – walking or running every day, taking half an hour every evening to practise mindfulness exercises.
- You can begin to establish a good and positive routine – a routine that takes your limitations into consideration, doesn't rush you, but still challenges you.

- You can get a good idea of whether your current medication or treatment plan is having an overall positive or negative effect on your life. In a month you can also come a long way in weaning yourself off a medication that you've decided is no good for you.
- You can form and consolidate several good habits.
- You can begin to plan a big change, you can seek and implement the help of friends and family, and then you can get the wheels in motion.

Things that help me

Trigger warning: mentions of exercise.

♣ Taking a long walk along the canal, or the coast, or by any body of water, actually. Water has magical properties and almost always makes me feel a little better.

♣ Taking deep breaths in and out until I can trick my body into feeling calmer and more able to deal with the day ahead.

♣ Talking to myself like a precious and cared-for thing, even if every other firing impulse is self-destructive and hateful. Using the language of encouragement and support even on days where I really don't feel like it helps me get back on track.

♣ Identifying something that's really troubling me and then taking steps to be brave and address it.

♣ Making my bed every day before I leave my room, or even just before I sit back down on top of it to work (or nap). Any deliberate action to look after myself works wonders.

♣ Doing all of my washing and taking all the rubbish out of my room. When I'm at my most depressed and low-functioning, I find the messes and the dirty clothes pile up first in the corner of the room, and then all over the floor, and then over every surface. And it acts as a constant reminder that I'm not well, that I'm feeling too dreadful to make any effort. And that makes me feel worse. So even just gathering all of the clutter and spending a few minutes organising and stacking it makes a big difference to my mood.

♣ Reaching the end of a workout, whether that's a long walk or a yoga tutorial or twenty minutes on the treadmill. I love that moment of slowing down, adrenaline still cresting, and knowing I don't have to work out any more is so nice. I get to sit down. I get to lie down. I get to have a biscuit.

♣ Cleansing, toning and moisturising my face. Just doing the most basic steps of a more advanced skincare routine is enough to make me feel slightly better about myself and my life.

♣ Reading something by someone who's been where I've been before and survived. If someone hasn't existed in the rock-bottom swamp place, I don't want any part of what they're selling.

♣ Getting to spend time alone after I've spent a lot of time around other people. This recharging time is vital to my overall mental health and ability to continue being a passable person on Earth. When I get time alone there's finally no pressure to say the right thing, do the right thing, wear the correct kind of clogs. It's wonderful and guiltless and I embrace it.

Healthy, boring advice

♣ Getting a good night's sleep and establishing a routine can do the most incredible world of good for your overall mental well-being.

♣ Keeping hydrated and regularly fed (with a mixture of foods that you genuinely like eating and that don't feel like punishment or deprivation) will help keep you feeling more stable and steady day to day. Your body needs energy and it needs calories and it needs variety and it absolutely needs the things that you love eating, regardless of whether they grew in a field or were squashed together in a factory.

♣ A weekly pill box can save you from missing a dose or accidentally doubling your dose because you can't remember whether you've taken your medication or not. Similarly, a few silent daily alarms or reminders on your phone can help you to take your medication regularly and at the same time every day.

♣ Avoid drinking alcohol until you're sick or incapacitated, which can put you in a massively vulnerable mental state – either that day or the day after. A hangover can trigger all sorts of unpleasantness that you could really do without, and a day of being unable to stick to a healthy or regular routine can throw you off in your recovery for even longer than the hangover lasts. So maybe try to drink a little less if this keeps happening, and definitely make an effort not to go to bed after a night out until you've properly hydrated, eaten something substantial and prepared for a hangover the next morning (banana in reach, rehydration sachet and whatever soft drink or snack you normally crave after a heavy night).

♣ A vitamin-D spray can be a helpful shortcut if you find yourself unable to get regular time outside in the sun. A vitamin-D deficiency can make you feel just as drained as the depression, which isn't ideal. So get yourself a tiny, delicious, pocket-sized spray and see what happens.

♣ Try batch cooking once or twice a week. Making enough food to last a few meals means that even on days where you can't be bothered to cook, you will have food on hand that can be easily reheated and enjoyed. Food is good. Food is necessary. Food is non-optional. So make acquiring and eating the food as simple as possible for future-you.

♣ Take a bottle of water wherever you go. If you can afford to get one of those cool, spill-proof reusable bottles, I'd recommend it. I spill all the time because I'm a charming idiot, so mine has probably saved me hours of wiping-up time. Plastic bottles are fine but they're less eco-friendly, get easily dented and if you forget to put the lid on then it's a whole wet mess of wet, wet water. Studies show that water is almost always bad news when let loose in a bag or a pocket. And you don't have to use your new bottle just for water. You can put juice in there. The possibilities really are endless.

♣ Put your clean clothes in one place and your dirty clothes in another place – ideally straight into a bag or a basket designed for such a purpose. The floor is not a neutral zone any more. The floor is off limits from now on. Even two piles on two different chairs is a better system than the floor. The floor is depressed-people kryptonite. You are a good and worthy person and you deserve a floor that isn't covered in depression detritus.

♣ Try to always have a spare set of clean bedding for when you need to change yours but can't face the whole washing, drying and replacing it thing. Chances are if you try to change your bedding in the deepest dip of your depression then you WILL hit a snag and either leave it to rot in the machine or just sleep on your bare mattress for three weeks. Which is not ideal. It is not ideal at all. Also, please consider buying bed linen that doesn't need ironing. Ironing bedsheets is a terrible hideous fate that I wouldn't wish on anybody. It's a scam. Don't disrespect yourself or your time any longer, sweetie. Buy easy-iron.

♣ Carry a small notebook and a pen around with you everywhere. Because let's be real: mental notes are fake and they do not work. They're cancelled. So going forward, try to act as though if you don't automatically write something down you're going to forget it. Write that down, actually. It's worth remembering.

Things I never thought I'd be able to do (but I did do)

- Live by myself.
- Travel abroad on my own without totally falling to pieces.
- Survive into my twenties.
- Make money doing what I love.
- Date and actually enjoy it.
- Have healthy and fulfilling romantic relationships.
- Make and maintain new friendships as an adult.
- Get my panic attacks under control.
- Speak aloud to a group of people without passing out.
- Write a whole book.
- Talk honestly and unashamedly about my mental illness.

How to help someone having an anxiety or panic attack

When you're having an anxiety or panic attack, communicating to your friends and family what you need is near impossible. So I've written up a handy little guide here. If any of this advice isn't applicable to you, then feel free to amend it.

1. The first step to helping your anxious pal is being able to recognise the signs of an attack as early as possible. Anxiety attacks can show themselves in subtler ways than full-blown panic attacks, and can therefore sneak right by you unless you know what you're looking for. Common signs that someone's having an anxiety attack can include a change in complexion (they might look a little green or grey or pale), sweating or shaking, behaving in a more withdrawn way than usual or not speaking as much.

2. If any of these signs are present, then it's time for you to subtly dig a little deeper and ask them if they're okay. Please make sure not to ask them in front of anyone else, or make a big deal out of it. Just quietly ask if they're all right, or maybe send them a text asking if they're maybe feeling anxious and if they'd like you to get them out of the situation and somewhere a little better. They may only be able to nod, or just give a strained look. Take the initiative here and ask them to come and give you a hand with something elsewhere.

3. The next step is getting them somewhere that's quieter. Don't grab them by the leg and drag them urgently away while honking loudly like a goose. No. This will probably make things worse. Try to be relaxed and measured about the whole thing. Just

gently guide them out of the current space and into somewhere more suited for helping them calm down. You can afford to do everything at the same controlled pace, so please do. Rushing and hurrying and acting with urgency is only going to make the anxious person feel more on edge.

Get them somewhere they can sit down, where they can have all the space they need and not feel worried that other people are going to see and judge them. If they're sitting, try to sit, too, so you're not towering above them like some haunted spaghetti that got cursed by a witch and grew enormous. That's the last thing that anyone needs to see, especially not someone having an anxiety attack.

4. Try communicating with them, but make sure they know they're under no obligation to respond. Talk in simple sentences and don't ask them anything complex or difficult. This is not the time to ask them to have a quick look at your tax return. Try to keep it to questions that they can answer with a nod or a shake of the head. Also remember to give them plenty of time to answer, because their brain will be busy zapping around and won't be working as smoothly as it normally would. Be endlessly patient. If they don't have the answer to a question, tell them that's fine. Tell them you're there for them and there's no rush to get back to normal. They'll no doubt be feeling incredibly embarrassed and ashamed, and anything you can do to lighten the mood or alleviate this feeling will go a long way.

Keep your tone light and friendly and don't express any frustration at their lack of engagement or ability to process or make decisions – it isn't their fault and they're doing the very best that they can. Be as consistent as you can in terms of pace of speaking, tone of voice and the helpfulness of your suggestions. Don't feel offended if you suggest something and they shake their head, or get an exasperated look. It's a very exasperating time for them. Just wait and be patient.

Tips for friends and family

I've struggled to express my needs or my mental health experiences to my loved ones. Not because they aren't wonderful and understanding people! Not by any stretch. But it's a scary thing to bring up. So I've put together some suggestions for things your friends and family can do to help when you're in the deepest darkest depths of depression, and you can share this list with those people (with any amendments or additions you can think of).

To a sceptic or a mental health non-believer, some of these things might seem ridiculous, as if we're just pretending to be ill because we can't be arsed. Depressed people often get characterised as lazy, which isn't the case at all. So what I want to say to the people reading this list in the hope of helping their mentally ill loved one is: if you're truly serious about being a good friend and ally and partner through all of this, then the very least you can do here is commit to not confusing our inability to act with laziness. Don't assume that we're being weak. Instead, try to consider that we're just up against a different set of obstacles. Start there, and the things I'm going to ask you to do won't seem as ridiculous. They'll be as understandable as handing someone something from a shelf that's too high for them to reach, but that you can reach with ease. It's that simple. Help us do things that are easy for you and hard for us.

Make appointments or phone calls for us

I can't explain why this is as difficult as it is. Maybe because nothing really feels as though it matters, maybe because speaking aloud to a human that we don't know is terrifying for no real or tangible reason. Whatever it is, it's fucking hard, often bordering on literally impossible. So do this for us if you can. Don't make a big deal out of it, maybe agree with us that you'll do it for us in exchange for a promise from us that we'll attend. Whatever works. But if you can vow to make our doctor's appointment when we're really not doing well (or call in to work or school or college to explain why we can't be there), then you'll be doing us a big huge massive bloody solid. The most solid of all solids. A big concrete high five.

Help us do our laundry

It's the same as above: moving and functioning are so difficult that mostly we're like 'nah' and go back to bed. Maintaining a basic level of existence is a devastatingly hard task, and as embarrassing as that is, it isn't enough to make us able to do it. Even standing up and getting a glass of water can be draining. Our bodies are full of lead, our heads are buzzing and lurching and we just CAN'T right now. So any help with getting these domestic tasks done can be day-saving. Even just gently reminding us to do them helps, or offering to do them alongside us, or promising to buy us a little yoghurt pot when we've successfully completed a few things on the to-do list.

Tidy our immediate area

Even if you just pick up all the cups and plates and food wrappers and other bits of rubbish and put them in a place we can deal with later, that's a helpful thing. Even if you just straighten the bed a bit and fluff the pillows up, put our dirty washing into the basket and our clean washing into a pile on the sofa – this is one less thing that we have to deal with in our current miserable state. Maybe just wipe down some surfaces. Anything that you can do in a quarter of an hour or less that makes our immediate living space less disgusting and more pleasant to exist in is well worth doing and exactly the kind of gesture that we need.

Pick up some shopping for us

Maybe grab some simple ingredients for meals, or some fruits we can snack on when we're too low to go outside. Maybe some toiletries, or a little apple pie to cheer us up. Domestic necessities are always a good shout – laundry tabs or bin bags that we've let run out because it hasn't occurred to us to do a wash or take out the rubbish in weeks. Basically the kind of boring, helpful shit that we couldn't give a fuck about when we're in the deep depths of depression but will actually allow us to cling on to a bit of humanity. Help us bridge that gap if you can.

Make food for us

When we get really depressed, the task of eating becomes a sporadic chore rather than a thing we do regularly or with any thought or enjoyment. We'll probably exist on the most simple, low-hassle option – inevitably cereal or something that can be blasted in the microwave and eaten out of the container with a spoon or some kind of improvised shovelling device. Nutrition or variety goes out of the window. Balance goes out of the window. Any desire to try goes out of the stratosphere. If it has more than two ingredients, forget it.

Listen to us talk and don't make uninformed suggestions about our treatment or illness

We don't need someone who hasn't suffered from an illness telling us how best to manage it. Even when you're trying to help, even when you have the most wonderful intentions – all this does is make us feel more alone and miserable than we already did. So forget good intentions if they aren't paired with a genuine effort to do the work and learn what our illness can do to us. Centre us in the conversation. If you've found out some information, or you have questions or ideas, bring them to us. We'll be as receptive as we can. I promise that we do all want to learn and we do all want to get better, and our frustration is rooted in exhaustion and isolation – not a refusal to accept reality or try harder.

Get us out of the house

Outside is a terrifying concept during a spell of depression or severe anxiety. The world seems big and odd and loud and scary and Entirely Too Much from our safe and familiar inside-space. But once we're out in it, we often find that it's fine out there, and actually quite a pleasant place to be. Going outside, even once a day, can help immensely in making us feel more human and get us back on the way to feeling back to normal. So encourage us to go for a walk with you, or just for a coffee around the corner, or to run errands. It's important to start local, so if we do have a weird turn or we feel suddenly very anxious or exhausted, home isn't too far away. But invite us to the cinema too, to dinner, or for a walk in a park that's a bus ride away. And try not to take it personally if we flake, or if we say no outright.

Understand that we're grateful even if we're too depressed to show it

You're being a literal life raft and we appreciate it more than our exhausted, flattened-out selves can even begin to express. It's like when you bring soup and medicine to someone in the grips of the worst and most terrible winter flu you can imagine. They might grumble and whinge and be all snotty in your general direction, but they are also truly grateful for the effort and will feel better because of what you're doing. The same applies here. We might be unable to be enthusiastically grateful until much later, and we might remain vacant and expressionless while you tell us you're here for us, that you care, that you want to help, but it really does mean the world.

Don't rush us

There's absolutely no long-lasting quick fix for depression or anxiety or any of the other tasty little mental disorders. The things that might make us feel briefly really good are also usually the things that'll damage us most in the long run – drugs, alcohol, spending millions of pounds on decorative crystals, whatever. Laying the groundwork for long-lasting wellness and happiness involves a lot of reprogramming and practice and weeding out bad behaviours that we maybe didn't even know were holding us back. It can involve years of work finding the right doctor, the right therapy, the right combination of medication, the right exercise regime. It's a long process to wellness. So day to day, just meet us where we are and be as understanding and accepting of it as you can.

Don't tell us to look on the bright side

Recovery is not a case of looking on the bright side until we're just normal and functional and not ill any more. That's like telling someone with chronic leg pain to eat a magical onion and dream about running a marathon. It's just an absolute OUTRAGE, and you are honestly being ridiculous. Depression makes us feel flat and awful and broken down and sick. It doesn't allow us to 'look on the bright side'. There's no switch to flip.

In fact, ditch the platitudes altogether

Instead of telling us, 'Everything happens for a reason,' say, 'That sounds really frustrating. I'm proud of you for getting through it.' Instead of saying, 'Just be glad it wasn't worse,' say, 'That sounds like it was really difficult. I'm glad it's over.'

Do your research

Having been sad before is not a good enough reference point for understanding depression. The two are only very tenuously connected. The same goes for feeling worried or scared – it doesn't give you any real understanding of how anxiety or trauma operates. So do your reading. Read this book. Read another book. Ask your loved one who's suffering if they have any recommendations. Read articles written by people who know what they're talking about. Learn and then use that learning to be a more empathetic and informed friend and ally to those people who need you. And don't treat this learning like an inconvenient task, either. It's a way to make life easier for us all.

Don't try to diagnose us

People love an armchair diagnosis. They love to look at someone with their wise and knowing eyes and tell them, 'That sounds like bipolar. I saw it on a TV show once.' Unless you're a doctor spending time with us, building a case, exploring the options, listening to us tell you things that our friends and family probably don't know – you can't diagnose us. So don't try. Mental illness is complex, and even a doctor's diagnoses can change over time; symptoms come and go. We hide things from our loved ones for a reason – we want to protect you from the whole picture. So don't diagnose us. Ask us what we think. Ask us what the doctors are saying. Ask us how you can help.

Don't feel defeated if you don't know how to handle it all straight away

The most well-meaning people mess this up. It's a really difficult thing to get the hang of, and nobody is blaming you for not representing a full and flawless support system off the bat (even if we're total brats and act as if everything is the worst). This whole process is about trial and error for us all and every one of us on every side will mess up. This is to be expected and accepted and not pushed back against. You've not failed us if you're still learning and don't say the perfect thing every time. Just learn from it. So long as you're open to changing your approach and listening to sufferers, then you're doing things exactly right.

Remember that it's not your job to fix us or save us

You're not here to make everything better. You're here to help, if you want, in any way that you can. But you're not a doctor or a magician. You can't love us all better and you can't sacrifice yourself and your happiness to give us a little bit of peace. Never could and never will. So give that up. Give it up and just focus on doing your very best to be there for us and reassure us and be kind to us when we can't be kind to ourselves. But keep yourself afloat, too. Your problems don't automatically take second place because someone you love happens to have an illness. Your life has to be enjoyable and it has to be good and you need support and balance too.

Believe us when we say we can't

When we tell you that we can't do something, it's tempting to want to jump in and reassure us that we can do absolutely anything we put our mind to, and that we just have to get up and try. It's tempting to try to inspire us through it. And this is well intentioned, I know, but it can be crushing. Because when we say we can't do something, we might be saying that we're close to burnout or an anxiety attack and doing this particular thing will probably push us over the edge. We've done the maths, we've weighed up the pros and cons and we've decided that this time, it's a firm no. Or we might just as easily mean that we're physically unable to do it, and that trying is just going to be embarrassing and disappointing and make us feel way worse. Or we could just mean: we cannot do the thing full stop.

So please don't outwardly disagree with us. Don't push us to do something that we're telling you that we can't do. Accept it, believe us, and continue to be supportive. Tell us that it's fine, not to worry, and that if we want to try again later, then we have your support.

None of this will be as simple as we want it to be

Properly and effectively supporting someone with a mental illness takes work and it takes learning. Going in blind with your own assumptions of what we need will rarely work out for anybody. You'll get frustrated and then we'll get frustrated, and nobody will win. So stay open to learning, and be patient with us and with yourself. Things work differently with mentally ill brains. Something that you think will be inspiring and encouraging for us to hear may actually be the same bullshit we've heard time and time again from people who haven't really grasped what we're going through.

Do the kind and corny stuff that might help but that we almost definitely won't do for ourselves

Make your loved one a self-care/bad day box. Fill it with snacks and funny notes and cute games for them to play. Maybe some letters and inspiring phrases written on Post-it notes. A bath bomb or face mask or tub of Play-Doh to distract them. If you can afford to buy things for a depressed or struggling loved one – do! It's a tangible way for us to see that we're cared for and important. Even very small things – a bag of our favourite sweets, some fancy biscuits and teabags, really soft socks. Corny, smooshy nonsense that we're way too cool and hardcore to bother with ourselves.

Consider how you phrase things

Offerings of help mean very little if they're said in a way that's confrontational or exasperated, or if they frame us as inconveniences or burdens. It's far better to say nothing, to be silent and gather yourself until you have enough energy to be sincere. It can also be useful to talk to the person in question and actually ask them what language they find helpful. Ask 'What do you need?' instead of something broad like 'Do you need help?' A question like that, with a yes or no answer, will often be met with, 'No, I'm fine.' When you ask them 'what', they'll be more inclined to actually tell you what might help.

Some things that I know

♣ Doing the wrong thing is not just okay, it's necessary. You have to go wrong. You have to choose poorly. In the mistake is the learning and in the learning is the doing better.

♣ If your recovery is stalling or none of the things that are supposed to help are helping, try changing the order that you do things in. Try shifting focus from one treatment or therapy to another.

♣ You won't ever arrive. The future is not for arriving at. You'll always get there a minute too late to meet it. The seat where it was sitting will still be warm, and there will be a half-drunk cup of coffee on the side, but it will be gone and it will not be coming back. The present, however, that's there for touching. The present is here, at your side, eager to go where you go, ready to walk with you anywhere, to change in any way you want it to. Look at the present if you want an equal. The past is no longer here and the future is an untouchable and indefinable quantity. Forget them. Be here.

♣ Healing is painful. Healing is agony. Healing is regrowth – new tissue, new bone, new cells. It really fucking hurts when it's happening. It's not all peaceful realisation and resolution. It's traumatic and it's gradual and it always takes longer than you think it will. This is okay. You will survive it. Keep going.

♣ The person that you are now is not the person that you're always going to be. And that might seem scary and it might seem impossible, but it is a basic and simple truth. It is also a lovely, brilliant thing, and as much as it might hurt you, it's the only thing that'll really help you survive this place. You're becoming someone who can make it out.

♣ The world will often ask you to feel guilty for not being traditionally competent or good at things. The world wants constant productivity and conformity. The world's plan is flawed. The way out is to embrace the imperfect, the stumbling, the clumsy. You don't have to wipe out all signs of incompetence to be worthy of respect or love or life. You can lean fully and unapologetically into whatever dysfunctional person you are. You can do that even while actively working on changing certain things about yourself. This is all possible.

♣ Uncompleted or abandoned projects aren't a sign of incompetence or failure. They're a normal part of being a person – especially a creative one. Every single person you admire has their own graveyard of projects that they couldn't quite wrestle with. Sometimes these projects are resurrected, like brilliant zombies. Other times they lie happily untouched forever, and somewhere along the way – maybe long after you die – someone else picks up the same idea, and makes something incredible.

How to use breathing to help reduce anxiety

I've always been very sceptical about the whole 'meditation and breathing for calm' malarkey. It seemed to me that my anxiety went much deeper than physiology, deeper than any good breathing technique could touch. It seemed like a waste of time that I could otherwise be spending staring at the ceiling or avoiding my responsibilities.

But then I tried it. Because I got desperate. And you'll try anything after weeks of daily panic attacks.

Breathing exercises are easy and accessible. You're breathing right now, aren't you? And NOW you're breathing kind of weirdly, because you're suddenly aware of it. It's super uncomfortable. Is it one big puff out, then pause? Or do you hold your breath and then breathe super quickly? Nope. You've forgotten. It's fine. Think about narwhals again and you'll be okay in a minute.

There are a few common things that people with anxiety might find they're doing with their breathing that make anxiety attacks more likely. There's monitored breathing, which is what I mentioned above, where you're VERY AWARE of your breathing and it starts to feel uncomfortable or unnatural. There's shallow breathing, which is breathing in too quickly. And then there's the breathing you do when you suddenly feel as though you're not getting enough air – the enormous breaths in and frantic, panicked breaths out.

You can start by just being mindful of your breathing – notice that it's happening. Try putting a hand on your chest or your stomach so you can feel your own breathing. Now take a normal-sized breath in through your nose and fill your lower lungs with air (you'll know this is working because when you breathe into your lower lungs they push down onto your diaphragm, which causes your stomach to get pushed out a little). Then exhale in the same calm and measured way. Keep this up and see if you start to feel a little calmer.

When you're panicking and your breathing begins to increase and become more erratic, using a breathing technique can help to calm you back down. Controlling and deliberately slowing your breathing can cause your oxygen consumption to decrease, your heart rate to slow, your blood pressure and muscle tension to decrease and return you to a safer and calmer state of mind. That's science, baby.

Take a long and measured breath in through your nose, letting your lower lungs fill first. Hold this breath for three or four seconds before exhaling very slightly through a pursed mouth. Try to let all of the tension leave your body as you do this.

Deep breathing can be a great tool in very stressful situations, but it's not always ideal for anxiety attacks. It can also lower blood pressure. It might take a bit more practice than other techniques to feel comfortable and natural, so stick with it. Sit down, ideally in a chair that allows your back to be very straight. Rest your arms out in front of you. Take a deep and slow breath in through your nose for about six seconds and then hold it for a few beats before releasing the breath slowly through your mouth. Repeat the exercise seven to ten times (more once you're well practised at it).

When people breathe into paper bags in movies, they're doing CO_2 rebreathing. It can work to control hyperventilation. When you're having a panic attack, you start to breathe very heavily, worried that you're not getting enough oxygen. In fact, you've got plenty of oxygen – too much. It's actually your carbon dioxide that's low, and so this breathing technique can help to rebalance these levels and calm you down a little.

Cup your hands around your mouth (or use a small paper bag if you have one) and try to breathe as normally as possible.

Practise these breathing techniques whenever you can. Don't just do it right now because a book is telling you to. Commit to practising them a few times a day for several weeks. Try to monitor your progress so you can see what's working and what isn't. Try to remember that this isn't just to improve your day-to-day mood and anxiety level – although that should happen too. It's also so that when the next panic or anxiety attack strikes, you're familiar with the technique, and not desperately and anxiously racking your brain for what the steps are. That'll make things worse! Get familiar. Have them written down on your phone or in a journal so you have them to hand if and when they're needed.

How to apologise better

Mental illness can make you feel so awful that you do shitty and unfair things to people. This isn't pleasant, but it's also not automatically excusable just because you were having a really rough time and you're mentally ill. You might be so exhausted from feeling dreadful that you snap at someone, or say something rude or unkind. You may say something that's manipulative or upsetting because you're scared to be alone or of rejection. Whatever it is, once we've recognised that it's shitty, we need to say sorry. We need to make amends. We also need to brace ourselves for the possibility that we won't be forgiven, that we crossed a line that can't be uncrossed, that we made another person feel so disrespected or hurt that there's no longer space for us in their lives. But first: the apology.

♣ Focus on the person who's been hurt. If you're the one who fucked up and needs to apologise, then here's a piping-hot tip: it isn't you who's been hurt. Don't centre yourself and your pain in your apology – this is manipulative and coercive and you might as well not bother apologising at all. You might as well go and get a smoothie and pour it into the toilet.

♣ Avoid justifications and excuses. You can give context and explain why you were in the state you were, but trying to reject blame and culpability helps nobody. Try asking the hurt party whether or not they'd like to know why you did what you did or said what you said. If they're not ready to hear it, respect that and don't get into it.

♣ Respect any boundaries or requests for space. If they ask to be left alone, leave them alone. This might mean that you need to do some serious self-soothing on your end. That's okay. Hurting someone else's feelings doesn't mean you have to self-destruct. But do what you need to do to give them the space that they've asked for.

♣ Don't threaten to hurt yourself if they can't forgive you. Forgiveness is not something that can be coerced. You'll just frighten them and put yourself in a worse position going forward. Most of the time there are healthy ways to get through hurt or betrayal – and when we take our time and commit to doing the work of behaving better, things turn out for the best. But nobody is obligated to forgive us or let us back into their lives right away.

How to use the DEARMAN skill for better social interactions

DEARMAN is an interpersonal effectiveness skill set. That sounds stupid and fake and like something you'd work on at a corporate woodland retreat. But it can actually be very good! Go figure! DEARMAN is a skill set to help you work through difficult and unpleasant social interactions and get a good overall outcome. Pretty groovy, right? Here it is.

Describe: Describe the situation factually. Avoid emotions and opinions and be non-judgemental. If you're struggling, try to imagine that it's someone else besides you who's in this situation and go from there.

Express: Express the emotions that you're feeling in relation to this situation. It can help to write these down in a list.

Assert: Ask for what you want. Ask clearly and remember that the other person has a choice about whether they do what you're asking or not. Don't shout, threaten, or tell them they have to do what you're telling them. Be direct and make no assumptions about what they're thinking or what they're going to do.

Reinforce: Restate your point in the best way you can. Try explaining why they might benefit from listening to what you're asking for and why you think it's a good and fair idea.

Mindful: Use mindfulness skills to try to stay on course and on topic here. Notice when the other person might be trying to steer you off course and calmly return to what you're talking about. Visualise what you want from the situation and the reason that you're having the conversation at all. Be mindful of your tone, the volume of your voice, and the words that you're using. Don't resort to insults or attacks. Repeat what you've said previously if necessary, and ignore any distractions or attacks against you.

Appear confident: Focus on your voice again. Make sure it is as calm and steady as it can be. Make eye contact and consider your body language – are you presenting yourself defensively, as though you have something to hide or be ashamed of, or are you open and relaxed and ready to engage fairly?

Negotiate: Consider a potential compromise if you're unable to get exactly what you want. Ask them for their opinion on how to move forward and how to solve the existing problem.

How to use self-validation

Self-validation is allowing yourself to experience feelings, emotions and desires without invalidating yourself, or treating yourself unkindly or judgementally. Invalidation happens to a lot of us for a very long time before we realise it's even a thing. It's an even longer time after that before we can start to do anything about it. Invalidation in childhood could be constantly being told that you're not good enough or clever enough to do things, and being treated with frustration or anger when you make a natural or understandable mistake. Basically it's whenever your normal existence and natural mistake-making are treated like abject and horrifying failures by the adults who are meant to be looking after you and your development. Growing up in an unstable or abusive home may mean invalidating messages are communicated through inconsistent levels of care, or unpredictable bursts of anger or frustration.

The result of childhood invalidation is often an adult whose sense of themselves and their own worth is almost entirely dependent on the validation and approval of others – and without that approval they feel unreal or absent or altogether worthless. We learn to self-invalidate in place of the original source of the invalidation. When something goes wrong, we're straight on the case with negative self-talk and self-abuse. A slip-up at work or a perceived social error can trigger a barrage of violent and invalidating statements:

'You're useless.'

'You can't do anything right.'

'You're a fuck-up and everyone knows it.'

But it's not always this extreme. Invalidating statements can seem like innocuous scolding. 'You need to work harder. Other people do this easily and you really shouldn't struggle this much.' This is an invalidating experience because you're asking too much of yourself. You're setting yourself up for a fall. You're judging yourself by the harshest of standards. You're not giving yourself a break and you're constantly telling yourself off for the smallest and most insignificant shit.

When we brush off other people's mistreatment of us, we're also invalidating ourselves and our worth. This is called minimising, like in that movie where that man makes his children very tiny.

Honey, I Shrunk My Self-Worth To The Point Where I Let Other People Treat Me Carelessly Because I Think I Deserve It. A classic film that we all know and love. Anyway, it's the same mess as above, and it has the same grisly, miserable end where we don't value our time and we let people treat us badly because we've decided that that's just what we deserve. We end up sad and beaten down and too defeated to really try in any aspect of our lives. We just give up because we think that's what we're meant to do. It's a spiral of absolute shit and I want us all to figure out just how to pull our way out of it and learn to do better. Here are some things to try.

♣ Locate your self-esteem in more than one location, and from more than one source. Practise self-talk that celebrates and recognises all of your skills and positive attributes, not just your ability to please, entertain or cater to the people around you. Maybe you're really good at making salads, or drawing erotic cartoons, or convincing squirrels to eat right out of your hands.

♣ When feeling invalidated, try talking to yourself like you'd talk to a loved one who was feeling the same way. This may be a struggle and it may seem like a waste of time, but practise it anyway. Teach yourself to automatically say something kind and reassuring to yourself in tricky times.

♣ Practise any self-soothing exercises that have helped ease negative feelings or bad episodes before. Try some new ones. Practise them not only in the worst and more difficult moments, but also just when you need a little steadying.

♣ Try talking to yourself out loud. Yes, it's weird and kind of creepy and silly and what have you. But it can help! It can help to hear a voice saying to you: 'You're doing well, you're okay, you're absolutely fine.' On the days where your friends or loved ones are busy and unable to be that reassuring voice, you can do it for yourself.

♣ Actually celebrate and commend yourself when you succeed at something. No more breezing by it, or chalking it up to good fortune. Take a moment after every victory to tell yourself very firmly: 'I've achieved something. I've done something impressive and it's worth being very proud of.' And treat yourself! Order your favourite food, or buy yourself something small, or go out for a drink with a friend to celebrate properly.

Forgiving your past self

Forgiving your past self can be very important for recovery. Forgiving yourself doesn't mean that you have to celebrate or agree with everything that past-you did. You can objectively recognise that past-you made some pretty serious mistakes, and didn't consider your (or other people's) best interests, and perhaps behaved in a very, very unhealthy and toxic way.

But change happens when we recognise what fundamentally hurts us and puts us in danger. This involves drawing out our worst impulses and figuring out ways to do things differently. This can be very difficult but can be taken one step at a time.

Often the faulty ways that we've behaved have actually kept us alive through the worst of days, so labelling them as useless or wrong doesn't make immediate sense. Instead it may make more sense to non-judgementally and gradually move away from them by honouring and accepting their purpose, but being firm with ourselves and saying, 'This behaviour has no place in my life going forward.'

So forgive what you can forgive, and leave the rest at the edges, and refuse to bring that poison with you as you go.

This is how it gets better

It gets better like this.

If you work on something every day, you get better at it. Like if you were really terrible at roller-skating but then you started strapping yourself into a pair of skates every single morning – you'd get better at it eventually. You'd stop flailing and falling over and flying into bins and you might even start being able to go in a fairly straight line, and maybe one day you could do a little twirl without breaking both your hips.

It's the same principle for recovery and wellness. You get better at things you practise at. Sometimes you only improve enough to be passable, but sometimes you get really good. They become the things that you know, the things that you instinctively do in a crisis. So work on your mental health every day that you're able to and things will change. And no, they won't change as quickly as you – or other people – might initially want, and you may have to painstakingly discover the things that aren't so easily fixed. But change will happen. It will be for the best.

Just keep putting those skates on.

Do your best

On some days your best will be getting up and brushing your teeth. On other days you will smash previous personal bests, you will do brave shit and slay your to-do list like it's the monster in a fairy tale. On others, your best will be just existing and doing as little harm as possible. My point is, your best wears so many different faces. Your best might be big and bright and shining one day, and then the next day it might be small and humble, like Shakira's breasts. So you can't hold yourself to one single standard all the time and expect to be able to always meet it.

Deciding that every single day has to count in the same way is a quick and easy way to make yourself feel like a miserable, stinking failure. Deciding that any day unseized or not wrung dry of all possible accomplishment is wasted is cognitive nonsense. Because some days you simply won't have the energy to do any seizing or smashing or slaying. Some days you won't squeeze every ounce of goodness out and make the day into delicious wholesome orange juice. On these days you won't have failed. You will just have been a human person on Earth. You will have done the best that you were able to do in that particular twenty-four-hour slot of time. And it definitely won't always match other people's perception or idea of what the best possible effort looks like. But ultimately that isn't your problem. Other people's expectations of life can stay with them. That's their business. Your business is staying alive, and you're already plenty busy with that.

So I'll say it again, because I want you to really hear it: your best is good enough. Your best has always been good enough. Your best continues to be good even when you yourself aren't feeling that fantastic.

Where's the lesson?

Depression hurts. Anxiety can stop us from doing things that we really, really want to do. Personality disorders make it painfully hard to maintain relationships. Mental illness does so much terrific damage to us that it's really any wonder we're able to get up in the morning and eat our toast and go on with our lives.

There can be a lot of wonderful moments in wellness and recovery, sure. There's ample opportunity to feel proud of ourselves for our strength, progress and endurance through the very worst of it. There's also our gratitude for the people who've helped us, who've learned with us along the way and who've held us up when we weren't able to hold ourselves up. These are our opportunities to celebrate ourselves and what we endured. When it isn't immediately threatening our lives and our ability to exist, we can look misery in the eye and say, 'You tried to get the better of me. You really tried it.'

But I'm starting to feel more okay with the fact that maybe there's not always some deep and profound meaning – that sometimes you suffer and it just sucks, and it doesn't really teach you anything much at all. I'm starting to find it easier to put that suffering behind me and keep walking, to not desperately tear into it all in search of significance. Sometimes the most significant and meaningful move is to shake your head and just be bloody glad that it's over.

You're allowed not to see any deep meaning in your bad days. Mental illness can be no more than a vast delaying force, a horrible, frustrating reality. And when you're getting better, when you're working on recovery, people will urge you to seek silver linings and be grateful for your struggle. But here's the thing: you don't have to do that. It might help you very much to, and that's totally valid. But it's just as valid to say, 'Actually, nope. That just really, really hurt. I'm here in spite of what happened, and yes I guess I'm pretty strong, but I do still wish it had never happened.' It doesn't make you ungrateful or uninspiring to fall on this side of things. It just makes you a person.

Everyone is pretending

I'm absolutely one million per cent making it up as I go along. Nod if you're doing the same. Yeah, I thought so. We're all nodding right now. IT'S ALL OF US. We're huge pretenders. And sometimes I think I'm pulling it off quite well. Other times I'm convinced I'm doing terribly and everyone knows I'm a fraud. But in reality nobody really cares about what I'm up to. People are so busy with their own lives and their own feet and their own hands and deciding what to watch next on their own Netflix accounts. They're worried about lunch. Or their dog. Or their own brain hiccups. That leaves very little room for worrying about you or judging you for the minutiae of your life.

This is the time to be honest. To be real. To be totally without pretence. It's just us here. And also ghosts. And insects. Because insects are ALWAYS here. *Always.*

Anyway. It's time to come clean. You're probably pretending that you're doing a lot better than you are. You're also probably doing a lot of things to make other people happy, or to make them think that you're a certain way when you're really another, different way. Maybe you spend money to go places that you don't really want to be and you say things you don't totally agree with to please people that may not even really be your people. This is human stuff and we're all guilty of it. The trick is learning to catch ourselves when we do it, and understand why, and then eventually figuring out how to do it less. That's all it involves – not beating ourselves up for doing it, or feeling guilty for doing it – just noting it and non-judgementally learning to cut it out.

You are worthy and you are deserving even when you're not all there yet. Nobody's all there yet! Everyone's guessing. Everyone's pretending. Everyone's just taking it one day at a time out here in the world. Some people are better at hiding it than others, but we're all very much making it up as we go along.

No, you're not a totally finished pie, but you're also not supposed to be. We're all crumbly pastry babies forging ahead regardless.

'This doesn't work for me'

'This doesn't work for me' is a more powerful sentence every time you say it aloud. Every time you say it without regret, every time you say it and mean it, every time you say it calmly and without anger or self-judgement, it makes you stronger. It makes itself stronger, too, ready for the next time you need to say it. It's like a prayer, or a spell, or an antidote.

'This doesn't work for me' means freedom. It means making a commitment to saying no to the things that you really don't want to do. It means being strong enough to accept that not all treatments or methods or medications will work for you, and that you won't be bullied or pressured into anything that doesn't feel right. It means opening yourself up to the idea that your life doesn't have to be how it is now, that it can be even better, even more free, even more of everything that you want. It means accepting that you're going to change. It means accepting change as something that might tear through your life like a hurricane, but that might also leave everything a lot better for it.

A life's work

Nobody saves you.

You're loved, and that doesn't save you.

You're talented, and that doesn't save you either.

You fuck up, and you pretend you didn't. You fuck up again and act like you don't care. You fuck up in secret. Outwardly you're fine. You're normal. You're doing great.

In secret you aren't coping.

You keep fucking up.

Maybe it almost kills you, and maybe that's enough to scare you into doing something about it. Something small at first. A single step, a call to the doctor, a text message to someone who loves you.

It's this that saves you. It's you. You admitting that there's a problem. You asking for help, you seeking out resources, you learning more about your illness, you connecting with others who go through the same thing. You being patient, and enduring the really bad days.

You starting to look more closely at your actions, and the consequences of those actions, and your subsequent quality of life. And you, in turn, deciding to act differently going forward. You'll see a doctor, you'll be firm and honest about what's been happening and you'll ask for help. Maybe you'll stop drinking for a while, just to see how you feel. Or you'll buy a book about depression, or anxiety, or whatever mental illness you're suffering from. You might download a DBT handbook and read one chapter every morning. You might practise mindfulness or meditation every single evening without fail. You might start going for long walks, changing your bedsheets more than once a month, forcing yourself to leave the house to see friends or family. You might just take out the bins for the first time in weeks.

All of these things will be what save you. Small daily commitments to wellness, curiosity, recovery and generally not being a total arsehole to yourself.

Nobody saves you but you. And you're better placed than anyone to do what you need to do to get that done.

It's figuring out what you need to live a happy and healthy life, and then going towards those things.

You save yourself, and it's a life's work.

It's today and tomorrow and then every day after that.

It's a life. It's your life. It's everything you want it to be.

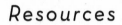

Resources

Recommended reading

This is a list of books that I've read and loved and learned from. A suggestion for anyone who can't afford to get all of these books or who isn't able to take them out from a library: how about you and a group of friends agree to buy one book each? When you and a friend finish a book – you swap.

Eat Up by Ruby Tandoh (For wonderful advice about reclaiming your joy of food; great for anyone struggling to eat and make joyful choices with food.)

The Highly Sensitive Person by Elaine Aron (For anyone who feels that they might be among the many of us who are very acutely sensitive and suffer with it.)

Big Magic by Elizabeth Gilbert (For creative people who don't know how to just be, or how to recapture the excitement that comes with being a creative person.)

A Beginner's Guide to Losing Your Mind by Emily Reynolds (For people who want to feel less alone and who need some more practical tips for dealing with depression, getting help and managing their own lives.)

The Body Keeps the Score by Bessel van der Kolk (For anyone who wants to understand more about the effects of trauma.)

How to Be a Person in the World by Heather Havrilesky (For anyone who could do with remembering that everyone is struggling, and wants to read some tremendous advice.)

Glossary/useful terms

ABC Skill A DBT technique to help you with emotional regulation. It stands for **A**ccumulate positive experiences/emotions, **B**uild mastery and **C**ope ahead.

All-or-nothing thinking This involves going all in with your thoughts. A good experience means that everything will be good forever – you're cured of your illness and you will be happy from now on. A bad day or a bad experience is evidence that you're screwed – things will only keep getting worse and there's no chance you'll ever feel good or happy again. Neither are based in reality.

Anhedonia An inability to feel happiness or pleasure in situations that would usually be happy or pleasurable. This can be a temporary symptom of major depression or burnout, but can also be caused by certain prescription medications. This can be similar to depression apathy, where you feel indifferent and unbothered by people or things that usually matter very much to you. Both can be incredibly challenging and disruptive, but both are usually temporary.

Aubergine An elongated-egg-shaped vegetable, deep purple in colour. Technically a berry, but would be terrible in a fruit salad. Great in curries, though.

Bipolar disorder Once known as manic depression, bipolar disorder is a mood disorder that can cause significant fluctuations between mania (a feeling of overactivity, excitement or euphoria) and depression (extremely low mood).

Black-and-white thinking Also known as 'splitting' or 'all-or-nothing thinking', this is a failure in someone's thinking to bring together all aspects of a person's personality – the positive, the negative – and consider them as a cohesive and flawed whole person. Instead, only the positive or the negative will be considered at a time, which can cause intense fluctuations between idolising a person or despising them, or an inability to accept that motivations or actions can be anything other than entirely good or bad. It's a common symptom of several personality disorders such as BPD (see below), and can function as a defence mechanism.

BPD A common abbreviation for borderline personality disorder, though often it's confused with bipolar disorder. It can also be known as emotionally unstable personality disorder. BPD is frequently misrepresented by the media, with female sufferers being hypersexualised and male sufferers ignored completely. This disorder can affect how a person relates to or perceives other people and relationships, and can cause significant emotional distress.

Brain fog A feeling of mental cloudiness or sluggishness, and an inability to think straight or with any clarity. It can be caused by lifestyle or environment – stress, burnout, lack of fresh air or physical movement – but it can also be a side effect of certain medications. Often it can be alleviated by going outside more often, changing aspects of your routine, eating differently, drinking more water.

Burnout An extended period of exhaustion – whether physical, emotional or psychological. Burnout can be caused by a prolonged period of high stress, or feeling unsupported while working on something big.

Catastrophising A kind of magnification – this is the act of predicting the worst-case scenario and deciding that that is definitely the one that's going to happen. For example, you may be worried about the outcome of a test or exam, and therefore conclude that not only are you going to totally fail, but that you're also going to be doomed for the rest of your life because of it. Catastrophising feeds on itself and can be automatic.

Cognitive behavioural therapy (CBT) A talking treatment that focuses on damaging thoughts, behaviours and beliefs and teaches ways to cope with and change them. The cognitive aspect works with the healthy and unhealthy ways we think, and the behaviour aspect works with the way we act and the things we do.

Cognitive restructuring A psychotherapeutic process or learning to spot, name and then dispute cognitive distortions such as all-or-nothing thinking, catastrophising or emotional reasoning. Cognitive restructuring may be something that you work on with a counsellor or therapist, with the goal of being aware of your own flaws in thinking and the overall negative effect that this has on your happiness and mental health.

Comorbidity Relating to a medical condition that occurs with another. For example, depression is often comorbid with anxiety. It's a really ominous-sounding word but it's actually quite chill when you get to know it.

Cyclothymia A more mild mood disorder than bipolar, but with many similar characteristics.

DEARMAN A DBT skill and mnemonic device to help people to better achieve a healthy and satisfactory result within conflicts. It stands for *D*escribe, *E*xpress, *A*ssert, *R*einforce, stay *M*indful, *A*ppear confident and *N*egotiate.

Depersonalisation Feeling as though you're watching your thoughts and feelings from the outside, and that they don't really belong to you. Your movements or actions or even the things you're saying may feel outside of your control, or automated.

Depression apathy An overwhelming feeling of indifference due to depression. This might manifest as a total lack of interest in all of the things that would usually bring joy, or feeling unable to connect with loved ones or usually pleasurable things – such as eating delicious foods, or watching something funny.

Derealisation A sensation of losing reality in one's surroundings – or being unable to verify what's really there and what isn't. This can often occur as a result of trauma, drug use or several common mental illnesses. It can also be a symptom of exhaustion or a side effect of certain medications.

Dialectical behaviour therapy (DBT) Based on CBT, it's a kind of talking therapy or treatment often used to treat people who aren't able to properly regulate their moods or emotions. It's similar to CBT in that it works to change unhelpful or toxic behaviours, but it also has a more specific focus on self-acceptance. 'Dialectical' refers to the idea of bringing together two seemingly opposing things, in this case acceptance and change.

Disqualifying the positive This is when you pass off successes or otherwise pleasant or positive things as flukes, or luck, and tell yourself that they have nothing to do with your talent or ability. For example, you may do well in a quiz, and then reason with yourself that it was a one-off, and definitely not representative of you being clever or good at something.

Dissociation An experience of mental disconnect, often triggered by stress or feeling overwhelmed. Dissociation can be experienced in short and infrequent episodes. A dissociative disorder is more often characterised by longer spells of dissociation.

Distress tolerance A set of skills often used in DBT to help someone learn to cope with distress during a crisis or situation that they're unable to immediately change. These skills can include radical acceptance (see below), using distraction techniques, meditation – really anything that does the job and isn't something you've previously identified as being harmful or toxic behaviour (e.g. heavy drinking or drug use).

Emotional permanence Knowing that emotions don't cease to exist simply because you aren't observing them. A lack of emotional permanence is a symptom often present in BPD or bipolar disorder, and can present as terror or panic upon realising that a person important to the sufferer is upset or annoyed.

Emotional reasoning A flaw in thinking or perception where a person believes that their emotional reaction to something must mean it's true, whether or not evidence supports this belief. Often the 'truth' of a person's feelings will trump the 'real' truth. You consider your emotions to be factual and always indicative of the truth. For example, you may *feel* afraid of a certain situation or place, and conclude that you shouldn't go because it's dangerous, despite you being totally safe there. You may *feel* that someone hates you and thinks that you're annoying, when in fact they like you and enjoy spending time with you.

Emotional regulation Your ability to respond reasonably and proportionately to emotional situations. Healthy emotional regulation tactics may include soothing self-talk, removing yourself from a stressful situation, or an automatic ability to stay calm and process difficult news. An inability to emotionally regulate can result in use of unhealthy coping strategies – such as self-harm, frequent begging to be reassured, or engaging in dangerous or risk-taking behaviours.

Executive function A term for the skill set used by a person to complete tasks and get things done. These skills include time management, the ability to focus attention when needed, having a working memory, and processing information properly. For someone living with a neurodevelopmental disorder such as ADHD or dyspraxia, or perhaps a head injury, this skill set is compromised and many apparently 'easy' tasks are rendered incredibly difficult.

Flexibility control The ability to take each situation as it comes and figure out a way through it.

Gaslighting An abusive manipulation tactic often used within relationships to cause one partner to doubt their own sanity or perception of the world. This allows the abuser to gain more control, and even become the gatekeeper of reality for their distressed partner. The effects of gaslighting can be far-reaching, and continue long after the relationship has ended. Self-worth, self-perception, trust and the ability to feel at ease can all be affected.

Generalised anxiety disorder (GAD) A disorder characterised by excessive or life-interrupting worry and anxiety about many things. Someone suffering with GAD may be extremely concerned about most aspects of their life – money, friends, work, relationships – and fear disaster acutely. Controlling said worry is very difficult.

Grounding A technique designed to help people remain in the present. It can be a useful tool when dealing with distress or anxiety, as both may trigger a distancing from reality – which can be harmful. Grounding encourages both a physical and sensory awareness with an awareness of mind and spirit.

Hypersensitivity Often described as being without emotional skin, hypersensitivity means feeling criticism or emotional pain very acutely. Often a hypersensitive person perceives rejection or criticism in places where is none.

Hypomania A milder form of mania, with many similar features, but never severe enough to represent a significant impairment.

Imposter syndrome Often a reaction to success or praise, imposter syndrome manifests as an inability to accept or internalise one's accomplishments as products or proof of their own talent or hard work. Instead they may chalk it up to luck or good timing, and feel irrationally afraid of being exposed as an imposter.

Intrusive thoughts Involuntary and often unpleasant thoughts that seem to arise out of nowhere but can be very vivid and distressing. These can be thoughts that are violent or sexually inappropriate and can often trigger extreme distress or anxiety, and can cause the thinker to worry that these thoughts are somehow indicative of who they really are and what they want – which isn't true at all.

Labelling The use of extreme and overgeneralising language to give a fixed term to a situation or person in your life. For example, you might forget your phone charger and from this instance you may conclude: 'I am clearly TOTALLY useless in every aspect of my life, as evidenced here by my forgetting my phone charger.'

Mania A mental illness marked by periods of excessive euphoria, delusions and overactivity.

Mental filtering A learned response to what you hear, mental filtering essentially means you'll selectively (and without realising) choose to focus on the negative things that you encounter. The positive things (of which there can be many) will not automatically stand out to you, and thus they'll be ignored. For example, you may have received lots of praise from a particular teacher or tutor during the term, but one critique or bad grade from them will lead you to conclude: 'The evidence clearly shows I'm doing badly in this class and my professor doesn't think I'm any good at all.'

Mindfulness A practice where someone's mind and awareness are trained to focus only on the present moment. Often used in mental health treatment to help those suffering with anxiety or depression or severe phobias. Very basic mindfulness techniques include having the sufferer identify what is happening around them at that moment, or focus only on their breathing for several minutes.

Mind reading This one is pretty much exactly what is sounds like – it's assuming that you know exactly what someone else is thinking about you and your worth. You'll tell yourself that someone who you're meeting definitely thinks that you're boring or weird, despite them saying or doing nothing to indicate this.

Obsessive-compulsive disorder (OCD) An anxiety disorder that causes people to have repeated and unwanted thoughts, feelings and mental images. It's an extremely distressing and unpleasant disorder, and can cause the sufferer to engage in repetitive or compulsive actions in an attempt to lessen this distress. Co-opted in the cultural lexicon to mean 'organised' or 'liking things a certain way', it's inconsiderate and damaging to use the term OCD outside of the context of the actual disorder.

One-mindfulness A DBT skill whose purpose is to help us to learn to focus only on the here and now, and the task or the moment at hand. When doing something one-mindfully, you will do that thing and only that thing. When eating, you'll just eat. You won't be watching TV or reading or scrolling on your phone. The purpose of this is so that you feel totally present and alert, and your focus won't be compromised and fragmented.

Overgeneralisation A cognitive distortion where the sufferer will take one experience and then generalise it to all experiences – even those that have yet to happen. For example, if you make one mistake when driving or have a small accident, you might think to yourself: 'I'm a terrible driver and if I ever get in a car again I will cause an accident.' It's often present in people who have depression or anxiety.

Perfection paralysis Being unable to act or make any moves to complete a task due to the fear of failing or making a wrong move. Rather than starting and learning as they go, or accepting missteps as a part of any process, somebody feeling perfection paralysis will view any potential failure as terrifying.

Personalisation A distortion that causes you to blame yourself or see yourself as having caused things that have absolutely nothing to do with you. For example, when a stranger is rude out of nowhere, you assume that you did something to deserve or trigger it.

Psychosis A mental illness often characterised by a separation from reality. Symptoms may include hallucinations and delusions and a general feeling of unrealness. The term 'psychotic' is not to be confused with being murderous or inhuman or evil. This is a strange and harmful misunderstanding perpetuated by people who don't know what they're talking about.

Radical acceptance A DBT skill that requires you to accept the reality of a situation without fighting or denying it. It has nothing to do with approval, and it doesn't require you to live with things as they are. It can help to lessen the immediate pain and remove very hurtful feelings of blame or denial, sometimes making it easier to find a way to change it and survive it.

Rejection sensitivity A tendency to react strongly and often with disproportionate distress to any real or perceived rejection.

Relapse A setback in someone's mental health recovery where they are unable to manage or control their symptoms, and they feel as though they've returned to a point earlier in their recovery where they were unable to cope with things that they've since learned how to manage. This might last a few days or a week, and it can be severe enough that it requires hospitalisation. It happens to everyone in recovery and never means that wellness is unattainable.

Self-concept A full idea of yourself based on what you believe, what you like, what you've done and want to do and other people's response to you. A person's self-concept can often be interrupted or warped, especially in cases of trauma or as a symptom of a personality disorder.

Self-harm/self-injury The act of deliberately harming your own body, often by cutting or burning. It's not normally intended to seriously harm, but is rather a way to cope with emotional distress.

Self-soothing The ability to comfort yourself in moments of distress or sadness. Healthy self-soothing exercises are things that alleviate the distress without causing more distress down the line. For example, it may momentarily make you feel extremely good to spend a lot of money on something, but later, when you're unable to pay bills, you'll feel terrible again.

Sensory overload What happens when one or more of your senses gets extremely stimulated by changes or factors in your environment. It can feel like a loss of control, like everything is happening all at once and very fast, and you're unable to stop any of it. This overstimulation can trigger anger and irritability, or a total refusal (or inability) to speak.

'Should' statements These happen when you have a very fixed or rigid idea of yourself, others, or the world around you, and overestimate the negative outcome if these ideas or expectations aren't met. For example, you may say, 'I should stop crying so much. Crying is weak. If I'm weak I won't ever succeed at anything.'

Suicidal ideation Unusually common thoughts of suicide. These can be imagined plans or thoughts of potential attempts. Though it can be an indicator of risk, suicidal ideation is not normally followed by a suicide attempt.

The three minds A concept created by Dr Marsha Linehan, the three minds are Wise Mind, Emotion Mind and Rational Mind.

Trauma bonding A strong emotional attachment between the abused person and their abuser. Often even when a person can recognise that the behaviour of the abuser was violent and wrong, feelings of sexual and emotional attachment may remain for a long time.

Working memory The ability to retain information and then use it to complete tasks.

Shopping list

♣ A set of pyjamas that you only wear on especially distressed and depressed occasions. This doesn't mean that your regular set of pyjamas have to be scratchy potato sacks that you cut arm and leg holes in. You can be fully comfortable at all times – your special PJs just have to be ones you don't wear all the time. They'll stay super soft and they'll retain their special and exclusive significance. Celebrity pyjamas. VIPJs, if you will.

♣ An extra-large packet of baby wipes. Being able to freshen up without having to get out of bed can be a lifeline on days where you really can't face it. The cleaner you feel, the more human you feel. You deserve to feel human, even on the days where you can't do anything at all.

♣ Dry shampoo, again for the days when you can't face a shower but also need your hair to not look like you can't face a shower.

♣ A plastic laundry basket for taking things from your room to the machine in one trip. Also very handy for actual washing if you're feeling adventurous.

♣ A few extra wastepaper bins for dry, non-perishable rubbish. If you spend a lot of time in bed, put a bin next to your bed. That way you won't be throwing rubbish across the room in a feeble attempt to get it into the bin like I do every single day of my ridiculous life.

♣ Disposable cutlery and crockery. YES, I KNOW IT'S NOT GOOD FOR THE ENVIRONMENT, MARGARET. But if you're depressed or disabled and have absolutely no spare energy for washing-up, this is a very, very reasonable option. Washing-up is harder for some people than others. Don't argue with me about this. I am a plate scientist and I am FAR too busy and important to talk about this.

♣ Mouthwash and mints for the side of your bed or your drawer. Wanting to brush your teeth but being unable to face getting up is a crappy feeling, so cheat a little bit with some minty-fresh accomplices. It's the right thing to do.

♣ One of those washing-up sponges that has a handle that you fill up with washing-up liquid. Way easier to use when you're low on energy but need to get some dishes cleaned. Also, who wants to have to put the washing-up liquid on the sponge every time like some kind of CHUMP? That's not how we live any more. Anything that makes cleaning or house maintenance easier and more accessible on the down days is worth investing in.

Websites

www.drugsand.me Non-judgemental and practical advice about how to most safely use drugs. It also has a function where you can check potential drug interactions so you don't accidentally mix something lethal with prescribed or recreational drugs when you're just trying to have a good time.

www.mind.org.uk A charity that provides information and support for anyone suffering from mental illness. A great resource for friends and family of sufferers, or anyone looking for easy-to-understand information.

www.lifesigns.org.uk A website aimed at anyone struggling with self-injury. It provides helpful and non-judgemental advice and safety tips and doesn't pressure the reader to stop self-injuring before they're ready, but has all of the resources for when they are.

Acknowledgements

Thank you to Julia, who reminds me that there is nothing so bad it can't be fixed. To Ray, who does when others only say they will do. To Archie, Callum and Charlotte, my ka-tet forever. To Jackie, who is so small and so brilliant. Why are you so small, Jackie? Did a wizard put a curse on you? Blink twice if yes. To Maureen, John, Jean, George and Robert, who all made sure I grew up laughing. To the Prattens, the Fells, the Willises. To Millie, Liv, Molly, Issy. To Jess. To Toby. To everyone who I've ever loved and shared years of my life with, even if we'd cross the street to avoid one another now. To Jonny and Emily. To my Peach friends. To my huge, loud, brilliant family. To everyone who's felt the world coming down around them and had to pretend that it wasn't. To everyone who's still here and everyone who isn't. To everyone who bought the book and everyone who helped to make this happen. Thank you.

Acknowledgments

Unbound is the world's first crowdfunding publisher, established in 2011.

We believe that wonderful things can happen when you clear a path for people who share a passion. That's why we've built a platform that brings together readers and authors to crowdfund books they believe in – and give fresh ideas that don't fit the traditional mould the chance they deserve.

This book is in your hands because readers made it possible. Everyone who pledged their support is listed below. Join them by visiting unbound.com and supporting a book today.

Allison Abbott
Sally Abraham
Amanda Ach
Tiffany Ackroyd
Oliwia Adamczyk
Geoff Adams
Zegir Aga
Rebecca Agatstein
Ariana Agouridis
Sarah Ahmadzai
Kat Aitken
Folu Akinkuotu
Folarin Akinmade
Chris Alais
Chantelle Albion
Isabella Albright
Jason Aldous
Emme Alexandra
Alison Alston

Jenny Alston
Dino Alvarado
Alissa Anderson
H.B.A. Anderson
James Andrewartha
Carter Andrews
Rachel Ann
Liz Anne
Hayley Anthony
Llia Apostolou
Nicole Aragona
Joaquin Ardiles
Sandra Armor
Christine Arrowsmith
Kunaal Arya
Andrea Ashburn
Chris Ashford
Ciara Ataliotis
Shael Atia

Sarah Atkins
Becca Auster
David Austin
Robbie Avey
Rachel Ayers
James Aylett
Amanda Azmi
Phoebe B
B K
Bridget Badore
Hanna Bailey
Laura Bailey
Bailey
Olivia Baker
Phil Baker
Cristina Barba
Barking@lambs
Tanya Barlow
Paul Barnes

Lily Barrett

Louise Barrett

Simon Barrett

Abi Barrington

Richard Barrow

Fiona Barry

Steven Bartels

Jacob Bartynski

Lily Battino

Allison Baughman

Alaina Bbbyluvz

Jess Beard

Corey Beasley

Arden Beckwith

Daisy Bee

Katie Beech

Martha Behan

Gaz Beirne

Brett Beletz

Ian Bell

Melody Bell

Scott Bell

Sophie Lily Bell

Stephen Bell

Chloe Bemrose

Adam Bennett

Stephen Bennett

Emelie Bergstedt

Ashley Berlin

Noah Berman

Violeta Bermudez

Jack Bernhardt

Brie Berry

Matt Bertsch

Stephanie Bethune

Zoey Bevington

Hi Bich

Cat Bills

Hunter Bishop

Sam Blanchard

Sonnet Blanton

Stefan Blaser

Celia Blundo

Bryce Boltjes

Becky Bolton

Tom Borcherds

Caitlin Bosco

Chris Bosman

Amy Bottrill

Keelin Bourke

Becky Boxx

Sam Boyce

David Boyle

Stephanie Boyle

Emily Boynton

Adam Brain

Bianca Brandon

Stephanie Brannen

Janey Brant-Beswick

Matt Braunscheidel

Peter Breeden

Ailill Breffni

Linnea Brett

Jo Brewer

Hannah Brletich

Rebecca Broad

Fred Bromley

Sophie Brooks

Amy Brown

Andy Brown

Dalton Brown

Georgie Brown

Lisa Brown

Martin Brown

Matt Brown

Rosie Brown

Amy Brown's Mom

Emily Brummer

Ryan Brushett

Kathryn Buchanan

Luke Buckler

Blake Buckley

Max Bucknell

Lu Bug

Sebastian Bunyan

Sara Burch

Nick Burgess

Emily Burian

Julie Burling

Mary Burns

Jonathan Burr

Stephen Burridge

Paul C

Becca Caddy

Mark Cahill

Jeff Cameron

Sam Cameron

Sophie Campbell

Martin Carr

Carrie Fisher's Ghost

Ann Carrier

Danielle Carrington

Laura Carter
Elizabeth Casey
Alexander Casimir
Cass
Joe Castle
Your Cat
Tom Cavanaugh
LeeAnn Celapino
Alex Censullo
Ollie Chamberlain
Emily Chapman
Gray Chapman
Pascal Chatterjee
Chickylala
Dimitris Chiras
Lisa Chisholm
Dominika
   Chmurzynska
Claudia Cho
Peter Chomko
Pamela Chozen
Nick Christian
Jill Clairo
Tim Clark
Abi Clarke
James Clarke
Pete Clasby
Evelyn Clegg
Dr Cleghorn
Paul Clifford
Garrett Coakley
Aryeh Cohen-Wade
Ollie Cole
Emma Coleman

Shannon Collier
Sarah Collins
Josie Comber
Sinclair Combs
Frankie Condon
Thomas Connell
Ashley Connick
Paige Connors
Caroline Conrad
Emily Cook
Georgia Cookson
Charlotte Cooper
D.B. Cooper
Keziah Cooper
Lucy Cooper
Bethan Copeland
Dylan Copeland
Michael Corbisiero
Jaime Cordova
   Mustafa
Emily Corner
Hannah Corner
Adam Corrie
Phillip Cotterill
Laura Courtney
Kristy Coventry
Lee Cox
Anna Cragg
Dave Cranwell
Becy Crawford
John Crawford
Adam Cresser
Doug Cresswell
Grace Cridland

John Crocker
Zach Crook
Kevin Crooks
Stchoo Blofeld
   Crossley III
Julia Croyden
Marilyn Crump
Anjelina Cruz
Antonio Cruz
Julie Csaki
Rebecca Cuddihy
Mark Cumisky
Erica Cumming
Aidan Cusack
Jennifer L. Cuzzocreo
Andreas D.
Courtney Dagger
Matthew Dale
Maegan Daley
Dan Dalton
Rory Daniel
Jane Darvill
Erin Davenport
Brian Davidson
Suzanne Davidson
Elizabeth Davies
Meg Davies
Julia Davis
Becca Day-Preston
Grace de Bláca
Marielle de Geest
Carmen De Pascual
Frederik de Ridder
Jim Dean

Austyn Degelman
Lily Dellar
Dominic Delzompo
Philippe Demeur
Derek Deposit
Clara Devaud
Callie Di Nello
Jonathan Dill
Sheila Dillon
Hannah Dingwall
Lauren DJ
Don't vote!
Victoria Donahoe
Dennis F. Donnelly
Emily Donohoe
Freddie Doust
Emily Dove
Ollie Dove
Sophie Dowdy
Bradley Down
Ellie Dowse
AJ Draper
Andrew Draper
Jon Dueck
Charlotte Duff
Hacksaw' Jim Duggan
Stuart Duke
Keith Dunbar
Naomi Dundon
James Dunne
Bethany Dyba
Kimberley Eady
Dave Eagle
Aaron Earley

Philip Eastman
Ashley Eaton
Rachel Eble
Maya Ebsworth
Jordan Ecarma
Zack Eccleston
Katherine Edwards
Phil Edwards
Heiko Egeler
Sami El-Hadi
Charlotte Eleanor
Meredith Eliot
Carter Marie Elliott
Kelly Ellis
Peter Ellis
Rachel Ellis
Ben Emmens
Jessica Enid
Flo Entwistle
EPM
Anna Erkers
Jade Esson
Cath Evans
EyeQuestOn (Ian)
Holly Fallows
Kata Farkas
Finbarr Farragher
Claire Farrell
Amberly Farris
Rebecca Fasciano
Tom Fassnidge
Hannah Faye
Helen Fee
Gill Fell

Olivia Fell
A fellow sufferer
Kaycee Felton-Lui
Paul Ferguson
Dee Fidge
Heather Filyaw
Craig Fincham
Anthony Fischer
Kira Fisher
Laura Fisher
Vickye Fisher
Claire Fishman
Meredith Fitzsimons
Allie Flessner
Anton Flynn
Dara Fontein
Dom Ford
Jessie Ford
Suzanne Ford
Fiona Forde
John John Forde
Christy Forrest
Josh Forte
Decklin Foster
Jamiee Foster
Eline Foulger
Rachel Foulkes
Julia Fox
Jack Fozard
Sophie Franks-
    Staub
Jess Fraser
Matthew Fratiani
Darcy Frear

Kim Freeman

Jessica French

David Frew

Minka Fromonline

Katie Frost

Timothy Frost

Simon Fullard

Lauren Furey

Sally Furminger

Pauline G. L. B.

Ben Gallatin

Bianca Galukande

Vivienne Gao

Mike Garnell

Henry Garner

Shea Garner

Sarah Garnham

Callie Gartland

Ola Gasidlo

Ciara Gavurin

James Gay

Kirbey Geissler

Kevin George

Stacey Gerasimov

Emily Giannelli

Ryan Gibberd

Millie Gibbs

Chace Gilbertson

Issy Gill

Bethany Gladson

Hattie Gladwell

Olivia Glazner

Christina Gleason

Amber Gleeson

Jolie London
Glickman

Paris London
Glickman

James Gloyn

Melissa Godin

Madeline Goetz

Alex Goodfred

Heather Goodlett

Anna Goodman

Steven Goodwin

Vivek Gopal

Don Gordon

Hannah Benn
Gordon

Keith Gori

Simon Gott

Dian Maisie Otter
Grace

Michael Grace

TheoJane Graham

Jason Gray

Matt Gray

Scarlett Gray

Hannah Greeley

Alex Green

Tim Greene

Jonny Greenfield

Grace Grieve-Carlson

Emily Griffin

George Griffin

Meagan Griffith

Ben Griffiths

Bryony Gundy

Amiya Gupta

Rowland Gwynne

Deniece H @
coldsoup3000

Missy H.

Alex Haag

Vic Habersmith

Haley Hagearty

Alex Hall

Molly Hall

Ryan Hamilton

Will Hamilton

Paul Hancock

Jim Hanner

India Hannon

Melanie Hanson

Mike Hardcastle

Ross Hardy

Pete Harris

Stephen Harris

Sophie Harrop

Sandra Hart

Nathan L Hartland

Jordan Hartley

Alex Hartline

Meike Hartmann

Caitlin Harvey

Ella Harvey

Max Harvey

Savannah Harvey

Sameer Hasaan
Naeem

Ramsey Hassan

Ryan Hauptman

Stuart Hawkes

Midath Hayder

Tori Haydon

Jessica Hayes

Katherine Haylett

Michelle Hayner

Lindsay Haynes

Sam Haysom

Katie Heaney

Jacqueline Hedge

Ally Hellyer

Helmi Henkin

Madeleine Hennessy

Kyra Herning

Corey Hersch

Jen Hester

Jeddy Higgins

Sean Higgins

Rosie Hilton

Sally Hilton

Katharine Raymond
  Hinton

Elisa Hoard

Caitlin Hobbs

Carla Hoffman

Tory Hoffman

Zoe Hollinger

Pan Hollingworth

Cameron Holt

Amy Hooper

Katie Hooper

Jessica-Lee Hopkins

Albert Hor

Andre Hordagoda

Alison Horder

Jeff Horne

Natalie Hornyak

Jenna Horton

Tash Horton

Lydia House

Kaj-khan
  Hrynczenko

Emma Huddy

Jamie Hughes

Claire Hugman

Ella Hungerford

Lauren Hunter

Kelly Hyde

Rachel Hyman

Dalia Icedo

Idapida

Sam Iles

Emily Ingram

Edward Irvine

Marcie Irving

Megan Irwin

Taibah Jabin

Tarang Jacob

Sarah Jacotine

Louise James

James from Twitter

Amy Jane

Eric Janec

Cornelle Janse Van
  Rensburg

Hanna Jansen

Kate Jay

Jenifer Jelinek

Cathie Jenkins

Daniel Jenkins

Kelsey Jenkins

Helena Jerrome

Jervas

Elena Joannides

Dominik Johann

John

Marjorie Johns

Jessica Johnson

Lauren Johnson

Sarah Johnson

Darren Jones

Matt Jones

Ian Karmel

Sara Kathleen

Anastasia Kaufmann

Nikhil Kaul

Eishar Kaur

Georgie Kay

Kristyn Kay

Michael Keane

Melissa Kearns

Simon Keating

Jade Keena

Janea Kelly

Rosie Kelly

Becca Kemp

Chelsea Kemp

Chi Kennedy

Christina Kennedy

Aisling Kett

Dan Kieran

Ferdie Kingsley

KK
Jana Gestörtiii Klengel
Greg Knabel
Charlotte Knight
Christopher Knotts
Joe Knowles
Michaela Knowles
Suzy Knox
Melanie Kohls
Daniel Kontos
Matthew Kosic
Albert Kovacs
Gavi Kovacs
Justin Krajeski
David Krieg
Cameron Krim
Brian F Krnc
Kathryn Kuchin
Roshan Kumar
Kurarin
Olivia L
Kel Lakin
Lalalalilly
Rebecca Lally
Daniel Laman
Benedict Lane
Cam Lasovich
Carina Mae Lawrie
Emma Leath
Ryan Lee
Brendan LeFebvre
Leilani
Charity Lenfest
Georgia Lennie

Stephanie Lenz
Mary Lewis
Sean Lewis
Olivia Li
Ben Libert
Chloe Lightfoot
Lena Lindblad
Laura Lindsay
Tracey Lindsay
Linda Lingham
Antoine Linguine
Emma Linnane
Margaret Linskey
Katherine Litman
Helen Liu
Joel Llewellyn
Nina Lloyd
Katherine Lofthouse
Grant Looper
Salinna Lor
Amy Lord
Mom Loves
Bailey Lowe
Kevin Luong
Nanna Lynggaard
Kira M
Christian Mackie
John MacLeod
Megan Macleod
Imogen MacMillan
Tallulah MacMillan
Sophie Macnair
Emily Macomber
Murdoch MacPhee

Max Madsen
Xander Madsen
Dana Mahar
Anushka Mahendran
Rachael Maher
Ruta Makaraite
Catherine Makin
Alexander Manley
Harriet Mann
John Manoogian
Kate Marciano
Christopher Marsh
Bethany Mart
Alex Martin
Lindsey Martin
Aisling Mary
Alex Maryan-Instone
Abbie Mason
Brian Mason
Katherine Mason
Hannah Matheson
Melissa Matias
Josef Matschy
Kelli McAdams
John McAfee
Holly McAlister
Zenia McAllister
Hank Ulysses
   McAnallen
Kate McAuley
Bethan Mcavan
Laura McCallion
Alex McCarthy
Kevin McCarthy

Ellie McCarty
Archie McColl
Callum McColl
Julia & Ray McColl
Maureen McColl
Sion Mccormick
Aimi McCroccoli-
    Francis
Kayla McDaniel
Cailin McDermott
Jimmy McDermott
Orlaith McDonagh
Caitlin McEvoy
Mitchell McEwan
Ashleigh McFarland
Keiran Mcgaughey
Millie McGovern
Lukas McIlhaney
Andrew Mckay
Joe McLean
Scott McLean
Mia McTigue-
    Rodriguez
Grace Medford
Hannah Jane Meehan
Laura Menmuir
Anya Metzer
Julia Middleton
H. Miller
Jacob Miller
Tyson Miller
Andrew Mills
Saima Mir
John Mitchinson

Louise Modarresse
Sarah Moffat
Sarah Moffatt
Cameron Moitt
Toni Montana
Zoe Moorcroft
Alvaro Morales
Dominique Moran
Alexandria Moretti
Cassia Morgan
Mark Morley
Laura Morris
Madeline Morris
John Morse-Brown
Brad Mott
Katherine Mott
Samuel Mottershaw
Matt Mower
Brianna Moynihan
Erin Muenter
Stephanie Mullen
Linda Muller
Annemieke Mumford
Ian Munk
Nikolaj Munk
Carmen Muñoz
    Torres
Katie Murgatroyd
Helen Murphy
Jennifer Murphy
Sean Murphy
Jurnee Murray
Corinne Nako
Brooke Nasa

Carlo Navato
Lucinda Naylor
Amy Nelson
Anton Nelson
Jeff Nelson
Renae Neumann
Rebecca Newland
Kathryn Newman
Darienne Nicholas
Debbie Nicol
Jack Nicoll
Phoebe Nightingale
Megan Niquette
Joanne Noble
Hannah Nolan
    Tierney
Kirsten Nolle
Hans Nowak
Paul Nunes
Anna Nymos
Rebecca O' Sullivan
Caitlin O'Connell
Megan O'Hara
Mark O'Neill
Erin O'Reilly
Cat Oakes
Catey Oakley
Georgia Odd
Wendy Oiseau
Laura Oliva
Natalie Olivas
Gregory Olver
Matthew Onorato

Justine Orlovsky-
   Schnitzler
Katie Orr
Alexandra Ortiz
Phoebe Oswald
Sasha Otanez
Rebecca Owen
Alex Owen-
   Goldsmith
Joelle Owusu
Keri P
Mike P.
Sarah Page
Nicky Painter
Luigi Palooza
Veronica Pålsson
Maris Panjada
Emma Pankratz
Brandyn Pantano
Brandon Pasqual
Shilpa Patel
Ruth Patten
Emily Patton
Steven Paul
Kirsten Pauli
Laura Pauli
Luke Pauli
Stephanie Pavona
Ashly Payne
David Payne
Princess Peach
Poppy Peacock
Ross Peacock
Anne Pearson

Gwyneth Peaty
Wilson Peery
Mirela Pencheva
Ed Peppiatt
Helen Perry
Jim Perry
Tyler Peschel
Dan Peters
Rachel Peterson
Joshua Philpott
Sophie Piercey
Char Pignatelli
Amy Pike
Yomaira Poblano
Kinga Podlaszewska
Justin Pollard
Simon Pooni
Tim Pope
Catherine Power
Matt Powers
Rebecca Powers
Emily Pratten
Joe Pratten
Sarah Pratten
M Prescott
Dany Prettyman
Brayden Price
Samantha Price
Cameron Price-
   Austin
Kellie M. Priebe
Jordan Prior
Rachael Prior
Alys Pritchard

Tony Quattro
Haley Quinn
Kate Quinn
Naomi Quinn
Ariana 'Bee' Raad
Marleen Raaijmakers
Rachel The Boat That
   Rocked
Amir Ragui
Rahmat
Danielle Ramirez
Marco Rampin
Denise Ratliff
Jess Ravenhill
Ray @SirEviscerate
Will Rayner
Leon Real-Vaughan
Kuber Reddy
Jenny Redhead
Owen Reed
James Reekie
Clare Rees
Andie Reeves
Elle Reid
Jack Reid
Yasmin Reid
Alyssa Reinhart
Mark Rendle
Stefanie Reville
Ben Reynolds
Noah Richards
Emily Richardson
Kyle Ridolfo
Nicole Rimando

Simon Ritchie
Chiara Rizzi
Susana L. Roa
Kai Roberts
Wyn Roberts
Hannah Robinson
Michael Darnell
    Robinson
Rachael Robinson
Rebecca Robinson
Richard Robinson
Matt Robson
Charlie Rodgers
Christopher
    Rodriguez
Egg Rolls
Martin Rombouts
Chess Romeo
Romeo
Adrienne Rose
Alisa Rose
Emma Ross
Dean Roth
Pippa Rous
Jamie Rowe
Emma Rukeyser
Zoë Rurangirwa
Jennifer Ryan
Matt S
Rachel S
Esther Saavedra
Robert Sadler
Matthew Sadorf
Nikki Sage

Lisa Salerno
Karla Saller
Jeremy Salmon
Christoph Sander
Erin Sanders
Kerry Sansbury
Mary Sansom
Kimberley Santos
Sarah
Christopher
    Sarnowski
Nicole Sarrocco
Richard Saunders
Marykate Scanlon
Elizabeth Scheibel
Ephraim Schoenbrun
Katy Schram
Jon Schwarz
Rachel Sciacca
Ellen Scott
Ashley Scotting
Simon Scriver
Claire Seaman
Daisy Searle
Tara Seddon
Jessika "The Realest"
    Selter
Sam Shah
Laurence Shapiro
Francesca Shaw
Darcy Shea
Katie Shearer
Brynna Sherley
Nicole Shero

Adrianna Shevlin
Caroline Sidman
Michael Siem
Lindsay Sipma
Brit Sippola
Daniel Skupski
Chloe Slack
Alasdair Smith
Benjamin Smith
Danika Smith
Emma Smith
Haley Smith
Jade Smith
Jake Smith
James R.C. Smith
Katharine Smith
Kevin Smith
Nanny Smith
Sam Smith
Stephanie Smith
Adam Snape
R Sneddon
Kerry Sommer
Reema Sood
Joe Souder
Kelly Hannah South
Frank Sowerby
    Thomas
Cath Spence
Stephanie Spencer
Vinnie Srihaput
Ewa Sroka
Terra Stagg
Brent Stanley

Nick Stenning

AR Stephens

Alison Stewart

Emily Stoddard

Hope Stone

Rebecca Ann Stone

Alessandra Straccia

Izzy Sullivan

James Sutherland

Anne Sutter

T Swan

Abigail Swann

Emily Sweet

Drew Swinburne

Elijah Swiney

Nida Syed

T L

Minori Takahashi

Daniel Takamori

Jessica Tanguy

Callie Tansill-Suddath

James Taylor

Keely Taylor

Kerry Taylor

Martha Taylor

Ella Teeley

James Temple

James Tennyson

Benjamin Thapa

Brandon Thomas

Lisa Thomas

Shelby Thomason

Dave Thompson

Patrick Thomson

Felicity Thow

Danson Thunderbolt

James Till

Anthony Timoti

Crispy Tofu

Keith Tokoly

Connor Tomasko

Keely Toozer

Cem Topcam

Devon Torrence

Carlos Torres

Alice Towler

Robyn Townsend

Richard Tran

Emrys Travis

Chloe Traynor

Jacqueline Truong

Beth Tucker

Allison Tuckerman

Keith Tudge

James Tufenkdjian

Matt Tulloch

Kate Turgoose

James Turnbull

Jem Turner

Steve Turner

Wendy Tuxworth

Ragnar Ulricson

Cara Usher

Nathan Usher

Rachel Valentine

Brandon Valosek

Merel van der Pas

Holly Van Dessel

Harald van Dijk

Emily Van Loan

Eric Van Uffelen

Jamen Vandehoef

Bobby Vanecko

Stephen Vann

Ana Vargas

Craig Vaughton

Ruth Veevers

Celeste Vela

Tom Victor

Laura Vincent

@Virjiggle

Baylee Vivian

Kate Vogel

Lucia Voll

Wouter Vos

Thien Vuong

Regan Wagner

Amy Wagstaff

Caroline Walden

Amy Walker

Dean Walker

Katie Walker

Steve Walker

Ellie Walmsley

Brendan Walsh

Madeline Walsh

Krysti Walters

Karen Walton

Kristen Wangsness

Chris Ward

Melanie Ward

Susie Ward

Liv Waresk

Chris Warnes

Aliyah Warshow

Holly Watkins

James Watkins

Jemma Watkins

Kathryn Watson

Victoria Watson

Alexander Watts

Andrew Watts

Nick Watts

Amanda Webb

Samantha Webster

Luke Weisbrot

Elliott Wellnitz

Nicole Wenger

Ehren Wessel

Rich A West

Hannah Whelan

Abigail White

Alice White

Caitlin White

Chris White

Camilla Whitehill

Charlotte Whitelaw

Chloé Whitmore

Scott Whitty

Taylor Wiens

Joe Wilcock

Mark Wilkins

Dale Wilkinson

Barton Willage

Beth Williams

Kristen Williams

Pip Williams

Ruari Williams

Claudia Willis

Sally Willis

Ludger Wilmott

Jo Wilson

Keeley Wilson

Rebecca Wilson

Skye Wilson

Whitney Winters

Anne Wolff

Mad Wolff

Connor Wood

Jasmin Woodward

Savannah Wooten

Lottie Wotton

Steve Wright

Charlotte Wyatt

Jack Yon

Madeleine Young

David Youngblood

April Yourdesky

Ameer Youssef